THE PURGE

THE PURGE

HERBERT R. LOTTMAN

WILLIAM MORROW AND COMPANY, INC.

New York

Library of Congress Cataloging-in-Publication Data

Lottman, Herbert R.
  The purge.

  Includes index.
  1. World War, 1939–1945—Collaborationists—
France. 2. France—History—1945-   . 3. Revenge.
4. Violence—France. I. Title.
D802.F8L58   1986   940.53′44   86-2370
ISBN 0-688-04940-0

Printed in the United States of America

First Edition

1 2 3 4 5 6 7 8 9 10

BOOK DESIGN BY BERNARD SCHLEIFER

Acknowledgments

THE AUTHOR IS GRATEFUL to many persons whose cooperation and guidance made this work possible, above all to the Archives de France, and personally to Mme. Chantal de Tourtier-Bonazzi, director of the Section Contemporaine, and Mme. Sylvie Nicolas; to Mme. Françoise Mercier and Mme. Lucienne Nouveau of the Institut d'Histoire du Temps Présent, where the author also had fruitful discussions with Marcel Baudot and Jean Leclerc. To the Fondation Nationale des Sciences Politiques (and Mme. Nicole Richard), the Archives Départementales du Rhône in Lyon, the Archives Départementales de la Haute-Savoie in Annecy, the Commission d'Histoire de la Guerre 1939–1945 in Lyon. Special thanks to the Société des Gens de Lettres, the Archives de l'Assemblée Nationale, the Ministère des Relations Extérieures, and the Service Historique de l'Armée de Terre (all in Paris).

Among others who offered testimony, or opened their files, may I thank Raymond Aubrac, André Bay, Jean Bernard and Roland Blayo in Lyon, André Cellard, Jean Chaintron, Pierre de Chevigné, Jean Comet, Geoffroy de Courcel, Jacques Debû-Bridel, Michel-Henry Fabre, Charles Fournier-Bocquet, Adrien Galliot, Renato Grispo, Serge Klarsfeld, Henri Krischer, Joseph Lambroschini, Gilles de La Rocque, Pierre Laroque, Raymond Lindon, François de Menthon, Pierre Mouthon, Joë Nordmann, Pierre Péré, Roger Peyrefitte, Robert Poirson, Maurice Rolland, René Tavernier, Pierre-Henri Teitgen, Alexis Thomas, Adolphe Touffait, Raymond Triboulet, Claude Urman, Robert Vassart, Charles Zambeaux.

Note on Usage

OFFICIAL DOCUMENTS refer either to a Comité Départemental de Libération or to a Comité Départemental de *la* Libération (emphasis mine); I have used the shorter form except in direct quotation. The abbreviation is CDL.

FFI, standing for Forces Françaises de l'Intérieur, was often used to refer to the non-Communist resistance only, i.e., to all combat units except the Francs-Tireurs et Partisans Français (FTP). In the later stages of the liberation the FFI included the FTP. In some places the non-Communist elements of the FFI were referred to as the Secret Army (Armée Secrète).

Among other frequently used abbreviations:

CNR—Conseil National de la Résistance
PPF—Parti Populaire Français (Jacques Doriot)
RNF—Rassemblement National Populaire (Marcel Déat)
LVF—Légion des Volontaires Français contre le Bolchevisme, a French unit which fought with the German army; not to be confused with the Légion Française des Combattants, Vichy's veterans' movement

Contents

THE PURGE

Prologue

THE OCCUPATION OF FRANCE by the hereditary enemy during the Second World War obliged nearly everyone to choose. One could choose not to alter one's routine existence at all, and then one was lucky if routine existence did not require daily contact with the enemy. One could avoid choice by removing oneself from the enemy's presence, say by voluntary exile abroad, or in a rural and remote hiding place; obviously not every French man or woman had the ability to move at will. A minority, whose ranks grew in the final months before liberation, discovered or even created opportunities to resist the occupation army and its French helpers, almost always at the risk of life or liberty.

But another minority thought it necessary, or found it profitable, to collaborate with the occupation authorities. Some contributed to the German war effort through sympathy with Nazi ideology. Others saw collaboration as an outlet for revenge against detested prewar policies, parties, politicians, since the Nazis and their French supporters in Paris and Vichy persecuted Communists, Freemasons, Jews just as some French would have liked to. Many of those later accused of collaboration were to say that they had served in the Vichy government to save what could be saved, to reduce the harm being done by the German invaders. At the beginning of the occupation old Marshal Philippe Pétain was seen as a protector. That was the time when (in the phrase of a popular historian) there were 40 million Pétainists, i.e., when everybody in France was one.

The coexistence of determined resistance fighters on one hand,

13

of equally resolute collaborationists on the other—and even if both groups were minorities—set off a civil war as the German occupation of France continued, a civil war more often like smoldering coals than an open fire. Some French men and women cooperated with the Germans in arresting, torturing, killing. When they could, opponents of the occupation attacked and executed collaborationists. When the Free French led by Charles de Gaulle returned to the mainland with their Anglo-American allies to reclaim the country from Germany, a symbol of the enemy remained on French soil in the hard core of collaborationists. To identify and punish them was the order of the day.

A rage which had stuck in the throat, a long-suppressed plaint, now mounted to the surface. A people which had lived under what historians concede to be one of the most horrible of conditions—subjugation to a cruel enemy—was free to take its destiny in hand, and to take revenge. The intensity of feeling at that moment is recalled by one of the resistance chiefs responsible for carrying out the punishment, Yves Farge, Commissioner of the Republic for the Rhône-Alpes region of southeast France: "I knew quite well what the people's anger consisted of. It was fed by revelations which were beyond the bounds of human understanding."[1]

Any history of the German occupation to which one turns will furnish examples of the revelations to which Farge refers. In his own southeast region we can pick up a sober chronicle of the industrial city of Saint-Etienne to read about the French who worked for the Gestapo. "There were rewards for denunciations, and an estimated three hundred persons worked for the Nazis." Their victims were tortured, then transferred to Lyon (where notorious Gestapo officer Klaus Barbie took over). In the region of Saint-Etienne alone the Gestapo and its French auxiliaries were responsible for seven hundred arrests. And then the German army's intelligence service, the Abwehr, employed young French men and women who belonged to an extremist movement called the Francistes; here some fifty persons wearing German uniforms sought out and denounced Jews, resistance fighters, made arrests, manned roadblocks. Finally there was the feared Militia, which had an estimated five hundred members in the district, three hundred of them full-time. "Armed by the Germans," says this chronicle, "the Militia behaved as the SS shock troops had done in Germany: arrests, torture, summary executions, looting their victims' property." After the D-Day landings in Normandy the Militia was mobilized to participate in operations against resistance partisans, with the bloody results one might have expected.[2]

These were extreme cases, hardest of the hard-line collaborators. But "the people's anger" was kindled every day of the week by abuses of power. "Grocers became little princes," we read in a popular account of those grim times. "The feudal lords of that new society were the farmers and shopkeepers, wholesalers and suppliers, with an unsavory cohort of intermediaries. . . . The curve of bankruptcies dropped almost to zero." The true masters, the Germans, let the French administration do their dirty work. The author of this account stresses the helplessness of townspeople: "Farmers hid most of their reserves: Often threats were necessary, especially in industrial areas, to get them to deliver. On the other hand they never opposed the requisitioning of their produce by the German occupying forces for they paid well. . . . From 1942 on, agricultural districts were the only ones in which births exceeded deaths; indeed, with the farm population eating better than it did before the war, its mortality rate declined."[3]

So the liberation of France also liberated anger. At first it must have seemed as if anywhere one looked one could find a culprit deserving punishment. Had the Germans succeeded in defending their own homeland and maintaining a Nazi regime in power the fate of many collaborators might have been different, for they could have crossed the border with the retreating Germans to remain under their protection. But the Third Reich collapsed, and many of the French collaborators who had taken refuge there were brought home for trial.

The punishment of persons known or suspected to have assisted the enemy is known as *épuration,* which can be translated as purge, or purification—the latter word particularly appropriate, since the purge was often carried out in the spirit of reform. The purge was not limited to courtroom prosecutions, such as the ones which sent Vichy's chief of state, Philippe Pétain, to prison for life and his premier Pierre Laval before a firing squad. And so this book will deal with all the forms punishment was to assume: the frontier justice before, during, and just after the liberation—when collaborators were sometimes executed on the street or in their own homes; the underground courts martial of the resistance; and then the ad hoc courts which operated in the immediate wake of liberation. But also with the mass arrests, the shaving of heads of women accused of "horizontal collaboration" (sexual relations with Germans), the more orderly vetting of the city, district, national governments, of parliament, the professions, and trades.

In recent years the postwar purge has had a bad press. Few Frenchmen now admit to personal experience of it. In the immediate postwar years some of the purged and their advocates published accounts of their ordeal (often privately printed). But the people who did the purging seldom wrote about their achievement, and official records have been secret until now. Some persons made it a point of honor not to speak of what they had seen or what they had done, while others apparently feared to admit participation in field courts martial, summary executions, and similar acts located in a twilight zone between legal and illegal. Many purge abuses were blamed on the Communist resistance, whose fighting arm was the Francs-Tireurs et Partisans Français (FTP); clearly it would help to have the FTP version of these events. But FTP fighters don't talk. They don't talk, their veterans' association tells us, because too many of them were prosecuted as criminals despite the amnesty which covers acts carried out to liberate France.[4] Certainly this process of forgetting was helped along by successive amnesty laws. So that most of what we can know about the purge comes from those who felt themselves to be its victims. Necessarily the picture is one-sided.

The events of the liberation were traumatic, and the scars have scarcely healed. Still, a story of such dimensions cannot be kept under wraps forever. Now, thanks to the comprehension of the custodians of official and unofficial records, it is possible to write this story.

When the author began his work firsthand information on the purge most readily available consisted of those memoirs by the purged themselves just referred to, or polemics written in their defense, one of which compared the fate of imprisoned collaborators to that of Captain Alfred Dreyfus.[5] In the decade following the liberation the purge was often compared to the reign of terror during the French Revolution, and its excesses were described as atrocities of the sort usually attributed to the enemy in wartime. In one of these accounts a husband is killed, his wife is raped and then murdered, together with their eleven-year-old son (so that he cannot serve as a witness). A bound man is forced to look on while his virgin daughter is raped a dozen times.[6] In another story a mother is raped, her infant thrown brutally aside.[7] Torture often precedes execution in these accounts—e.g., an accused collaborator is stabbed in the eyes, his genitals are torn off, or he is made to lie on a bed of burning sawdust.[8] A priest is forced to dig his own grave, then is buried alive after being shot in the genitals.[9] Another priest—aged sixty-five—has his chest crushed, ribs broken, nails and hair torn out, flesh ripped off with pincers.[10]

Sex and sadism are combined in many hostile accounts of the purge. Women have their breasts sliced off.[11] Collaborators are forced to walk barefoot in a pit filled with broken glass, while the women among them must strip naked to serve their captors, and some are made to copulate with animals.[12] We are also told of women who help commit these atrocities—e.g., in the mountainous Auvergne region, two resistance women punish collaborators while dressed only in brassieres and panties.[13] In southwest France women defecate on the bodies of executed collaborators.[14] Whatever we may wish to make of these unverifiable stories, it is certain that women were punished, occasionally by death, often by humiliation, for women did take part in the secret war, and on both sides. Many distinguished themselves in the resistance, and at the liberation their new status would be consecrated, for they became eligible to vote for the first time.

It would serve no purpose to throw a veil over charges such as these, but how judge them, when the witnesses all come from one side? Even well-intentioned survivors of the period recall feverish hours at the liberation. We have photographs of resistance veterans herding uniformed Militiamen and grim-faced women with shaved heads along village streets. What no memory, no photograph shows are the jurists in the act of writing purge legislation, the committees of civil servants sitting in judgment on those of their peers who had taken the wrong path, magistrates deciding the fate of generals and admirals, although the purge consisted of these things too.

It does sometimes seem as if a conspiracy of silence, based on a curious consensus of purgers and purged, blocks objective inquiry into the events of the immediate postwar. It is time for such an inquiry all the same. For the French who experienced these events are often still with us; some of them, with their sons and daughters, are now in responsible positions in government, business, the media, and the arts. They, and the rest of us, have been living in the shadow of these events without quite knowing what they were.

1

GAULLISTS AND MAQUIS

"Summary executions are like bowling—a French game."

—JEAN ANOUILH, *Pauvre Bitos*

ONE

Resistance Justice

THE FIRST PURIFICATION was carried out on the battlefield, and this battlefield was everywhere in France. The purifiers—call them law enforcers, executioners—were resistance partisans, some of them strictly disciplined, others informally organized, untrained. Their targets were first of all the enemy occupation forces—army, police, when possible agents of the Gestapo; but French men and women believed to be collaborating with the enemy were also fair game. Sometimes these targets were clearly identifiable by their uniforms, or by their presence in the headquarters of German or collaborationist units. But at other times the persons to be punished were isolated individuals considered dangerous to the resistance or to the Free French cause. Often, but not always, candidates for this battlefield purification were investigated, interrogated when captured, even tried by field court martial. In a few cases alleged collaborators were the subjects of secret indictments, in absentia trials. Whatever the procedure, the death sentences subsequently carried out were summary executions. Because of the secrecy, the uncertain legality of the procedure, these summary executions have given birth to myths which have drowned out attempts to present a sober record.

But let us try.

Two events were largely responsible for transforming isolated acts during the German occupation of France into guerrilla war. One was the drafting of French citizens to work in German factories, first on a "voluntary" basis, then beginning in 1942 via Vichy's Compulsory Labor Service (Service du Travail Obligatoire),

21

which sent increasing numbers of young Frenchmen to serve Germany's war. The scope of this draft, its brutality, led many eligible workers to take refuge in clandestinity, swelling the ranks of the resistance with angry young men. The other event was the establishment of the Militia (Milice), a paramilitary force created by the Pétain regime in Vichy with German encouragement, to combat their common enemies.

The enthusiasm of young Militia recruits was raised to fever pitch by Vichy's hard-line collaborators, and the Militia quickly acquired a reputation for ferocity as it maintained order in the name of Marshal Pétain, under the orders of Pierre Laval and Militia chief Joseph Darnand; in practice Militiamen often served as auxiliaries to the German occupation forces, chanting Nazis songs as they marched. Before the disappearance of the Vichy regime even the customarily imperturbable Pétain himself was to protest against the "evil behavior" of the Militia, denouncing (in a letter to Premier Laval) "inadmissible and odious acts" carried out in the name of the crackdown on terrorism. In addition to abuse of power, arbitrary arrests, collusion with the German police, the Militia (in Pétain's words) had "employed procedures which have caused public opinion to rise up against it everywhere it operates." The old marshal spelled out his complaint: "Farms and even entire villages have been burned down in reprisal raids, innocent hostages have been arrested, murders committed. . . . Kidnappings and robberies are regularly reported." More, Pétain blamed his own regime's Militia for the assassination of Georges Mandel, a cabinet minister in prewar France and a Jew; the Militia was also responsible, "without doubt," for the murder of another prewar minister, both a member of the Popular Front cabinet and a Jew, Jean Zay. The Militia, as Pétain went on to say in this document dated August 6, 1944, tortured "often innocent victims," creating "an atmosphere of police terror unknown until now in our country."[1]

So we have, on one side, young men who refused compulsory labor in Germany, loosely organized into resistance groups (these were the *maquis*), sometimes but not always led by seasoned officers who had opted for Free France, more often by Communist Party leaders; and on the other, another army of young men, Vichy's Militia. In the final year of German occupation the villages and towns of occupied France, the countryside between them, were frequently the theaters of acts of violence, sometimes of front-line fighting. And just as the resistance fighter in the hands of Militiamen was tortured, beaten, executed, or handed over to the Germans for disposal, the fate of a Militiaman captured by the resistance was predictable.[2]

Frontier justice inevitably brought the risk of injustice. Was every suspected Gestapo agent or informer of the German or Vichy police really guilty of crimes against fellow Frenchmen? The resistance side lacked means of finding out, and often there was no time to try. Surely many of the men and women who were executed, or whose homes or farms or other property were damaged or destroyed in the name of resistance to the enemy, could have furnished satisfactory explanations for their behavior. Often local rivalries, preexisting political differences, intensified the hostility of resistants to suspected collaborators. Under peacetime conditions dispassionate legal proceedings might have settled matters. While war was in progress there was no time for that, no opportunity.

The archives of the resistance are singularly reticent with respect to the punishment of collaborators; much of what we know comes from their targets. For example, from the confidential reports of the Vichy regime's national police—the gendarmerie of Vichy's prefects. Thus in a summary of the monthly reports of prefects in the spring of 1943 we can read of "acts of terrorism—the chief means of Communist activity—which demonstrate singular daring on the part of their instigators," in the regions of Limoges (in southwest France), Lyon (in southeast France), "centers of the gravest attacks." Among incidents reported: the murder of a high gendarmerie officer, the bomb attack against the home of a local representative of Vichy's propaganda services. In one region another such representative escaped an attempt on his life, while the chief of the Gestapo in the town of Chalon-sur-Saône was not so lucky, for he was killed in the act of arresting a suspect.[3]

Reports sent to Vichy by the prefect of the Lyon region, Alexandre Angeli (whose own purge trial was to be an event in liberated Lyon), indicate the severity with which the French police and the Germans dealt with resistance activity in southeast France. Still, "Communists and terrorists"—the term used by Vichy and the Germans to describe resistance partisans—were on the offensive "nearly everywhere." A report in August 1943 tells of the murder of a member of the Légion des Volontaires Français contre le Bolchevisme (a French detachment of the German army) in Chambéry, a large town in the Alps; of the execution of the president of the Pétainist Légion Française des Combattants of Verdun-sur-le-Doubs, of another member of the Légion des Volontaires Français in Lyon, along with a German noncommissioned officer. Prefect Angeli's report for August describes the killing of two Militiamen in Grenoble, the wounding of five others in the Rhône, Isère, and Haute-Saône districts, while an official of the Légion Française des Combattants was killed in the Drôme district. In September 1943, twenty-three persons were killed, thirty-one wounded, at the hands of "terrorists"; eight of the victims were Militiamen, three officials of the Légion Française des Combattants, eleven police or gendarmes, four members of Jacques Doriot's pro-Nazi Parti Populaire Français, and so on.[4]

In Lyon itself the district prefect was soon to alert Vichy to the climate of insecurity created by "terrorist attacks." There were nine murders or attempted murders in the two-month period from September 1 to October 31, 1943, and this did not include attacks on German soldiers. There were nine more in November, eleven in December, including the killing of Jacques Faure-Pinguely, an appeals court judge and chief magistrate of the notorious Special Section, a German-inspired tribunal which sent political prisoners to death. Lyon Prefect Jean Dissard reported that Faure-Pinguely had been shot in his home by four persons, two of them wearing German uniforms.[5]

It is rare to come upon an account of a resistance execution as seen from the resistance side, but we do have one for the Faure-Pinguely affair. For in this case the avengers were a tough group attached to but acting independently of the Francs-Tireurs et Partisans (FTP)—literally, Irregulars and Guerrillas, the Communist-controlled resistance partisans. They were members of FTP-MOI, MOI standing for Main-d'Oeuvre Immigré, a prewar Communist organization of refugee workers. Faure-Pinguely had prosecuted an FTP member, Emile Bertrand, who was found guilty and then guillotined on November 2, 1943, as well as FTP-MOI member Simon Fryd, a Polish Jewish refugee who had been wounded and arrested while commanding a group of partisans who were appropriating ration tickets required for their underground group; Fryd was guillotined on December 4. So the FTP, sitting as an underground tribunal, "sentenced" prosecutor Faure-Pinguely to death. In the words of a report by a FTP-MOI agent:

> We alert our intelligence service. . . . We must obtain the criminal's photograph, his personal address or addresses; we

need information on the cars he uses, his itineraries, his protection. . . . Our choice of men was easy: Fryd's comrades were all volunteers; ever since the death of their heroic fellow fighter they thought of nothing but revenge. . . .

On December 12, 1943, at 6 A.M. the battalion chief gives last instructions, places the men who will cover the retreat. Four comrades dressed in German uniform and two civilians make their way to Faure-Pinguely's address. Two of the comrades in uniform stay outdoors as protection. The others ring at Faure-Pinguely's door and he shows them to his office without suspicion. With a perfect German accent our chief says to him: "Sir, we need some information on the executions you ordered, particularly those of a Bertrand and a Fryd." Faure-Pinguely exclaims: "How can you doubt my good intentions? I work in close collaboration with you . . . and I can assure you that the arrogance with which Fryd answered my questions would have been enough." He could not say more; at his left, in German uniform, was a childhood friend of Fryd who was trembling with anger and who, disobeying orders, struck the criminal's head with a rifle butt.

Faure-Pinguely got up again, stumbled, fell over his desk, his head falling on the knees of the chief who drew his pistol, placing the barrel on the prosecutor's temple. A shot. Justice is done.[6]

In Lyon the FTP-MOI group took the name Carmagnole (the dance of the French Revolution); in Grenoble it was Liberté. In both places young men who had little to lose carried out assaults against individual collaborators, although their principal target was installations such as railroad lines, factories producing goods for the Germans. The men of FTP-MOI were Jewish refugees from Hitler's Europe, or (especially in southwest France) refugees from Spain's Civil War, sometimes anti-Fascist Italian migrant workers. Many had prewar clandestine experience, and their chiefs were battle hardened. They accepted strict discipline, practiced tight security. When a member of the group came upon a target of opportunity, say a contingent of German soldiers who passed a certain point regularly, he would take no action, but pass the information to a higher echelon. Or an order might come down to kill an enemy soldier, at random, near a Gestapo office (to show that it was possible to defy the Germans). One objective was to create insecurity among occupation troops so that they would have to keep men in France who would otherwise be at the front. Another was to obtain weapons. (These weapons often came from the French police; when things went well the police agent offered no resistance and was not harmed.) FTP-MOI received no weapons from the non-Communist resistance, nor from the Allies.[7]

One young member of FTP-MOI had lived in Paris until the German invaders approached the city, with parents who had migrated from Poland before the war. He left Paris to find work in the Vichy zone, eventually reached Grenoble, where he distributed tracts for a Communist youth movement. When an FTP-MOI section was created there he was transferred to it (he was then nineteen). In Grenoble the small Liberté group sent threatening letters to notorious collaborators, following up with physical attacks when possible, although here too most action involved impersonal targets such as railroad tracks. But one spectacular event took place during the young man's stay in Grenoble. Vichy propagandist Philippe Henriot came to town, and all Militia brigades of the region gathered in town to hear him speak. The Liberté group first hoped to kill Henriot, but discovered that his heavy police protection would not allow that. Instead, they decided to go off in parties of two to harass individual Militia leaders. This particular young activist carried two grenades on his bicycle, a pistol in his pocket. Near the railway station he spotted a Militia chief with a bodyguard, jumped off his bike, and began shooting with his six-shot Colt. He wasn't sure whether he had hit anyone but had to get away fast; his bicycle chain broke and he threw a grenade to cover his retreat on foot. Then he discovered that he had left a book with a library card in his bike bag; next morning other members of Liberté were to hold up the town library and remove the whole file of loan cards. From the newspapers the young activist learned that he had shot and killed the secretary-general of the Militia for the Drôme district.

The young man was arrested in September 1943 but managed to slip out of the hands of the Militia. His group sent him up to Lyon, where on the day of his arrival—November 10—he was assigned to blow up electric transformers to shut down factories on Armistice Day. The following spring he moved on to a third FTP-MOI action group in Toulouse. This group already had some impressive achievements behind it. The leader, Marcel Langer, had been arrested at a railway station carrying a valise filled with explosives. He was tried by a Special Section, whose prosecutor was one Pierre Lespinasse. The prosecutor called for Langer's death and Langer was guillotined; henceforth the prosecutor himself was a marked man. Even the BBC French-language service beamed to France had a word for him. In an angry broadcast on September 23, 1943, Free French spokesman Maurice Schumann denounced the bloodthirsty servility of Vichy's judges, identifying some of them by name, warning that their prosecution of patriots would not be forgotten. "As your colleagues in Toulouse will be called to account for the blood of the partisan Langer. . . ."[8]

On October 10 a member of the Toulouse FTP-MOI gunned down prosecutor Lespinasse. A member of Pétain's staff attended his funeral. But the partisans were convinced that henceforth resistance activists would escape the guillotine, and indeed one of their FTP comrades who had killed a Militiaman got twenty years of hard labor instead.[9]

At the end of 1943 the Vichy regime authorized the publication of the names of victims of the resistance—and there had been 709 of them in the last four months of that year: 230 gendarmes, 147 members of a national police force called the Gardes Mobiles, 152 policemen, 30 Militiamen, 150 civilians. There had been 9,000 bombings of factories and other installations, 150 attacks on town halls; 686 farms had been destroyed, 3,714 haystacks burned down, 600 trains derailed.[10] In Algiers the Free French press headlined:

CONDEMNED UNANIMOUSLY BY THE FRENCH PEOPLE

LAVAL'S MILITIA CAN DO NOTHING

AGAINST THE ACTION OF PATRIOTS[11]

They couldn't say that they hadn't been warned. From the start the Free French in London, via those BBC radio broadcasts nearly everyone listened to, the underground press which most of those concerned could read, wall inscriptions, anonymous letters, made it clear that the day of reckoning was not far off. As early as July 13, 1940, in the very week that a pared and chastened parliament sitting in Vichy voted constituent powers to Marshal Pétain, Charles de Gaulle in a London broadcast promised that "liberated France will punish those responsible for its disasters and the artisans of its servitude."[12]

In 1941 the warning became more specific. On London radio, in the broadcast *The French Speak to the French,* a commentator advised fellow Frenchmen: "To the Gestapo of Hitler and the Gestapo of [Vichy chief Admiral François] Darlan, you must use your own secret police, your own secret terror." Resistance revenge was already in progress, he added. Thus a man in the Calvados district of Normandy had committed suicide after denouncing someone to the Germans, for he had been afraid "to face the censure and the possible reprisals of other Frenchmen."[13] Warned Maurice Schumann, in another London broadcast directed across the Channel on September 1, 1941: "We possess and we are holding on to a list of all those—squealers, miserable judges, dishonored soldiers—who have sentenced themselves to death in contributing to the death of a patriot." He added: "Let this warning be remembered by those who would still save their conscience . . . and their head."[14] A fortnight later Schumann took note of a reward the Germans were offering to anyone who denounced resistance people. Those who accepted this reward, he promised, would be inscribed on a list of persons sentenced to death. "Let me add that this time the sentence will be carried out before the war is over."[15]

The resistance press of mainland France, written and printed and distributed under constant threat of discovery, punishment without appeal, made it clear that liberated France would settle scores with traitors. *Libération,* organ of the movement of that name in the south zone, regularly published blacklists of collaborators. Thus on January 10, 1943, it identified a member of the board of the group called Collaboration in Toulouse, together with the president of the Légion Française des Combattants in the Haute-Garonne district, a high school teacher in the same district, three black marketeers in Périgueux, a leader of the Service d'Ordre Légionnaire (predecessor of the Militia), and so on. "These names are only a sample," explained *Libération.* "Those who are named here are invited to think it over. *Libération* has its eyes and ears everywhere."[16]

A tract was addressed to police and gendarme officers by the Combat resistance movement. It instructed them to warn resistance activists when they were in danger of being apprehended, and told them that when they were ordered to undertake house or body searches to do them superficially. "Slow down your investigations— don't go too far in your interrogations—cover over the tracks—reduce the impact of your reports." Otherwise, for the few traitors among the police, "they will be inscribed on our lists. Liberated France will carry out the punishment!"[17]

Henceforth the punishment of traitors was a leitmotif of Free French propaganda. Marx Dormoy, Minister of the Interior in the prewar Popular Front government, had been killed by collaborators; when Vichy freed his murderers the Socialist Party underground newspaper announced: "We have sworn to avenge Marx Dormoy."[18] The blacklist in one underground paper, *Bir Hakeim*, was a veritable who's who. It led off with high-ranking Vichy officials, e.g., "General [Henri-Fernand] Dentz. Has, by his attitude, collaborated directly with the enemy in giving the order to resist and to fire on our men during the Syrian campaign. *Sentenced to death.*" Then followed a list of writers and journalists, many of them "sentenced to death" (and indeed some of them were to be sentenced to death by liberation courts). For lesser offenders, among them the authors Henry de Montherlant and Jean Giono, only their arrest and trial were demanded. But *Bir Hakeim* "sentenced" showman Sacha Guitry to death. Trials were requested for Edith Piaf, Fernandel, Danielle Darrieux, Pierre Fresnay, movie directors Henri-Georges Clouzot and Henri Decoin.[19]

Could collaborators hope for due process of law? The Gaullists warned that those who harmed French patriots were under an immediate threat of death. Thus the Socialist journalist Pierre Brossolette—later to be a resistance martyr himself—speaking on London radio in July 1943 warned that police guilty of acts against the resistance would meet the fate of Nazi leader Reinhard Heydrich, who had been shot down in Prague a year earlier. Already, he added, several French police officers had been killed by the Free French. "The only chance the others have to escape the same summary treatment is to abandon their criminal activity at once." He named names: leaders of torture brigades in Paris, the director of Paris's municipal police force, the head of police intelligence, as well as local policemen who worked with the Germans in Marseille, Lyon, Montpellier, and Nice. "All these men . . . must disappear from the scene; they can only choose the means of doing so."[20] (After a mission to occupied France, Brossolette was arrested in Brittany en route back to England, and was tortured: He then threw himself out of a window so as not to reveal secrets.)

On September 3, 1943, the Free French in Algiers took the formal decision to bring to trial Philippe Pétain and "those who belonged or belong to the pseudogovernments created by him which capitulated, destroyed the constitution, collaborated with the enemy, delivered French workers to the Germans, and ordered French forces to fight against the Allies or against other Frenchmen who continued the war."[21] The Free French Commissariat for Justice issued a warning that collaborators would not be able to justify their deeds by hiding behind Vichy legislation (at best this would be considered "extenuating circumstances").[22]

As the ranks of the resistance grew and German and Vichy repression hardened, the warnings became harsher. For London radio the humorist Pierre Dac wrote new words for "Mack the Knife" from the Brecht-Weill *Threepenny Opera;* the final refrain, a warning to the Militia, can be translated this way:

> Sad creatures
> You must leave us,
> For the traitors
> No pity![23]

Dac addressed these traitors over the air in April 1944, "solely and in all good faith to reassure you and to give you some details about what's in store for you." No matter how they tried to hide, he said, collaborators would be tracked down. "You are known, catalogued, labeled." One day, or one night, they'd come to get you. "You'll turn green, sweat will pour from your forehead and down your back; you'll be taken away and, a few days after that, you'll be nothing more than a small heap of garbage."[24]

In the French heartland some of the warnings were even more precise. Thus an underground paper published in the Ardèche mountains reported that some women were showing too much interest in German soldiers. A few of these women had already had their heads shaved, and occasionally they had also been painted with Mercurochrome or ink. "A good technique," noted the paper, adding that it might be more difficult to do such things in large cities. And for women who coax resistance people into telling secrets in order to denounce them for a reward, "punishment will be more serious, as one can imagine."[25]

It reached the point, in the final year of German occupation, that the Conseil National de la Résistance (CNR), founded under Gaullist auspices as a coordinating agency for mainland resistance movements, criticized the circulation of blacklists, for they often confused "simple dupes of the Pétain myth" with true traitors, so that totally innocent people were being denounced as collaborators. The CNR took a stand against threatening letters, ad hoc tribunals. Justice would come at the close of the ordeal; it would be "pitiless justice," unassailable justice. But for today, concluded the CNR, the important thing was to win the war.[26]

TWO

The Battle
for France

BUT WINNING THE WAR meant dealing with the enemy here and now, and with the enemy's accomplices. In that final year of occupation the man who seemed to exemplify collaboration with all of its ideological implications was Philippe Henriot, then fifty-five, a prewar member of parliament and journalist of the extreme right, an ardent propagandist who when he addressed a meeting in German-occupied Paris wore an appropriately black shirt. In 1944 he became Vichy's secretary for information and propaganda; on Vichy radio his was the voice of violence, of unhesitating alliance with the Nazis. "The day the Germans are chased out of France, French anger and vengeance will break out against that handful of scoundrels," Free French spokesman Jean Oberlé declared on London radio. "Poor Philippe Henriot! His mind isn't quite at ease."[1] On his side, Henriot in his radio talks warned that liberation would bring "famine and despair," and added that most Frenchmen wouldn't live to see it. He addressed de Gaulle: "France deprived of its colonies, handed over to Bolshevism and occupied by Negroes, that's what your liberation would be." He denounced *judeo-gaullistes,* and "Jews who wanted, who lead, who finance this war and who expect to come out of it in charge of the universe."[2]

On June 28, 1944, three weeks after the Anglo-American landings along the Normandy coastline, Philippe Henriot opened the door of his Paris bedroom to a resistance commando, and was shot dead in his wife's presence. At once the Mouvement de la Libération Nationale, a coalition of Combat, Francs-Tireurs, Libération, and

32

other resistance groups, took credit for the killing. It had been carried out by the Mouvement's shock troops.[3] That very day the French on London radio proclaimed the news, reporting that Henriot's execution had caused "a strange joy." Speaker Jean-Jacques Mayoux quickly added that before the war no one would have thought of wishing the death of a fellow Frenchman but, with respect to traitors, "summary execution becomes the most sacred of rights, the only possible form of justice."[4] There is evidence that the CNR had second thoughts about the revelation over the airwaves: A communiqué exists in which the coalition expressed fear that this confession would lead to "an aggravation of the bloody reprisals exercised against those of our comrades who are in the hands of the enemy or of the Militia."[5]

They couldn't shoot a Henriot every day. Most targets of resistance attacks were less prominent. They might be village or town or district officials, representing a security threat to local operations, or an ideological challenge to the liberation struggle. Sometimes the victim had had the bad luck to be present when a British plane was parachuting arms to waiting partisans, and then it was his life or danger to a whole operation and its participants.[6] Most often the targets were declared enemies of the resistance. The archives allow us a look at an exchange of messages between the Comité de Libération of the Ain district and Captain Henri Romans-Petit, district military leader of the Forces Françaises de l'Intérieur (FFI). In early May 1944 the committee criticized Romans-Petit for failing to arrest ten Militiamen and Gestapo agents it had identified, and he replied angrily that he was doing the best he could. He produced his own list of persons executed during the previous week: a Militiaman at Bourg, five more at Coligny, another at Beaupont; two German agents had been killed at Saint Paul de Vanaxe, another at Villerevesure.[7]

Resistance historians have ventured the estimate that there were twenty-five hundred summary executions of collaborators, black marketeers, and other unsavory elements between the autumn of 1943 and June 6, 1944—D-Day. This represented a fourth of all such acts of unofficial punishment documented at the time the study was made (in 1974).[8]

D-Day, when at last the Allies landed on the beaches of Normandy, was the signal for pitched battle—national insurrection, in the phrase of resistance chiefs, who were quoting de Gaulle.[9] In an order issued in June 1944 the CNR's military arm informed the FFI that it should proceed (among other acts) "to arrest and, if necessary for the success of the insurrection, to execute traitors, Militiamen, members of the RNP, the PPF, Francistes, etc. . . ."[10] In a memorandum addressed to the Allies, the Free French Commissariat for the Interior stressed the role of the police in assuring military security and maintaining order in the early hours of liberation. Concerning "persons whose activity is dangerous for public order" the memorandum acknowledged that "in most cases the police will be confronted with a *fait accompli,* resistance people having already carried out the summary executions or arrests which the people had demanded." But the commissariat stressed that legality had to be restored rapidly.[11]

To what extent was this expeditious justice necessary? There is evidence that the question caused some sleepless nights among mainland resistance leaders. Judge from this note drawn up by a coalition of underground movements and circulated before June 1944 to all local leaders in preparation for the day when the Allied landings would set off an insurrection. The document opens with a bang: "Hostile elements other than those having taken part in combat—if there is combat—must be arrested immediately or shot in case they resist arrest." That meant Vichy civil servants, notorious collaborators, Gestapo agents, enemy soldiers "if any are still left." The planners of the insurrection were then drawing up lists of such persons, with both their home and office addresses, the locations of country homes "should they go into hiding." Further on the memorandum reads: "The period preceding the insurrection must necessarily be marked by a progressive intensification of executions of traitors. The question to be asked is whether it is desirable that the victorious insurrection be accompanied by executions without trial." So the planners asked the Free French in Algiers to ponder this troubling matter. It offered its own solution: that special tribunals be established, composed of resistance fighters and judges known for their integrity and patriotism.[12]

The instructions circulated by the Communist-controlled FTP were unambiguous. Each member of that formation was expected to subscribe to an engagement which included these promises:

> To avenge all crimes committed by the enemy and its police against patriots.

To track down all traitors guilty of denouncing patriots, who by such acts have sentenced themselves to death, sentences which must be carried out as quickly as possible and without appeal, even after liberation. . . .[13]

On July 11, 1944, a little over a month after the Allied beachhead had been established, a CNR statement issued to commemorate Bastille Day was read over London radio: "The hour has come to exterminate the Militia killers, on whom the enemy is counting to prevent France from rising up to free itself."[14]

After the June landings Allied forces spread across Normandy, taking Cherbourg on June 27, Caen on July 9. Down south on August 15, the Free French joined the Americans to attack Mediterranean beaches; Marseille and Grenoble were liberated on August 23, while Paris was clear of Germans on the twenty-fifth. The resistance played its part, attacking railroad lines and trains, harassing German troops moving to meet the advancing Allies, hitting electric lines, river and road transportation, telephone and telegraphic communications. Attacking Germany's helpers too—e.g., on June 17 FTP partisans "executed" a woman agent of the Gestapo in the Oise district; between June 1 and 19, ten Gestapo agents were killed in the Aube; on June 16 and 17, three Militiamen and two Gestapo agents were killed in the Saône-et-Loire; on June 24 a Militiaman was shot dead in Paris.[15]

It is not easy to obtain details concerning these summary executions. Often the actual execution was preceded by an interrogation or a field court martial, and at times records were made of proceedings, but where are they now? We do have the story of a former gendarme in the Lot-et-Garonne resistance whose war name was Lieutenant Edouard. Because of his experience he was appointed officer of military justice. He is seen interrogating a Militia captive, who is sentenced to death and executed. Then he interrogates "Miss Betsy," a young Englishwoman who has been in contact with the Germans, and whose frequent travel is unexplained; she does not confess, and is executed. But most of those questioned by Lieutenant Edouard, including a former Garde Mobile patrolman who had been a member of the pro-Fascist PPF, and twenty-five Militia members—men and women both—are *not* sentenced to death.[16] In the same district we have the story of a young dressmaker from Agen who has a German soldier boyfriend. She too moves around a great deal, and in a region where denunciations of partisans were frequent, where many had been killed. A resistance investigator introduces himself to the young woman, confesses to being a partisan leader, and she becomes interested at once, saying that she has dreamed of visiting the partisans; she loves outdoor life. Of course she asks questions: How many partisans are there, where are they camped? So she is abducted, found in possession of a map of partisan territory and a list of suspected partisans. When young partisans strike her during the interrogation their chief stops them. Finally she confesses that she is the mistress of a German who is investigating the resistance. The partisan chaplain is called in, and then she is shot together with her parents, for they were aware of her activity. "She was an attractive girl," the partisan chief remembers.[17]

Much later, analyzing those acts of expeditious justice of which he had been aware, Jean Chaintron, a key figure in FTP operations in southwest France as a member of the Communist Party's Central Committee, concluded that insofar as Communists were concerned, they had acted consistently with their tradition of revolutionary justice. In fact they could have gone further but they did not; this was because the leadership realized, as early as June 1944, that the liberation of France would not be accompanied by revolution.[18] London radio took pains to justify partisan justice as "French legality." "All the partisans of the united resistance obey precise orders," a commentator declared. "Radio Paris [the German-controlled station in occupied Paris] says: They murder. The partisans reply: We render justice." But London radio warned that partisans had to weigh their acts. It quoted a resistance newspaper which declared: "The time has come for evenhanded and efficacious action against Germany, but not for personal revenge."[19]

THREE

The Clandestine Planners

PLANNING FOR THE POSTWAR was always a priority for the Gaullists in London and Algiers, and for the mainland resistance. It was not only a matter of ridding France of the Germans and of the Germans' accomplices; postliberation France had to be better. In occupied France the goals of resistance movements were hammered out in studies circulated within individual groups and then between groups. They were to be summed up some months before liberation in the program of the Conseil National de la Résistance (CNR), a coalition whose membership ranged from the Communist-controlled Front National to movements inspired by the Christian Democrats, and including representatives of prewar political parties too. Its first formal meeting was held in May 1943 in Paris under the chairmanship of Charles de Gaulle's apostle to the resistance, Jean Moulin; just one month later Moulin was arrested, tortured, and left to die by the Gestapo.

Planning for the postwar included plans to punish. In the program of CNR as published in March 1944—published in the form of underground tracts, of insertions in underground newspapers—the first section contained a "plan for immediate action" which called for the creation of local liberation committees. One of the missions of these committees was "to track down and punish Gestapo agents, Militia members, informers and traitors." The FFI (Forces Françaises de l'Intérieur)—combined resistance fighting units—were to be reinforced by civilian volunteers operating under such names as the Patriotic Militia.

The CNR program also contained a list of measures to be taken during the fight for liberation; here the resistance coalition pledged "to see to the punishment of traitors and to the eviction from the civil service and the professions of all those who compromised themselves with the enemy or who cooperated with collaboration policy." It would also "demand the confiscation of property of traitors and of black marketeers."[1] The statutes of the Comités Départementaux de Libération (CDL)—the liberation committees operating in each of France's administrative districts—were also being circulated in the months preceding liberation; each CDL had a role in preparing "immediate measures to purge and neutralize traitors"; indeed, local committees were authorized "to arrest traitors and suspects."[2]

But the chief instrument of the liberation forces, of the Provisional Government headed by de Gaulle, was to be another invention of the Free French: the Regional Commissioners of the Republic, a corps of proconsuls who at the hour of liberation were vested with nearly all the power a president or even a king might have (for the power of pardon was a presidential and a royal prerogative). Thanks to this invention the Gaullists were able to impose their authority at the instant the enemy and his helpers disappeared from the scene, and sometimes even before that. Thanks to this concept France never got or needed an Anglo-American military government of the kind that had been conceived for territories liberated from Nazi rule. Nor did mainland Frenchmen get a chance to refuse the Gaullists. As conceived by Free French planners the Regional Commissioners—one for each large region of France, seventeen geographical units corresponding roughly to Vichy's regional prefectures—had to be men of action as much as administrators. They would be drawn not from the ranks of the civil service but from a variety of professions, and they were to represent a wide range of opinion; above all they were to represent the "new spirit" of post-Vichy France.

The decree which created this unique corps of proconsuls was drawn up and signed on January 10, 1944, five months before D-Day. But unlike most decrees issued by the Free French this one was kept secret, and not published until after D-Day, so as not to alarm France's allies unprepared for so thorough a takeover by the Gaullists.[3] The role of the Commissioners was revealed to occupied France by London radio's French program on June 3, to pave the way for the liberation transfer of power. The commentator made it clear that if communications were cut with the Provisional Government each Commissioner of the Republic "disposes of exceptionally broad powers." He could suspend any law, make any law, take any decision necessary "to assure order, the functioning of government . . . the security of the French and Allied armies." And so the powers of the Commissioners "have practically no other limitation than the purpose for which they were bestowed." A Commissioner could suspend any local official elected or appointed, launch police operations, block bank accounts. "Keep in mind," stressed Pierre Laroque, a prewar government officer who headed one of the Gaullist planning teams, "that there is practically no measure which can't be taken in case of need by a Regional Commissioner of the Republic."[4]

So it should be no surprise that Charles de Gaulle's proconsuls were to play a decisive role in the purge of collaborators. The decree which spelled out the powers of the Commissioners, finally published in Algiers's *Journal Officiel* on July 6, 1944, made it clear that they were responsible for assuring the security of the French and allied armies as well as to reestablish legality; the decree became applicable in each district or township at the moment of its liberation.[5] But even before that, the new Commissioners were to be on the scene as underground leaders of their regions. And just as the decree which had empowered them was kept secret for months, their identities were a secret as they took up their posts in enemy-occupied France. They came equipped with confidential instructions, often in draft. These instructions stressed the likelihood that Commissioners of the Republic would have to act alone, without being able to obtain help or advice from a central authority, for "hours, perhaps even days." On the subject of keeping order they were told: "You will not wait for government instructions before arresting individuals dangerous for public safety." While such arrests would satisfy the demands for justice in some regions, "elsewhere they would be inadequate by themselves. . . . And you cannot remain passive in the face of the people's anger. . . . Military tribunals sitting as courts martial according to law will try traitors."[6]

Not the least extraordinary aspect of Free French planning was the extent to which it was done not in the clubrooms of London or the hotels and government buildings of French Algeria, but in mainland France itself, often in German-occupied Paris, dangerously, and by men of the law one would not expect to find playing cloak-and-dagger roles. As part of the Gaullist effort to coordinate mainland discussions, a Committee of Experts was created in Lyon in 1942, which soon took a more formal title, Comité Général d'Etudes (CGE)—literally, General Committee of Studies. Its mission was triple: to prepare immediate measures to be carried out when the Gaullists replaced the retreating Germans and Vichy; to suggest general policies for the new regime; finally, to draw up a list of persons to be appointed to key posts in postwar France.

François de Menthon, then forty-two and a professor of political economy, took charge of the new study group with the endorsement of "Rex," the name then being used by Gaullist emissary Jean Moulin, who had arrived in France from London with the mission of coordinating mainland movements and people. Count de Menthon, heir to a family castle on Lake Annecy, was a respected Catholic layman. He had been wounded at the front in 1940 and taken prisoner; after escaping from a POW camp he received a university appointment from the Vichy regime but was eventually dismissed. In the meantime he was active in an underground movement with fellow Christian Democrats which they called Liberté, and which was to merge with another movement called Vérité to form one of the best-known and most effective resistance organizations, Combat. De Menthon's hope was to mobilize the expertise of all mainstream political groups in his General Committee of Studies. He also had the help of competent jurists such as attorney Jacques Charpentier, then head of the Paris bar; law professor Pierre-Henri Teitgen, a fellow Christian Democrat; and a thirty-year-old civil servant, Michel Debré.[7] At the outset the experts had no liaison with the Free French in London, where other jurists such as René Cassin, an authority on domestic and international law, were studying the same problems. But the job of the CGE was to determine what the mainland wanted.[8] In a meeting with a resistance coordinating committee in November 1942 the CGE agreed to draw up questionnaires and draft proposals for submission to resistance groups; the experts would then collate the results for transmission to London. The creation of the corps of proconsuls, the Regional Commissioners of the Republic, was one result of this dialogue between the Gaullists in exile, the resistance at home.[9]

The CGE could draw on the services of high-ranking civil servants in the judiciary when necessary. Early in 1943 it made contact with Maurice Rolland, then thirty-nine, deputy prosecutor for Paris: Would he draw up, for the committee, a study of the judicial consequences of liberation? During the occupation, while continuing to serve in Paris, Rolland was an intelligence agent for the resistance, and eventually was obliged to go into hiding. When told that he was needed by the Free French in Algiers to help put the finishing touches on postwar purge legislation he undertook a series of adventures in an effort to leave France. He waited on a Mediterranean beach for a submarine which was to pick him up, but German sentinels discovered his group; during the scramble he abandoned a pair of orthopedic shoes (made necessary by a hip deformation); henceforth the Germans examined the shoes of all suspects picked up in the region. After several trips across France, Rolland eventually took off for London from a clandestine landing strip near Compiègne, and reached Algiers only in April 1944, where he joined the task force which was drafting the purge laws. At the liberation we shall find him in charge of vetting the court system.[10]

While still in France Rolland created a committee of legal experts which included Charles Zambeaux, then an assistant prosecutor, and prosecutor Robert Vassart. They would meet at the home of a member of the group, which home had the advantage of possessing three entrances—to facilitate discreet comings and goings.[11]

In their study of the purge to come the Rolland group paid particular attention to procedure. They did not think it advisable to define new crimes, since that would mean trying collaborators for violating laws which had not been written when the acts were committed, and such retroactivity had been a characteristic of the despised Vichy regime. Collaboration, they felt, was a form of collusion with the enemy—a crime already covered by the penal code. Still, they recognized that some acts committed by collaborators were not crimes strictly speaking; for such acts a lesser sanction had to be found. They came up with the notion of *indignité nationale*—literally, unworthiness, to be punished by a range of sanctions including deprivation of civil rights and professional status. In this way, persons who had not committed definable crimes, but who had supported collaborationist movements, for example, would not have to be tried for the more serious crime of collusion with the enemy. It was a new concept, not really a new penal sanction. In legal practice, lowering a penalty may be retroactive, but since it is favorable to the defendant it is acceptable.[12]

And how to bring collaborators to trial? One of the conclusions of the Rolland group was that a new court would have to be created. They could not utilize regular military tribunals because too many officers had been collaborators, nor could they use existing criminal courts because too many judges had behaved badly under Vichy rule. These new courts would have to make use of fewer people: one judge instead of the traditional three (since it would be easier to find one noncollaborationist judge in a particular district than three); there would be juries of six instead of twelve (and of course collaborators would be excluded from them).[13]

When CGE Chairman François de Menthon went to London he carried with him the recommendations of the Rolland group. De Gaulle asked de Menthon to stay, and he became the liberation committee's Commissioner for Justice, and then Minister of Justice in the Provisional Government. And when Rolland himself arrived in Algiers he brought along the final draft of his group's proposals.[14] Meanwhile the CGE planners, in the absence of final decisions from Free French headquarters in Algiers, took a decision of their own: Pending definitive instructions the Commissioners of the Republic would carry out the draft proposals drawn up by the CGE.[15] Committee member Michel Debré had spent the summer of 1943 drawing up lists of Commissioners and prefects, comparing notes with Teitgen and other CGE members, but also with delegates of resistance movements (who had their own candidates). As they were collected the suggestions were hidden in the files of the Chamber of Deputies, and Debré had a still more secure cache for them: his own office at the Council of State (the administrative court of appeals in which he served); in that sleepy jurisdiction it was possible to meet at night or on Sundays without fear of being disturbed.

One of the group's early decisions was to choose district prefects from outside the official prefectoral corps. For one thing, the country expected new faces; for another, traditional prefects were trained to avoid political involvement, while liberated France would require a totally different kind of leader. It was also felt that the new prefects, like the Regional Commissioners, had to come from the resistance or be ratified by the resistance, for otherwise they would lack authority, and the previous holder of the post would remain in place with the support of the Allies.

Indeed, appointing and installing Commissioners and prefects *before* the liberation was seen by Teitgen and Debré as a "taking of power" which would prevent the United States from placing a puppet à la Admiral Darlan at the head of the state.[16]

And we now know the first Commissioners of the Republic were appointed even before the January 1944 decree which formally established this corps. Months earlier than that, mainland planners were informed that an Allied landing might take place as early as October 1943. So Michel Debré hastily prepared a draft decree setting up an Action Committee on the mainland, empowered to appoint Commissioners of the Republic. The draft appointments were hand-carried to Algiers and returned with signed decrees dated in early October. Each of these appointments carried the warning: "The present decree will not be published in the *Journal Officiel. . . .*"[17]

FOUR

Algiers

CHARLES DE GAULLE HAD rallied the Free French around him from a base in London. But after the Allied takeover of North Africa in November 1942 the Gaullists were able to make their home on a parcel of liberated French territory. De Gaulle himself arrived in Algiers on May 30, 1943, and on June 3 the Comité Français de Libération Nationale (CFLN) was founded; a year later it became the Provisional Government of the French Republic. As early as November 1943 a Provisional Consultative Assembly sat in Algiers to participate in drawing up the statutes which were to become the first laws of the postwar Republic. In fact Free French law was defined in decrees drafted by de Gaulle and his ministers (then called Commissioners), representing most of France's political families. For in de Gaulle's view national unity was the key to victory, and so the main political groupings had to be represented in the liberation government along with the resistance movements (some of whose leaders were identified with no political party at all). The Algiers cabinet contained Radical Socialists such as Pierre Mendès France, Socialists such as Adrien Tixier, Christian Democrat François de Menthon. The Commissioner for the Interior, Emmanuel d'Astier de la Vigerie, had been brought in from the resistance.[1]

In Algiers the Gaullists pursued the planning of the purge that would have to be launched as soon as mainland France was liberated. But in fact the purging could begin right then and there in North Africa, which had been ruled by Vichy until November 1942. Many Vichy administrators remained in place, and some Vichy people had actually crossed over from France hoping to join the Free French. One of the latter group was a singular personality, Pierre Pucheu, then forty-four. The son of a worker, he had trained himself to become a business leader, and it was as a technocrat that he joined the Pétain regime, moving into the dangerous job of Interior Minister (which in France controls the state police apparatus) in August 1941. Shortly after Pucheu's arrival in Morocco in May 1943 he was placed in forced residence; in August he was arrested and brought to Algiers for trial.[2]

This wasn't the first act of purging by the Gaullists in North Africa, but it was the most spectacular until that time. Soon after that, as has been noted, the Free French in a formal statement declared that Pétain and his ministers were guilty of treason as defined by the penal code, and announced their intention to "bring them to justice at the moment of liberation." Meanwhile civil servants were warned that they could not justify their activity by claiming that they had only been obeying Vichy's orders.[3]

Before the year ended the Gaullists had unveiled an impressive arsenal of measures to be ready for liberation day. On July 6 a decree had been directed against one particularly obnoxious collaborationist movement, the so-called Parti Populaire Français of the pro-Nazi Jacques Doriot; it was simply banned.[4] In August the Gaullists established a purge commission to investigate elected officials and civil servants; it could also deal with lawyers, doctors, and those in press or radio work who had been involved with censorship. Those found guilty of collaboration by the commission could be transferred, reduced in grade, discharged with or without pension, and they would still be subject to prosecution.[5] The next month the decree which set up the Provisional Consultative Assembly excluded from this body Vichy ministers and employees, as well as members of the prewar parliament who had voted constituent power to Pétain in July 1940.[6]

In October 1943 the Gaullists issued a decree on another thorny subject which would have to be faced soon enough: collaboration which was not necessarily political or military, but which served both the enemy and the offender. This was financial collaboration. Business relations with the Germans were subject to sanction unless the French party to the transaction could prove that he had been obliged to deal with the occupation authorities on Vichy orders.[7]

A number of these early purge measures could be applied at

once, for as has been noted, some of those who had served Vichy were now within reach. Indeed, the purge of the administration of French Algeria after the November 1942 Allied takeover had been severe. All three prefects had been replaced; of the eighteen deputy prefects, seven were called up or invited to enlist in the Free French forces, two were suspended and referred to the purge commission, one was allowed to retire, ten were transferred. Other high-level officials were suspended, referred to the commission, or permitted to retire; a few were interned. A similar purge at the top was carried out in the neighboring protectorates of Tunisia and Morocco.[8] By mid-December 1943, 352 French citizens and 233 Moslems had been interned by Algiers for collaboration or criminal acts, and the new Gaullist prefects had ordered the internment of 203 members of collaborationist organizations.[9]

But of course the chief concern of the Free French was their nation across the Mediterranean, now and at the hour of liberation. Justice Commissioner François de Menthon pursued the planning he had initiated while still in occupied France. He had come to the conclusion that the resistance jurists were right in advocating two distinct laws, one to punish acts of collaboration under penal law in force before the collapse of France in June 1940, and a second to deal with acts of collaboration which did not constitute violations of law; in other words, he was ratifying the concept of *indignité nationale*.[10] The decree containing the essence of the judicial purge was signed on June 26, 1944. A preamble circulated by the Justice Commissariat but not published argued that the Vichy government was not legitimate, and thus its orders did not excuse acts of collaboration. Crimes to be punished were those already defined in existing legislation; no new crime would be created. The only retroactivity would be in the direction of "benevolence and justice," since courts would be able to attenuate penalties. Finally, because there simply weren't enough courts for all the cases that would have to be heard, new courts would have to be set up so that justice could be meted out rapidly, "so that the Nation can proceed calmly to heal its wounds and rebuild."[11]

Much later, and in retirement, former Minister de Menthon was to describe Gaullist justice as a matter of *raison d'Etat*—national interest. In order to maintain France's rank among the Allies de Gaulle's government had to be the only legitimate one, and Marshal Pétain's had to be a "pseudogovernment"; this meant that participation in the latter constituted treason. De Menthon knew that it would not be easy to apply such criteria to the period before 1942, when the United States and even the mainland resistance had recognized Pétain as chief of state. But national interest required that the Gaullists condemn Vichy as a whole starting in 1943. The ambiguous legal situation, like the ambiguous political situation, justified the purge laws: "special legislation . . . appropriate to unusual circumstances."[12]

In the view of the Gaullists, then, the key to the purge was to be found in existing legislation. This meant reference to a series of decrees issued by the Edouard Daladier government in July 1939 on the eve of the war, designated as Articles 75 to 83 of the penal code. Article 75, the principal authority for the trials to come, defined as a traitor punishable by death

> Any French person who bears arms against France;
> Any French person who engages in collusion with a foreign power for the purpose of encouraging it to wage war against France. . . .
> Any French person who, in time of war, engages in collusion with a foreign power or with its agents for the purpose of assisting the acts of this power against France.

Article 76 goes on to deal with defense secrets, demoralization of the army or the nation; subsequent articles deal with attacks on the security of the nation (punishable by terms of hard labor), acts harmful to national defense (prison, fines, a five- to twenty-year loss of civil rights).[13]

Formal debate on the purge was scheduled by the Consultative Assembly for January 11, 1944. And it was lively. Communist delegate Fernand Grenier offered the example of a successful purge: the execution of a prosecuting attorney on mainland France three days after he had sent patriots to the guillotine. Justice Commissioner de Menthon observed that the Gaullists weren't waiting for France's liberation to begin the purge: Whenever possible, "proceedings will go forward in North Africa, execution of the sentence included. To do otherwise would be a sign of cowardice, since among the arms that we possess to defend our resistance comrades, one is the prosecution of traitors now in our hands." Nevertheless the Assembly voted—unanimously—a motion regretting the slowness of the administrative purge, the delay in punishing "traitors and collabora-tors."[14] Remembering these things later, de Gaulle admitted that he had understood the preoccupation of the "resistance assembly," yet he failed to be shaken from the policy he had set for himself: to limit sanctions to those who had played a significant role in Vichy, and to those who had been direct accomplices of the enemy. He added that the state of mind revealed by the Assembly debates had made it clear to him that it was not going to be easy, after the liberation of mainland France, "to contain vengeance and to leave it to justice to decide punishment."[15]

On April 21, 1944, de Gaulle's cabinet issued a decree provid-ing for the organization of government in France after the libera-tion. This was a basic text, and later decrees were to cite it as authority. What were the prospects for victory just then? The Allies now held much of southern Italy, the Red Army was pushing the Germans back from strategic centers (the siege of Leningrad had ended in February; Odessa had been liberated on April 11). Opera-tion Overlord, the Allied landings on the beaches of Normandy, was just six weeks away. The Gaullist decree of that April day pro-claimed: "The people of France will themselves decide on their fu-ture institutions." And so a constituent national assembly would be called together as soon as liberated France was in a position to hold elections—one year at the latest after the liberation. At that time Frenchmen—and for the first time, Frenchwomen—would vote by secret ballot for their representatives. Meanwhile the decree pro-vided for the organization of Free French power down to the village level. In each township mayors and council members elected in 1939—in the last elections before the war—were to return to their jobs. Town councils appointed by the Vichy regime, the "usurper," were dismissed. Officials who had favored Vichy or the Germans would also be dismissed. When necessary to obtain a quorum, pre-fects could appoint additional councilmen from the ranks of the re-sistance. Similar rules were established for the assemblies which sat in each French administrative district, while the principle of inelig-ibility for public office was introduced for former Vichy cabinet ministers and other collaborators, as well as for members of the pre-war parliament who voted constituent power to Pétain in 1940 (ineligibility would be waived for persons who could prove they had been active in the resistance).

Meanwhile each district of France would have its own Comité Départemental de Libération (CDL), composed of representatives of resistance movements, trade unions, and parties affiliated to the Conseil National de la Résistance. These committees would assist district prefects as representatives of the resistance, and they were to be consulted for replacements to town and district assemblies. (The CDLs would cease to exist after the election of new town and district assemblies.)[16]

The April 21 decree included the provision: "On its arrival in France, the Assembly will be consulted on the setting up of a High Court of Justice." The point was to be ready to bring to trial the "usurping" chief of state and his ministers. Such a court had existed before the war as a function of the Senate, the upper house of parliament. Meanwhile, the judicial apparatus available in Algiers was rudimentary. On October 2, 1943, a military tribunal was established to bring to court persons who had committed offenses against internees in detention centers; this was a limited measure, designed to punish Vichyite prison guards and other lower-echelon personnel.[17] But it was clear that a means would have to be devised to try high officials and military personnel already in Free French custody—Vichy's Interior Minister Pierre Pucheu for example. In a confidential memorandum to de Gaulle on October 18 François de Menthon complained that nothing had been done to follow up the September decision to prosecute Vichy officials. Treason was the competence of military tribunals, yet public opinion was blaming de Menthon personally. And so he appealed to de Gaulle to set up a tribunal of public safety, or to vest responsibility for these cases in the military tribunal which had been created earlier that month.

De Gaulle scribbled a reply. There should *not* be an extraordinary jurisdiction. De Menthon was to prepare a second decree authorizing the military tribunal to deal with Vichy.[18] That was done on October 21: Henceforth this tribunal could punish "crimes and offenses against the internal or external security of the State committed in the exercise of their functions by members or former members of the de facto organism calling itself the Government of the French State"—that was Vichy—and could also try governors general and other high officials, members of collaborationist groups and paramilitary formations.[19]

FIVE

The First Trials

INTERIOR MINISTER PUCHEU HAD been a symbol of collaborationist evil to the mainland resistance. From the moment of his arrest in the summer of 1943 there was pressure for his trial—and execution—although moderates among the Free French did feel that purge trials should be postponed until the liberation, when a new corps of judges and new legislation would be available. But the militant majority could not accept the idea that a Pucheu was in the hands of the Free French—a Pucheu considered responsible for tracking down resistance fighters, Communists—and that he was not yet standing before a firing squad. As early as August 30, 1943, the Conseil National de la Résistance declared that "Pucheu has been found guilty of complicity in murder and sentenced to death by the French people."[1]

General Jean Bergeret, another former Vichy minister, was arrested by the Free French on the charge of "collaboration with the enemy, treason, and compromising the security of the State." The Gaullist radio spelled out his role in assisting the Germans during the Anglo-Gaullist attack on Syria in June 1941: "He was the first to agree to the arrangement which was at the origin of this affair: placing landing fields in Syria at the disposal of German aircraft en route toward Iraq." He was also the first important Vichy official to be charged with treason following the extension of the competence of the military tribunal; indeed, his arrest was decided on the day the decree was signed.[2]

Before either Pucheu or Bergeret could be brought to trial, ad-

50

ditional—and more controversial—arrests were made. Marcel Peyrouton, who had been forced to leave the Vichy cabinet because of his opposition to Pierre Laval, had gone to Argentina as Pétain's ambassador; when he heard that Laval had been taken back into the Vichy government he resigned in protest. And when the Allies landed in North Africa and Admiral Darlan took over there with the Allies' endorsement, Peyrouton placed himself at Darlan's disposal as a reserve officer. After the assassination of Darlan, Peyrouton renewed his offer to General Henri Giraud, then senior Free French official in North Africa; soon he was informed by the U.S. military attaché in Buenos Aires that he was to proceed to Algiers to report to General Dwight D. Eisenhower. When he got there Giraud made him governor general of Algeria. But when Charles de Gaulle transferred his headquarters from London to Algiers, Peyrouton resigned; de Gaulle wrote him that "I am certain that the French will appreciate, as I do, your unselfish gesture." Peyrouton was taken into the Free French army.[3]

But the purge was gaining momentum. In November 1943 Peyrouton was summoned to appear before the purge commission in Algiers to be interrogated about his role in Vichy; from there he was sent to forced residence in Laghouat, an oasis town in the Sahara.[4] By now the Free French had decided (at a December 11 meeting) to proceed with the arrest of former ministers and high civil servants of the "pseudogovernment of Vichy" who were present in North Africa. That meant not only Pucheu, Bergeret, and Peyrouton, but Pierre-Etienne Flandin, a short-time Vichy minister, and another former governor general, Pierre Boisson.[5] Maurice Schumann told listeners to his London radio broadcast that Article 75 of the penal code concerning collusion with a foreign power "fits like a glove on these gentlemen belatedly repentant. . . ." He took Flandin as an example, accusing this former minister of having declared in November 1940 that "occult forces seeking to establish Judeo-Masonic domination" were responsible for the war. How could the Free French purge minor officials, asked Schumann, if they failed to punish the promoters of treason?[6]

But this first spectacular purge was being carried out in time of war, in a theater of operations, and it concerned persons of interest to France's allies, or at least they thought so. On December 21, at the first news of the arrest of Peyrouton, Boisson, and Flandin, Winston Churchill cabled Franklin D. Roosevelt that he was

shocked. "I consider that I have a certain obligation as, in supporting your policy and that of General Eisenhower, I did undoubtedly
in Algiers in February encourage these men to hold firm in their
posts and aid us in our struggle for Tunis, saying also in that case,
'Count on me,'" the British Prime Minister affirmed, adding: "It
seems to me the American obligation is even stronger because we
were admittedly following your general lines." Churchill asked
Roosevelt to "impress upon the French Committee the unwisdom of
their present proceedings," and wondered if Roosevelt intended to
offer asylum to the arrested men. In a subsequent message Churchill
explained the "strong" case in favor of these Allied protégés: "Boisson saved us the cost and diversion of a major expedition against
Dakar. Peyrouton returned voluntarily. . . . Flandin . . . prevented
an expedition from Dakar being sent to attack the Free French near
Lake Chad." Of course from the Gaullist point of view Boisson had
been "the first Frenchman to open fire on his countrymen," in resisting the Gaullists off Dakar in 1940.

Eisenhower, then in Tunis as commander in chief of Allied
forces in the Mediterranean theater of operations, cabled Roosevelt:
"I am profoundly disturbed, particularly in the case of Boisson who
acted for a time as my loyal subordinate." He warned of "serious
consequences." Roosevelt asked Eisenhower to inform the Gaullists
that "you are directed to take no action against these individuals
[Boisson, Peyrouton, Flandin] at the present time." He subsequently
amended his request, asking the Free French (through Eisenhower):
"If, in view of the charges made, it is necessary that these individuals should stand trial, their trials should not be held until after the
liberation of France and the establishment of constitutional government." Meanwhile the American President was telling Churchill: "It
seems to me that this is the proper time effectively to eliminate the
Jeanne d'Arc complex and to return to realism. I too am shocked by
the high-handed arrests at this time." And added privately, to Admiral William D. Leahy, a trusted adviser and former U.S. ambassador to Vichy, that he thought the time had come to eliminate
Charles de Gaulle. Churchill cabled Roosevelt on December 23,
1943: "France can only be liberated by British and American force
and bloodshed. To admit that a handful of émigrés are to have the
power behind this all-powerful shield to carry civil war into France
is to lose the future of that unfortunate country and prevent the ear-
liest expression of the will of the people as a whole. . . ."

The French, through René Massigli, Foreign Affairs Commissioner, confirmed to the U.S. representative attached to Free French headquarters, Edwin C. Wilson, that a decree was being drafted which would allow postponing trials until the liberation, and he assured the Allies that the three men under indictment would be housed in decent conditions in the meanwhile. On December 30 de Gaulle himself made the same promise.[7]

In London, in January 1944, in a meeting with Winston Churchill and Roosevelt's emissary Philip Reed, Gaullist Interior Commissioner Emmanuel d'Astier expressed concern that if Pétain and Laval were in a position to save American lives, the Allies might decide to reward them by keeping them in their present positions. He also feared that the Allies were holding back arms from the Free French to be able to bargain for the release of Boisson and Peyrouton.[8] Flandin, Boisson, and Peyrouton were soon moved to the best possible quarters within Algiers's military prison, and then to a proper villa.[9] They were eventually tried in liberated France, by the High Court of Justice.

Pierre Pucheu benefited from less protection. When he heard of the decree which permitted postponement of trials until the liberation, he feared that prisoners like himself would be "as good as sentenced, for an indefinite period, to prison and silence."[10] But his trial was not to wait. On January 7, 1944, the composition of the military tribunal was fixed by decree: It contained three officers and two civilian magistrates, and one of the latter presided (Léon Vérin, chief justice of the Court of Appeals of Tunisia).[11] The trial opened on March 4 in the criminal court chamber of Algiers's Palace of Justice; the indictment charged that Pucheu had belonged to the Vichy government and participated in its subversive acts. Specifically, it accused him of favoring the recruitment of French volunteers to fight in German uniform, of placing French police in the service of the Germans. When it was his turn at the bar Pucheu protested that he had not been given a fair pretrial examination, important witnesses weren't being heard, essential documents weren't available. He demanded to be tried not by temporary judges but by the people of France or its qualified representatives.[12]

In fact the prosecution had some hard evidence. In Algiers it had turned up the text of a directive Pucheu had signed in December 1941 to encourage recruitment for the Légion des Volontaires Français contre le Bolchevisme, that French auxiliary of the German army. It also possessed the text of a Vichy decree establishing the Special Sections (the courts which were issuing retroactive death sentences for political offenses), and another setting up a State Tribunal whose death sentences against resistance fighters could not be appealed.[13] "Only the people of France," declared Pucheu, "can decide whether it wasn't in the national interest to discourage incidents at that time." He added: "In any case the Marshal [Pétain] was alone responsible for policy. . . . All the actors in the drama must be available for an equitable judgment to be made."[14]

There was a third serious charge. As Interior Minister, Pucheu had placed the French police in the service of the enemy; at his order, resistance men had been tracked down, and then treated as Communists. Resistance witnesses testified to the ruthlessness of Pucheu's antiterrorist brigades.[15]

The summing up by the prosecutor, General Pierre Weiss, stressed the "conditions of absolute legality" under which the trial was taking place. "This is a regular criminal trial. There is neither a special punishment nor a special procedure here." He said that Pucheu's case was "an episode in a vast enterprise of subjection and Nazification of France. The head of this conspiracy is without any doubt the old man who, for its misfortune, our country found on its path in 1940." He dismissed the notion that Pucheu had played a double game, i.e., that he had tricked the Germans to gain time. "Some double game!" exclaimed the prosecutor, citing Vichy's surrender of the French fleet at Bizerta (the chief port of Tunisia), its arbitrary legal system, the deaths of Allied soldiers during the landings in Algeria and Morocco in November 1942. Pucheu's lawyers attacked the climate of hostility toward their client created by the Algiers press, and argued that prosecution of Pétain's ministers had to wait until a High Court was set up after the liberation of the mainland. Prosecutor Weiss pointed out that if Algiers wasn't serene, what kind of atmosphere would Pucheu find on the mainland, where there was only "suffering, despair, resentment and vengeance waiting to be released?"[16]

The court found Pucheu guilty on seven of fourteen counts, notably concerning recruiting for the Légion des Volontaires Français, collaboration with the Germans, placing the police at Germany's service. But it rejected broader charges implicating Pucheu in a plot against the Republic (and thus avoided the reproach that its decision was a political one). Pucheu's crimes—encouraging Frenchmen to serve in a foreign army, acting in collusion with a foreign power—were covered by Article 75 of the penal code, thus called for a death sentence.

Privately, two of the military judges suggested to Chief Justice Vérin that military justice permitted a suspension of execution. The other members of the court agreed, and Vérin conveyed their feeling to de Gaulle. At the same time, General Giraud wrote de Gaulle asking for clemency, for it was he who had authorized Pucheu to come to North Africa to join the fight against the enemy. Warned Giraud: "If French blood was to be spilled after a trial which has taken on the appearance, whether one likes it or not, of a political trial, we are in store for dangerous excesses."[17] De Gaulle replied with a reminder that Giraud had approved the decision to try Vichy ministers; if he refused to commute Pucheu's death sentence, added de Gaulle, it was because of the national interest, which only the government is qualified to define.[18] "His pardon would have scandalized and perhaps discouraged many resistance comrades," François de Menthon would say in recalling this moment. "His execution was a challenge to Vichy, which represented a direct threat to our families remaining in France."[19]

Pucheu was shot at dawn on March 20, 1944. Announcing the verdict over London radio Maurice Schumann reminded his listeners of what Pucheu himself had said when he was Interior Minister: "We shall be without pity."[20] This time the Allies were careful to stay out of the picture. From Washington, Secretary of State Cordell Hull instructed his Algiers representative, who was then Selden Chapin, to "scrupulously avoid any comment which could be interpreted as representing the views of this Government or which could even remotely be construed as an excuse to accuse us of intervening."[21]

On the mainland a unique experiment in opinion sampling was attempted by resistance militants in April and May 1944. They made a point of not polling known collaborators, and acknowledged the fact that their sample was weighted in favor of the middle and upper classes. Of the sample, 22 percent were in the resistance, 56 percent were resistance sympathizers, 22 percent were neutral. Of the 432 persons questioned, 60 percent approved the execution of Pucheu, although 75 percent felt that further executions should be postponed until liberation in order to avoid reprisals against Gaullists and their families in France. Among those who favored the execution of Pucheu comments followed three main lines: "He really deserved it, because he was a traitor." "If he was really guilty it was right to execute him." "Algiers wanted to give a lesson. They did it with the most representative person they had available." Among negative responses: "They should wait until the war is over." "It should be done on mainland soil."

In a second poll in May the question was asked of 384 persons: "After the liberation, the purge will be in the hands of justice. But in the first days the people's desire for revenge will explode. Should it be tolerated, kept within limits, or prevented?" The replies:

Tolerated	28 percent
Limited	28 percent
Prevented	44 percent

Those favoring toleration of public vengeance offered additional comments such as this one: "There are many guilty persons, justice is slow, and evidence is often impossible to bring to bear; we'll be buried in long-drawn-out trials which will lead to forgetting the whole thing."[22]

Beginning in March 1944 the Algiers Military Tribunal tried members of French military units which had fought alongside the Germans in North Africa. In the first such trial one defendant was sentenced to death, three others to hard labor or prison. (A Frenchman received the death sentence; the lesser penalties were for Moslems.)[23] In a second trial two persons were sentenced to death, one to hard labor for life, with lesser terms for five others.[24] Soon after that Lieutenant Colonel Pierre Cristofini, first commander of French forces in Tunisia who had been allied to the Germans, received a death sentence.[25]

But the next major case heard by the Military Tribunal—it was to be the last—was that of Admiral Edmond Derrien, accused of making the Bizerta naval base available to the Germans during the battle of Tunisia.[26] His defense, as expressed during pretrial interrogation, was that in allowing the Germans to enter Tunisia and in resisting the Allies he was following Vichy orders.[27] General Weiss remarked in his summing-up: "Every time that an unpatriotic act is committed, the chief criminal appears in broad daylight and he is always and everywhere the Marshal! Admiral Derrien would not be in the defendant's chair without Pétain. . . ." He accused the admiral:

"The marvelous day when our American and British friends landed in Africa to save us, the day when we had our only chance to be reborn, the admiral continued to obey the gravediggers." Had the same gesture been committed by a sentinel, the prosecutor observed, quick justice would already have been done.[28] The case was heard behind closed doors for reasons of national security, but the sentence was announced in open court on May 12, 1944: solitary confinement for life (for defendants over sixty, hard labor was automatically replaced by solitary confinement), reduction to the ranks, eviction from the Legion of Honor. In fact the court had found him not guilty of turning over Bizerta to the enemy but said that he had delivered French ships; the sentence should have been death but he was granted extenuating circumstances.[29] François de Menthon later revealed that a trade-off was also involved. On May 4 a Vichy court martial, in reprisal for the execution of Colonel Cristofini by Algiers, had tried nine resistance men caught in the Haute-Savoie. Five were executed immediately; the fate of the remaining four depended on the Algiers decision. So Derrien's life was spared, and so were the four resistance men on the mainland.[30]

II
LIBERATION

"National liberation cannot be
separated from national
insurrection."

—CHARLES DE GAULLE, 1942

ONE

Taking Over

HOWEVER PRECISELY THE PURGE could be planned for, or even carried out within the confines of France's North African territories, the necessities of the battlefield seemed to call for more expeditious measures in occupied France. We have many reports of summary executions in the final weeks before liberation. In the mountainous Ardèche, for example, where German operations had been particularly brutal, the estimate is that 255 such killings of suspected collaborators took place during the liberation period. Paradoxically, prosecutions in the regular courts (when the time came for them) were comparatively few: 1 in 1,600 inhabitants compared to the natonal average of 1 in 400; one can only guess that resistance action had made postliberation judicial action unnecessary.[1]

Often these unofficial executions followed field courts martial by partisans. We have, thanks to preserved records, details of some of them. Two men, one aged twenty and the other thirty-six, were picked up by the Ardèche resistance, accused of aiding the Germans who were fighting the resistance. They were interrogated on July 13, 1944, shot before dawn the following day.[2] The same partisan unit also arrested a particularly unsavory character and his mistress; the man confessed to black market dealings with the Germans, and to bringing his mistress along to facilitate these dealings (she would drink with the Germans, then strip and make love with them). The prisoner also admitted that he had stolen wine, and let it be believed that the partisans had done it. Both this man and his mistress had denounced resistance people to the Germans, although the woman

61

(aged twenty-three) could recall only one example of that. After lengthy interrogation both captives were shot. As in many such instances the officer in charge of the partisan unit—using the war name Lieutenant Yole—drew up an official report which, in the name of the French people, declared both prisoners guilty of theft, treason, and collusion with the enemy. As authority for the executions, the report cites the penal code and the code of military justice.[3]

Justice was swift, but according to available evidence it was carried out in the spirit of battlefield justice prevailing in all armies at all times. In those cases for which documents are available, resistance men are seen to have acted with a sense of discipline and responsibility. Because of the absence of defense, of appeal, we shall never know whether the captives would have been sentenced to death by peacetime courts, but this is a problem in all courts martial.

Statistics for one region—the six administrative districts grouped around Toulouse—show that while most summary executions took place in the weeks between the Normandy landings of June 6, 1944, and August 20 (by which time most of the region was liberated), a considerable number occurred before D-Day, and after liberation:

	Before June 6	June 6–Aug. 20	After Aug. 20	Total
Ariège	7	79	42	128
Gers	14	101	24	139
Haute-Garonne	39	49	16	104
Lot	43	47	24	114
Hautes-Pyrénées	15	76	24	115
Tarn	14	25	15	54

The compiler suggests that the high figures for the Haute-Garonne and Lot before D-Day may be explained by the early formation of partisan units in those districts, and to particularly efficient purgers. Most executions in the liberation period (June 6 to August 20) were preceded by field courts martial.[4]

We know how one fighting unit, the Bataillon de Guérilla de l'Armagnac, saw its role. The unit's chief, Maurice Parisot, in a directive dated August 10, 1944, made it clear that a military formation did not have the power to render formal justice; that would be the job of the postliberation courts. Meanwhile resistance justice had to "render harmless" or to "suppress" persons representing a danger to the resistance, while serving as a warning to those expressing hostility to the resistance in speech.[5] The Bataillon de Guérilla de l'Armagnac court martial operated from June 8 to August 23, 1944, applying the military code of justice in the battlefield, which called for death sentences for collusion with the enemy and other acts prejudicial to military action. Convicted prisoners were authorized to see a priest and to write a last letter before execution. The firing squad consisted of six men chosen by lot, one of them armed with blanks. During its ten weeks of activity this field court martial tried and executed three agents of the Germans, two resistance men who had agreed to cooperate with the Germans after capture, nine Militia members convicted of bearing arms against the resistance. Some forty persons, a fourth of them women, were held for trial after the liberation, at which time they were turned over to the police; three were subsequently executed after trial.[6] Thanks to records kept by one of the participants we can read the official minutes of a court martial held on August 17, presided by the battalion commander, with his deputy (a captain), a lieutenant, and one of their men chosen by lot:

> Whereas the proceedings indicate
> 1) That ———, traveling salesman residing at Eauze, Gers district, is by his own admission county chief of the Militia;
> 2) That in this capacity he participated in drawing up a list leading to the arrest of patriots in Eauze on May 17, 1944— also admitted to by the defendant;
> 3) That in this capacity he participated in operations against patriots in the Haute-Savoie;
> [The court] unanimously pronounces the sentence of death and declares the present judgment immediately enforceable.

The defendant had the help of a lawyer chosen by the resistance men; his personal effects and last letter were turned over to his family after the execution.[7]

We also know something about a people's tribunal set up in the Isère in July 1944 by the Comité Départemental de Libération, with the participation of representatives of the Communist and non-Communist resistance both. The purpose was to punish acts that the

FFI military tribunals were not competent to take on; decisions were "without appeal and immediately enforceable."[8] In agreement with the FFI the CDL had set up an internment camp called La Bérarde in a "semiliberated" area considered inaccessible to the enemy. On August 9, when the Germans were on the offensive nearby, the people's tribunal sat at La Bérarde to try a group of internees. Five, including one woman, were sentenced to death; two received suspended sentences; seventeen internments were confirmed (eight of the internees were women). Moreover, twenty-four persons, among them twelve women, were released. One man and one woman were assigned to unpaid work at La Bérarde; fifteen others were enlisted in the resistance.[9]

More spectacular was the execution of the prefect of the Isère, with the publisher of the district's principal daily newspaper. Both had been sentenced to death by the clandestine Comité Départemental de Libération. It happens that a detailed account of this action is available, drawn up by the resistance task force itself. On August 1 the task force learned that the prefect was visiting the country house of the newspaper's owner in the outskirts of Grenoble; their orders were to execute the prefect—condemned for his pro-German, antiresistance attitude—and the publisher (believed responsible for the newspaper's collaborationist line). Seven men crowded into an automobile; on arriving at the newspaper owner's estate they set up an automatic rifle to cover the operation. The resistance men announced their presence by a hail of bullets, wounding a local manufacturer (considered to be innocent of collaboration). To the question "Which one of you is the prefect?" the newspaper publisher replied, "I am," but the prefect interceded to identify himself. Both men were shot at once, and the newspaper owner was warned that he had better change his line. The prefect received a final shot; and the task force withdrew, this time utilizing the prefect's car as well as their own.[10]

The liberation of France was not a day, or a single event; it became possible on June 6, 1944, with the Anglo-American landings in the north, inevitable before the August landings in the south. Free French forces were increasingly engaged, and the mainland resistance gradually acquired the structures of an army, or of a loosely knit coalition of fighting units. In some regions liberation came with the arrival of Allied tanks; elsewhere, the German retreat was followed by a takeover by the FFI; sometimes FFI military action hastened the withdrawal, and made it costly for the enemy. As a consequence the liberation is celebrated on different days in different towns and regions. At the moment it was happening, it was often laced with danger; the enemy was gone but not always very far. Fighting in the streets, sniping from windows and rooftops, the lack of reliable information on enemy strength and movements, the presence even in liberated territory of armed auxiliaries of the Germans, all help explain the frenzy of those days, when pursuing the enemy and punishing the enemy's helpers seemed part of the same war.

Certainly punishment was not going to be postponed; the only question was, who would carry it out? Sometimes that seemed to depend on how a region was liberated, who was in charge. As early as mid-July, over a month before the insurrection in Paris, commentator Maurice Schumann, accompanying advancing Allied troops in Normandy, reported to the French via London radio a message designed to reassure: "From June 6 to today I haven't seen a single case, I repeat not a single case, of individual vengeance or reprisals exercised by the population of liberated France against a real or supposed collaborator." He attributed this discipline to both the resistance and the Provisional Government, citing as an example the way an FFI unit had rescued a man accused of having denounced seventeen persons to the Gestapo; a crowd had attempted to lynch him in Bayeux. In that Norman city in the month since the Free French had taken over, twenty-seven men and eleven women had been interned, said Schumann, after painstaking investigation. "Justice has been or will be done."[11] Indeed, the best available statistics for the Calvados district, the battlefield behind Omaha Beach, show only one summary execution in 1943, four in 1944 before D-Day, and only seven after that. There were no hastily improvised resistance courts martial or military tribunals before the postliberation Courts of Justice were ready to hear cases.[12]

Indeed, the assumption of power had been minutely planned for by the Justice Commissioner and his staff. And the Provisional Government of Charles de Gaulle had appointed representatives from each of the cabinet ministries to follow the Allied advance—a way to make sure that liberated territory would be Gaullist. The Justice Commissariat had attached its own representatives to the landing parties; its Normandy delegation was on the scene before the end of June 1944, although it found few court officials to talk to—they were all absent from home, on holiday, or in hiding.[13]

The takeover in Bayeux, just south of Omaha Beach, and in

other nearby villages and towns was orderly. The chief concern of the Commissioner of the Republic for the liberated Normandy beachhead, François Coulet, was the security of military operations. On moving in the Gaullists in Bayeux turned over some notorious collaborators to Allied military police and there were a few demonstrations against local Vichyites, but nothing worth worrying about. Vichy's representative in Bayeux was placed in forced residence (over the objection of the Allied commanders, to whom this official had offered his services).[14] But the local police and gendarmes were kept on their jobs because their attitudes were felt to have been satisfactory during the occupation.[15] Internment camps were set up, staffed by the French army, but police kept arrests to a minimum, although one police official pointed out that in a township of four hundred inhabitants it would be possible to arrest five or six persons for collaborationist activity—or ten times that number, and still remain moderate.[16]

Each village, each town has engraved the hour of its liberation in local history. But some of that history remains oral, as does an account of that moment in Marmande in the Lot-et-Garonne district. Resistance fighters entered the town, then clear of enemy troops, on Sunday afternoon, August 20, roused the village band, set up a flagpole; flags appeared everywhere. Three cars filled with partisans arrived to liberate Marmande symbolically, although local resistance people made it clear to them that their job was to pursue the retreating Germans. At a report that the Germans were coming back the crowded main square emptied. But the Germans did not come back. Resistance men entered the gendarmerie, arrested the captain and his deputy; on the main square where a crowd had gathered again they stood in formation as a flag was raised; a statue representing the Republic was set on a pedestal, with a wreath at the base. Resistance leaders moved into the town hall. At three in the afternoon the arrests began, and a woman with a shaved head was pursued by the crowd. To save her the local resistance chief ordered her arrest, announcing over a loudspeaker that the curfew would be continued and that anyone arrested after dark would be shot without warning.[17]

Women shorn of their hair: This seems to have been the first act of purging nearly everywhere; it accompanies arrests, shootings, sometimes replaces them. On arrival in the town of Montélimar on the heels of the liberators resistance writer Elsa Triolet (wife of

Communist poet Louis Aragon) found a crowd outside the Palace of Justice. Inside, she discovered a group of prisoners waiting to be interrogated. All the men looked like convicts and murderers, all the women like prostitutes. The women's heads were shaved, and the men who guarded them did so with disgust "but also with a certain sense of duty." Triolet noted that of two hundred suspects arrested, eight were held over for trial, the others being turned over to the resistance auxiliary, the Patriotic Militia, and of this latter group twenty-three went to jail and sixty to forced residence. Of the hundred or so remaining, twenty were women with shaved heads. The crowd waited for them outside the Palace of Justice, whistling and booing; next day Triolet saw some of the same women, their heads hidden under multicolored turbans.[18]

In liberated Paris, Jean-Paul Sartre encountered, on the Boulevard Saint-Michel not far from the Seine, another "sad cortege." But there was only one shaved head in the group; the woman was about fifty, and the shearing hadn't been thorough. "Some locks hung down to her puffed face; she was without shoes, had a stocking on one leg and nothing on the other; she walked slowly, shaking her head and repeating in a low voice: *'No, no, no!'* Around her several young and pretty girls sang and laughed loudly, but it seemed to me that the faces of the men who escorted her were without gaiety. . . ." Sartre himself felt uncomfortable. "Even if she were guilty this medieval sadism still was disgusting." He doubted that the crowd realized how cruel shearing was; their victim seemed to have gone mad, and he had heard that other victims of shearing had committed suicide.[19]

Shaving heads: It was certainly an attempt to devise a punishment to fit the crime. During the occupation some young and older women had been seen in the company of German soldiers; young women also took part in Militia activities. They could serve as informers against the resistance, against young men who refused compulsory labor in Germany—just as easily as men could. Some women appeared well fed, well dressed, flaunting and occasionally boasting of their liaisons with occupation soldiers or privileged collaborators. When liberation came, revenge was in the cards.

The Paris wit Jean Galtier-Boissière quotes (without telling how he heard her) a sheared woman during the liberation of Paris: "My ass is international, but my heart is French!"[20] Getting even with women who spoke like that became a priority. Another writer describes a scene in flag-draped Libourne at the hour of liberation, accompanied by rousing patriotic songs. A summary court is set up at the town hall, where a prostitute denies having "fooled around" with Germans. "Her hair is sheared off all the same; she is stripped naked and forced to run to the pedestal which supported the statue of the first duke Decazes, a statue which the Germans removed to melt down the bronze." She is raised to the duke's place, to be jeered by assembled townspeople.[21]

Was there a national directive to shear the heads of female collaborators? Apparently not, and yet the act was carried out in every corner of France. Certainly this particular form of punishment was announced to the nation at large by radio from London. Thus on August 20, when Paris and much of French territory remained to be liberated, a *Sunday Express* correspondent speaking on the BBC French program described the scene at Nogent-le-Rotrou, on the road to Chartres, where he found three thousand people on the town square looking on as sixteen women, aged from twenty to sixty, were lined up to be shorn. As each rose from the barber's chair with a shaved head the crowd laughed, booed. "There were good reasons for that," explained the broadcaster. These women had kept the Germans informed of the movements of local partisans. The correspondent concluded with a description of the bathing of these women in a tub before they were paraded through the streets; soon they would go to trial. "The guiltiest will be shot as traitors to their nation and to avenge the young men who were tortured."[22]

If shorn and stripped women served as expiatory objects, they had another and perhaps more immediately useful function: to sop up the anger that would otherwise have ended with bloodshed. At least one participant in the liberation fighting sensed this: Father Roger More, chaplain and member of the FTP resistance in the Savoie. When informed that some young women had been arrested and were to be sheared he told his partisans: "Let them do it." He felt that by allowing the shearing they'd be providing a firebreak— energies would be diverted from killing. "For a long time after that," he would later say, "women wearing turbans would no longer say hello to me. But blood didn't flow."[23] The scars lasted. Nearly four decades after the fact, in 1983, a woman was discovered living as a recluse in a town in the Auvergne. She had avoided public contact ever since her shearing at the liberation, hadn't been seen at all for thirty years, and had gradually sunk into madness.[24]

TWO

Swift
Punishment

BEFORE THE LIBERATION COURTS were quite ready to perform the tasks assigned to them by decree, a more expeditious form of justice settled the fate of many of the most conspicuous collaborators. On the grounds that the existing court system on the mainland had collaborated with Vichy, and because the Courts of Justice conceived by the Provisional Government to carry out the purge were not yet in place, liberated France improvised. Courts martial sprouted. Later it was assumed by some that the creation of these courts martial had been spontaneous, not to say illicit. And it is true that as soon as it was securely established the Gaullist government did what it could to shut down these improvised courts, and to transfer defendants to the jurisdiction of the Courts of Justice. But the courts martial were as legitimate as the Provisional Government which introduced them. And in many ways courts martial composed of recognized officers of the FFI were an improvement over the revolutionary people's tribunals which had been created in a number of liberated towns. As they took power, the Regional Commissioners of the Republic often closed down these people's tribunals—and set up courts martial in their place.[1] When they did so, it was under the broad powers granted them under the January 10, 1944, decree defining their authority.[2]

More than that. On July 29, 1944, on the eve of liberation, the Provisional Government in Algiers informed the Commissioners of the Republic (who were then in place, but operating clandestinely) that early experience in the first patches of reconquered mainland soil showed a need for courts martial to try "notorious traitors" such as "Militiamen captured with their arms, spies, looters." A draft decree setting up local courts martial accompanied this directive; it took as reference the prewar code of a military justice. The courts martial, so the confidential directive explained, should be composed of FFI officers and noncommissioned officers in uniform. Meanwhile people's tribunals and other temporary courts should not be allowed. And only those individuals whose activity represented immediate danger should be brought before a court martial; all others should simply be apprehended and held for later trial.[3]

An early experience was the court martial created on July 3, 1944, by Commissioner of the Republic Yves Farge—then known only as "Gregoire"—in the Vercors mountain partisan territory. Gregoire's secret decree called for a proper court respecting the code of military justice, trying prisoners under Articles 75 to 86 of the penal code. "The decisions of the court martial," read the decree, "are without appeal and enforceable within twenty-four hours."[4] Actually the "Vercors Republic" over which Commissioner Gregoire then presided was to have a short life, for the Germans attacked the mountain on July 19. Outnumbering the partisans six to one, they had soon dispersed them, after killing six hundred men.

A year later few Frenchmen would have accepted the quality of justice dealt out in the summer of 1944. But there were other questions to be asked. For example, would the collaborators handled so expeditiously by these courts have survived, in the absence of these courts, to stand trial in more tranquil jurisdictions? Would local opinion have exercised the hunger for justice, for revenge, on even more persons, with even less evidence? It was considerations such as these which occupied the thoughts of the liberation Commissioners and prefects, of local resistance leaders. "It is important . . . to avoid letting the mob carry out its own justice on the pretext that legal justice isn't ready," explained Henry Ingrand, Commissioner of the Republic of the Auvergne region, to justify the setting up of a court martial in Vichy on September 5, 1944, even before the liberation of the district capital (Moulins).[5]

What were these courts martial? The best way to discover how they worked is by reading local newspaper stories. For no stenographic records were made, and official minutes were sketchy—and few of them can be found in government archives. But in the press, in the small-format, single-sheet daily newspapers of the first weeks of liberated France, we can find more information on these trials than about most other events that were going on in the region at that moment. We learn something about the atmosphere of the courtrooms too, something no official document would reveal. Thus in the capital of the Haute-Loire, Le Puy, a newspaper called *L'Appel de la Haute-Loire,* organ of the Comité Départemental de Libération, was the only daily being published in the first days of liberation. In it we can read of the setting up of a court martial by decree (dated August 21) of Commissioner Ingrand. The judges were FFI officers, and the local bar had been asked to assign defense attorneys. The population was asked "not to take part in any hostile demonstration against the defendants, so that the hearings can take place with the calm and dignity which are a tradition of French justice."[6] The first session of the court opened in the Le Puy Palace of Justice on September 4 to try Frenchmen who had been captured in the company of German troops fighting the FFI, and so they were accused of having taken up arms against France and collusion with agents of the enemy.

As in a regular court, this court martial opened with a reading of the indictment. The head of the local bar took the floor to state that "never has the defense had to plead in such painful circumstances," but he promised that "it would remain worthy of its mission and serve justice." The chief justice, a colonel, who sat with two majors, a lieutenant, and a simple soldier, thanked the bar president and promised that the rights of the defense would be respected. And then the questioning of the defendants began. Each in turn sought to explain his or her presence in the German column, denying that they had shot at partisans—even when they were captured with their arms. One admitted membership in the Militia, of being district secretary of the PPF, even that he had sent a letter to German Ambassador Otto Abetz in Paris, expressing hope that Germany would win the war. Another, who was a local government officer, had close contacts with the Germans; his wife happened to be both German and pro-Nazi. A third defendant, a Militiaman, had been captured in a bus where eight submachine guns were discovered. Still another was an armed Militiaman, who begged to be allowed to join a fighting unit "to die more honorably than here." Then a whole family of Militia members—father, mother, sixteen-year-old son, eighteen-year-old daughter—came before the court.

After examination of the defendants the government prosecutor summed up the charges. "To fight one's father and to fight one's country are two criminal acts which are the most shocking to the human conscience," he began. "The accused who appear before you today collaborated with the enemy against patriotic Frenchmen. . . . I know that you will think of our comrades who fell in fighting for their country, or who died in Gestapo prisons after frightful tortures." The four defense attorneys pleaded extenuating circumstances, arguing that the defendants hadn't joined the German retreat to fight the FFI but to save their skins; some had rendered service to their fellow citizens. . . .

The court withdrew to deliberate. At 5 P.M. (the trial had begun that morning at 9) the military judges returned and the chief justice read the verdict—first quieting the turbulent spectators, threatening to evacuate the courtroom. Five defendants were sentenced to death: the PPF leader who had written to Abetz, the official whose wife was German, the Militiaman who had been found with the submachine guns, the man who had hoped to join the FFI, the father of the Militia family. Two men and two women were held for further investigation; two men and a woman were acquitted. The executions took place the following morning at a nearby camp.[7] "An urgent procedure, an exceptional procedure," admitted the CDL newspaper, "but not a hidden one. The session is public; legal defense is accepted; everything takes place in broad daylight." What a difference, commented the editorial, with the "nighttime executions in Vichy and German jails."[8]

On September 15 the court martial met again in Le Puy to try fifteen persons, including the district chief of the Militia, his wife, a seventeen-year-old Militia soldier who had joined only that summer, and the chief of the district security service who was described as a Militia torture expert. The prosecutor, an FFI captain, called for a distinction to be made between those who had quit the Militia in March 1944 after their chief, Joseph Darnand, had ordered their mobilization as an army, and those who stayed on. All the defendants were in the latter category. He asked for death for the district chief of the Militia, for the security chief, extenuating circumstances for their wives, and for a girl who had been a Militia typist (although a convinced collaborator). For the others, he left it to the wisdom of the court. The defense took the floor at 11:30 A.M.; that afternoon five persons were sentenced to death, and shot the next day.[9] On September 21 the court met a third and last time to try a particularly active Militia member accused of roughing up suspects at interrogations, and of close cooperation with the Germans; nine women also went before the court. The Militiaman was sentenced to death, along with the mistress of a German officer who had taken Gestapo money for denouncing partisans, and a waitress at a local hotel, mistress of a German policeman, who was also accused of denouncing partisans. A woman Militia member and the mistress of a German noncommissioned officer who had worked with the waitress were each given ten years of hard labor; a woman who denounced young men who had "prevented her from sleeping," and another woman whose son was a Militia member and who had denounced partisans, each received five years. Three other women, aged sixteen, seventeen, and twenty-eight, were acquitted. The executions took place the following day.[10]

Now listen to a source hostile to such proceedings. He was a witness against accused collaborators, at a court martial held in the Nîmes Palace of Justice; the chief justice was the district chief of the FFI, a young Communist attorney from Paris. "The criminal courtroom was filled to bursting. People were smoking, eating, shouting, exchanging comments in the pure tradition of the French Revolution. . . . The spectators were agitated; the tumult never died down." It continued even after the three FFI judges entered the courtroom. The witness tells us that these judges were "imaginary" officers of the FTP, and one had even held up the Banque de France as part of his resistance career. We are also asked to believe that the government prosecutor had formerly written for a collaborationist newspaper, and in 1942 he had even complained directly to Pierre Laval about the "Jewish terror" reigning in Nîmes. In the eyes of this source, the Communists were simply putting their class enemies on trial, making sure to sentence at least one person to death at each session to pacify opinion. The spectators were carpetbaggers, sadists. This author claims that he heard the judges say: "We have orders from the [Communist] Party. We must sentence X, Y, Z, to death." The prosecutor is heard to say: "Even if the defendant spent only five minutes in the Militia, I ask for death."[11]

Just how differently the courts martial were seen by Vichy sympathizers on one hand, by resistance people on the other, is clear from the first case tried in Grenoble at the beginning of September 1944. Later, in a complaint against the excesses of the purge addressed to the United Nations, an organization called Union pour la Restauration et la Défense du Service Public called the ten young defendants in the trial "nice French boys." The atmosphere of the court, of the city, was tense; even before the trial it was announced that the death sentences would be executed that very evening out of doors; we are even given an account of how the prison chaplain found the six young men sentenced to death on their knees in prayer.[12] Yet if we believe a contemporary account, the court could have been more severe than it was. "Four Militiamen out of ten escaped the supreme punishment," complained the local daily. "Four out of ten: When we were in school that wasn't a very good grade." The journalist went on: "The dead—those lying at the bottom of the Isère river, in the mass graves all over France, those still falling in the fighting zones—these dead ask us, demand of us that we do our duty."[13]

Apparently the protests were heard, for in its next session the court martial sentenced all the defendants to death. During its brief existence this Grenoble court ordered the execution of nine of the thirteen Militia members put on trial.

Was it a massacre? The best available research suggests that, considering the total number of suspected collaborators to be sanctioned by the purge process in one way or another, these courts martial were brisk and brutal but punished relatively few persons. While the more official judicial purge was under way Justice Minister François de Menthon confided to members of the Consultative Assembly in a secret session of its Justice and Purge Committee in May 1945 that in addition to the sixteen hundred death sentences which until then had been ordered by the Courts of Justice there had been—"but I can't publish this, especially because of foreign opinion"—some one thousand victims of summary executions during the liberation, and about a thousand others sentenced to death and executed by special tribunals, courts martial, resistance courts, during the months of September and October 1944.[14]

But then in 1951, in response to a question by Jacques Isorni, the member of parliament who led the fight for amnesty, the Justice Ministry was able to give a more precise figure, which turned out to be lower. There had been 766 death sentences ordered and carried out by liberation courts martial "set up either by civil or military authorities."[15]

THREE
Paris

As THE ALLIES ADVANCED from their Normandy base the German withdrawal from Paris began, harassed by the city's own resistance forces armed with rifles and Molotov cocktails. This premature insurrection was almost a cause of rupture between Communists and Gaullists, when the latter chose to defend a truce with the Germans to spare Paris. Finally on August 22 attacks on the remnants of the German occupation forces were resumed. On August 24 an advance detachment of General Philippe Leclerc's Second Armored Division entered the capital, followed the next day by Leclerc himself. The next afternoon Charles de Gaulle marched down the Avenue des Champs-Elysées with Leclerc and other heroes of Free France.

Controversy has never ceased concerning the significance of the contribution of the Paris resistance—dominated by the FTP and the Communist Party—in the liberation of the city. What is certain is that the popular uprising permitted the people of Paris to feel that they had beaten the enemy and liberated themselves, and in his public statements de Gaulle chose to endorse this version of events. Local resistance groups which had not had an opportunity to take part in real combat in the manner of the partisans of rural France, who had not been able to play much of a role against the occupation army, were now in a position to exercise their combativity against local collaborators—those who had not fled. Tension was exacerbated in the first hours of liberation by the reported action of isolated, unidentified snipers, who were believed to have fired into celebrating crowds. Meeting at the city hall under the chairmanship of Georges Bidault, the Conseil National de la Résistance called for "energetic measures" and warned that if any armed collaborators were caught they would be shot at once. And the CNR told the Provisional Government that responsibility for public order "should be confided only to unquestionably patriotic elements of the police . . . and above all to the experienced units of the Forces Françaises de l'Intérieur."[1]

It was, very precisely, the participation of resistance units in the rounding up of collaborators—sometimes arm in arm with uncompromised policemen, more often acting independently—which was to create the atmosphere later remembered as terror. Terror—the reference is to the phase of the French Revolution during which Robespierre and the Committee of Public Safety sent hundreds of persons before the Revolutionary Tribunal and then to the guillotine—came to the mind of at least one observer, the conservative writer Paul Léautaud. For Léautaud and his friends, the resistance was nothing but a "gang of Apaches," so he noted in his diary on August 24, on the eve of the liberation of Paris. "It's a chase; it's a bloodbath; it's a bloody hunting party." (That on August 25.) "I envy people who have the courage to kill themselves," he remarks at another point. He hears that things are a hundred times worse in the provinces, where Communists and Jews have taken power.[2]

In the recollections of defense attorney Isorni we can read how rough these liberation arrests could be. Collaborationist writer Robert Brasillach had gone into hiding, so police and FFI men raided his parents' apartment, took his mother and father away with them. Brasillach's mother was locked up, as she later recalled, with common criminals, but even this was considered too good for her, and she was transferred to a large cell containing thirty women accused of collaborating; she was released only when her son gave himself up.[3] In his impressionistic account of the liberation Jean-Paul Sartre gives us some snapshots of resistance action. On the Rue de Buci around the corner from Sartre's Left Bank hotel, the FFI rounds up a dozen Orientals (whom Sartre identifies as Japanese); they turn out to be Militiamen. As they are lined up on the street passersby throw themselves on the prisoners, remove their trousers, and spank them energetically; with trousers at their knees the prisoners hop into a police van.[4] After the celebrating crowd is fired on, Sartre is present when a woman accuses a hotel employee of responsibility for the shooting. He is arrested at once and would have been shot immediately, but the hotel manager succeeds in convincing an FFI captain to postpone the execution until he can produce an unimpeachable witness to the innocence of his employee.[5]

How many arrests in Paris, and—important—by whom? By the end of August the Justice Ministry felt it wise to inform the press that the number of accused collaborators apprehended and jailed was far less than imagined. There had been talk of twenty thousand arrests; the true figure was closer to thirty-five hundred. Lists of suspects had been drawn up by the ministries and the liberation committees, and passed on to the national security service, but this service was itself in the process of being purged; the FFI was rounding up suspects on the basis of signed denunciations. The Justice Ministry was aware that some resistants had acted without orders, that false resistants were even carrying out arbitrary searches. But there had been few instances of personal vengeance.[6]

In the Paris region the purge was in the hands of the Comité Parisien de Libération (CPL) and of local liberation committees. "An essential mission of each Local Liberation Committee," reads a CPL directive dated August 14, "is to carry out as quickly as possible the arrest of all persons who have collaborated or betrayed. It is your job to draw up the list." There were to be two categories of arrests: The first covered the Militia, Vichy propagandists, members of the PPF, judges on Vichy courts martial; the second concerned persons whose attitude or remarks had been "particularly scandalous." The directive made it clear that the role of the local committees in these arrests was to end with the installation of a liberation prefect. Meanwhile their task was render collaborators harmless, and to prepare the judicial stage of the purge by putting suspects into the custody of the law.[7]

In a report to the CPL on September 4 by Georges Marrane, a Communist member of this committee as well as the CPL liaison with the police, it was revealed that local committees of liberation, with the FFI and the Patriotic Militia, had carried out four thousand arrests by September 1 (a figure not very different from the government's estimate of thirty-five hundred). Marrane admitted that the massive arrests "by patriots belonging to various organizations and without police or judicial experience" posed urgent problems, for it was necessary to decide whether suspects deserved jailing, internment, or parole. Some arrested suspects had not yet been transferred to a proper prison, while others were still at large;

clearly mistakes had been made. But vetting groups were now functioning under the responsibility of the CPL, with the agreement of
the prefect. They would determine whether to send a suspect to jail
or internment or to release him on parole. Marrane cited an announcement of the Prefecture of Police which declared: "If a dangerous individual known to be an enemy agent or denounced by
public opinion is liable to seek to escape, it is the duty of citizens to
take him in hand and deliver him to the nearest police station." But
apart from such exceptional circumstances, "no arrest should be un-
dertaken except by qualified police authorities." Steps were also
being taken to control the bearing of arms; the CPL was issuing authorizations to individuals on the recommendation of their respective resistance units.[8]

The Paris press—limited to a single sheet for each daily during
this period—carried reports of arrests of collaborationist officials
and other well-known personalities (in *Le Figaro* these reports were
regularly published under the headline ARRESTS AND PURGING) One
such report described a solemn ceremony in Paris's Palace of Justice
to honor those who had died in the war. Four arrests were carried
out in the middle of the crowd of judges and attorneys in ceremonial
robes: three of the suspects were attorneys; the fourth was the prosecutor of the high court of appeals.[9] Among those picked up on one
of the early days of liberated Paris: the chancellor of the Legion of
Honor (a friend of Pétain), the manager of the famous restaurant
Maxim's, a well-known opera singer, a priest accused of working for
the Gestapo, a former president of the national employers' association.[10] *Le Figaro* made it clear to its readers that it had decided "to
publish only those lists of arrests released by the Ministries of Interior and Justice and the Prefecture of Police."[11]

However and by whomever they were arrested, no matter
where they spent their first hours of detention (in police stations, in
public or private buildings temporarily transformed into jails), suspects eventually found themselves at the Depot. Some things never
change: The Depot on Quai de l'Horloge seemed to be one of them,
contiguous to the medieval Conciergerie in the compound that was
once a royal palace on the Ile de la Cité. The royal prisoners of the
Revolution had been detained there, and now in August 1944 eminent personalities of the arts, high-ranking officials, found themselves (to quote one of them) "in this temporary prison in which, for

many centuries, thousands and thousands of criminals, minor offenders, and the unlucky had known oppression." This from Pierre Taittinger, member of an industrial dynasty and until that instant president of Paris's Municipal Council (equivalent to mayor). Taittinger describes the men who arrested him, whose uniform consisted of armbands bearing a hammer and sickle, of the revolvers and submachine guns they aimed at him; he speaks also of the "acts of savagery" he witnessed at the Prefecture of Police. He found himself in the cell which had once held Georges Darboy, archbishop of Paris, arrested by the Commune and shot in 1871; his cellmates were other members of the Paris Municipal Council, while the prefect of Paris and members of his staff shared an adjoining cell. Taittinger knew that these ground-floor cells, however badly lighted, were clean, and that he and his associates were among the privileged in that temporary prison. "Outside our prison refuge the tumult was intense. There were gunshots on the street, and even inside the Depot we heard cries of horror interrupted by rifle fire, machine gun spray . . ."[12]

A visitor, Claude Mauriac, soon to become the private secretary of Charles de Gaulle, observed that if there were 10 men to a cell in the overcrowded Depot on the September day he dropped in, 209 women slept on the damp floor (among whom he recognized a celebrity, singer Germaine Lubin).[13] The actress Mary Marquet, another prewar celebrity, leaving the Depot for the Drancy detention camp, found a crowd outside as she and other prisoners boarded a police van. "They shouldn't go to Drancy but to the firing squad!" someone shouted. "To the firing squad."[14]

But before Drancy, in the first days after Paris was liberated, suspected collaborators were transferred from the Depot to a covered sports arena called the Vélodrome d'Hiver, site of the Six-Day Bicycle Races. During the German occupation this popular stadium had acquired a sinister reputation, for it served as a temporary camp to detain persons waiting transfer to Germany or to camps in eastern Europe. In July 1942 it had been the temporary jail of Jews during the historic roundup by French police under German orders. Now, at the end of August 1944, it held arrested collaborators. Some two thousand persons were detained there on the last day of August. On that day a reporter noted the presence of stage and screen star Sacha Guitry, wearing pajamas and a panama hat, and there were some well-known actresses on the women's side of the stadium. The reporter felt that the detainees were well treated and well fed; they could receive packages too. "What a difference from Nazi jails," he concluded.[15]

Taittinger recorded his experience as a prisoner in this "concentration camp" which the Vélodrome d'Hiver had become. He himself had been taken there in a police van into which suspects had been piled; inside the van there were tiny cages, overheated in the August sun, and too small to allow either sitting or standing. While his van waited its turn to unload its charge of prisoners, Taittinger's guards provoked the waiting mob to commit violence against them. He quotes one of these guards: "You're about to see a gang of collaborators, agents of the Boches, traitors." Each internee was insulted as he descended from the vehicle, including the "dirty collaborator Sacha Guitry," who was hit on the back of his neck and on his buttocks as he leaped to the ground. Guitry apparently witnessed an assault on still another prisoner, Jérôme Carcopino, a distinguished scholar and former Vichy education minister, who was covered with blood when he fell into Guitry's arms. Taittinger also tells us that a former official of high rank was beaten severely at that time, and would never recover. Using skills he says he had acquired on the soccer field, Taittinger himself managed to avoid most of the blows intended for him, and even to give some. He notes that the wounded Carcopino won release from the stadium largely thanks to the arrival of a group of American reporters. One of them, a woman, publicly embraced one of the "martyrized" sheared women detained in the stadium, to the cheers of the other prisoners.[16]

Drancy was an unremarkable suburb on the northern outskirts of Paris. By 1944 it too had acquired a sinister reputation, for deported Jews had been held there en route to the extermination camps. The Drancy compound was actually a group of fourteen-story buildings originally put up to house low-rent families, converted into barracks for the Gardes Mobiles police force.[17] Now these buildings were to hold suspected collaborators until their release or transfer to a real prison—Fresnes for most of them—pending trial. For some hard-line resistance veterans, Drancy seemed too good for its present inmates. "Drancy Palace," the Communist Party daily *L'Humanité* was to call it, describing the life of the celebrities confined to its barracks as a party "where you flirt, a drawing room where you gossip." A photograph of "flirting" prisoners accompanied the article. "They don't serve tea, but they smoke good tobacco, they eat chicken, red apples—taken from the many packages they receive." They paid, said the reporter for *L'Humanité*, with the money they had stolen while serving the Boches. He felt that the soft treatment of the Drancy internees, who strolled on lawns in the sun, was scandalous. Free the innocent; try the others. And fifteen gendarmes to guard six thousand detainees were not enough.[18]

But in the same period an anonymous open letter called attention to the deplorable conditions experienced by Drancy inmates. Denying the claim of Justice Minister de Menthon that a sorting-out of prisoners had been done by committees which included court officers and attorneys, the letter insisted that neither group had been represented. "A favorite theme of reporters is to compare the idyllic Drancy of today to the tragic Drancy of the Jews. Certainly we bow our heads in respect to the martyrdom of Jews arrested and deported by the Gestapo." But, said the open letter, during their detention the Jews could heat their food on portable stoves, while such equipment was forbidden now. The Jews had had heating, which was gone. In a room where four Jews had been detained, there were now ten suspected collaborators. And the investigators had failed to notice the tattooed faces, shaved heads, burned feet, bruised limbs, and other traces of brutalities. Worse, after six weeks, many persons still didn't know why they were being held, could not correspond normally or consult lawyers. Those recommended for release weren't released, while the press published appeals for more evidence to justify arrests already made, and some persons after release were arrested a second time by the Patriotic Militia and brought back to Drancy.[19]

One of Drancy's women internees, actress Mary Marquet, provides a graphic description of the camp in its first hours of use to hold collaborators. In her room, among broken objects and overturned furniture, she discovers yellow spots on the ground like so many autumn leaves, and sees that they are yellow stars, which she guesses were ripped off their clothing by Jewish inmates at the hour of their liberation. She even finds some good things to say about her quarters. "The walls are whitewashed. Beams on the ceilings. A large bay window with a view of the whole camp." Only the armed guards, the three barbed-wire fences, spoil the illusion. She receives the visit of Pierre Taittinger, to whom she says: "As you can see, our room is now quite a pleasant flat!"[20]

Taittinger's arrival at Drancy was less pleasant. He receives a whiplash on his face from an FTP officer, responds with a fist to the jaw, but before the FTP man can grab a submachine gun they are separated by the arrival of another bus loaded with prisoners. Taittinger is assigned to a room with most of the high officers of the Seine prefecture. He describes the sorry state of these working-class apartments which are now cells, and the effort of himself and his friends to make life more agreeable in them. But the guards are fierce, punishing internees with heavy exercise, firing at the legs of other internees, including pregnant women, to force them off the lawn and back to their quarters. Cries are heard from the cellar of his building; he thinks resistance guards are beating up chained prisoners down there. Without claiming to have been an eyewitness, he says that women then in the infirmary have been tortured, burned, or have bleeding feet; some have been branded with hot irons or had the tips of their breasts cut off. Corpses are said to have been found in the cellar, supposedly of prisoners who had hanged themselves. Taittinger also says that all but 10 percent of the guards are Spaniards who fought in the Civil War, Communists, or even persons who served at Drancy when Jews were being interned—and tortured these Jews. One officer, he claims, was a Militia member and Gestapo agent.

As more and more suspects were rounded up and the population of Drancy grew—from three thousand to four thousand, then the six thousand already mentioned—the number of inmates in each barracks rose from forty to sixty. Mattresses disappeared; prisoners slept on straw on the ground. Taittinger hears that the total population of internment centers in the Paris region alone is sixty thousand.[21]

Paris was bristling with stories of the tracking of traitors. A useful source is the raconteur Jean Galtier-Boissière, who when he sees a list of prominent persons who have been arrested, published in *Le Figaro,* is reminded of a society column (for there are a countess and other eminent persons). He quotes the comment of the actress Arletty after her arrest for keeping company with a German officer: "What kind of government is this which worries about our sleeping arrangements!" While he acknowledges that most French stars were more or less compromised, he feels that jealousy and ambition explain some of the purging of important people by less important ones. He observes that second-string reporters gloat when a celebrity like the boxer Georges Carpentier is arrested, tells of a lady of high society called from her table by her maître d'hôtel while she is receiving guests such as the painter Marie Laurencin and the writer Paul Léautaud; the hostess fails to return, for she has been arrested. The atmosphere in Paris is exemplified by street-corner sale of a pamphlet which lists collaborators who deserve to be shot. Pétain is on the list, but so is the owner of a restaurant near the Champs-Elysées. Jean Cocteau tells Galtier-Boissière that persons attacked in the press are afraid to protest, just as they were during the German occupation.[22]

Someone used the name Jean-Pierre Abel to publish a book whose title translates as *The Age of Cain,* presented as the first eye-witness account of the hidden side of the liberation of Paris. Its author tells of the arrest of himself and his wife by young FTP men on August 30, 1944, their detention in the Dental Institute, transferred into an FTP prison, where "Abel" claims that torture and even death faced accused collaborators. When the police sought to take over the building the FTP (moved, says the author, by class hatred) threatened to kill their prisoners unless the police withdrew, and it took some time before the authorities were able to restore order.[23] Replying to "Abel," a writer in Sartre's monthly *Les Temps Modernes* admitted that he had served at the Dental Institute. He denied that prisoners were tortured, although some—Militia members, even German soldiers—had been executed against a wall outdoors. "The FTP couldn't be asked to trust the judges who had sentenced resistance men to death to avenge their own dead," explained this writer, referring to the judges who had served Vichy and who were apparently going to stay in place. He admitted that he himself had served in firing squads in which members of the Nazi SS and the Légion des Volontaires Français were shot. Such justice seemed natural to men who were neither sadists nor abnormal, but who had friends to avenge, and atrocities to punish.[24]

Quoted because it is a rare confession, a rare justification of the resistance side of the extrajudicial punishment of collaborators at the hour of victory.

FOUR

France Takes Charge

SLOWLY, STEP BY STEP, the central authority (which was now Charles de Gaulle and his ministers) transferred their headquarters from Algiers to Paris, curbed the anarchy, and dominated it. The likelihood of a national revolution or even of local insurrections disappeared.

There was no bloodbath in Vichy. Even a writer generally considered harsh on the purgers, popular historian Robert Aron, had to admit that conditions in the main detention camp in Pétain's capital, the horse track, were "not dramatic." Yet he says that over a thousand persons were held there, "a social and intellectual elite of a level seldom found in jail"—former cabinet officers, generals and admirals, scholars and writers. A court martial had been set up in the lobby of the Hôtel du Parc, a first-class tourist hotel which had served Pétain and Laval as seat of government; Aron notes that there were nine death sentences followed by execution, one of these victims being the head of Laval's security police. Yet in a later and still more severe account of the period, Aron will say that the worst punishment inflicted on the Vichy internees was moral: insults by their guards.[1] We now know from the official records that 650 persons were arrested in Vichy in the first month of liberation, of which number 114 were released at once. But in Clermont-Ferrand, seat of the Regional Commissioner of the Republic, there had been 1,106 arrests, and 180 released; in the four districts under the Commissioner's charge, there had been a total of 2,980 arrests, 746 releases.[2] Vichy hardly stands out in these statistics, and yet it was the capital of the collaborationist government.

Internment was not an improvised solution. Borrowed from decrees issued before the beginning of the war to deal with persons who might represent a security risk, it was seen by the Free French of Algiers as a means to hold on to the large number of suspects who would necessarily fall into their hands during the liberation of the mainland. An Algiers decree of November 18, 1943, made reference both to Vichy's regulations concerning internment and to the Daladier cabinet's 1939 provision for detention centers. Individuals who represented a threat to national defense or public security could be barred from their normal place of residence or assigned to special detention centers, and this until the end of the war.[3] Following the liberation, the Provisional Government in Paris issued a second decree (on October 4, 1944) which offered three possibilities: An arrested suspect could be barred from his normal place of residence, assigned to residence in a specified locality, or interned. Inspection commissions, each composed of a legal officer, a member of a Comité Départemental de Libération, and an officer of the security police, were to be informed within a week of each arrest, and had a month to dispose of the case. (The suspect's attorney could file a brief.)[4]

In all, 126,020 persons were interned by the liberators. Of that number, 36,377 were released as soon as conditions allowed, which often meant when public anger ceased to represent a danger to the internees. For one of the lessons soon learned by the Gaullists was that the arrest and detention of an accused collaborator might save him from lynching. It was in the weeks immediately following liberation that public opinion was most agitated, and it was then that the largest number of persons was held in the new camps.[5] Thus the regional chief of the Pétainist Légion Française des Combattants of Limoges was arrested and interned, on the order of the purge commission of the Comité Départemental de Libération. The CDL president described the move as "half sanction, half protection," for the anger aroused against this notorious collaborator might have led to lynching. He was kept in detention for a few months and then released, by which time he was able to return to a modest teaching job without danger.[6]

In each of twenty-two districts, the number of internments exceeded 1,000; in ten other districts, there were fewer than 200, fewer than 100 in six others, fewer than 50 in seven. The district with the highest number was the Seine, which included the city of Paris: 7,998 internments. Of 86,589 cases reviewed, 34,270 led to release,

36,852 to a recommendation that the subject be investigated by a Court of Justice for possible prosecution, 9,862 suspects were given parole, 1,758 were barred from their place of residence, 2,442 were turned over to military tribunals, 1,405 to ordinary criminal courts.[7]

Anything involving such large numbers can breed rumors of still higher numbers; there was even a claim that a million people had been locked up at the liberation.[8] Against the charges of widespread abuse of civil rights there exist confidential reports written at the time by and for those responsible for carrying out the arrests and internments. In a summary of the situation in his Auvergne region by Commissioner of the Republic Henry Ingrand we find an admission that some internees had been guilty of only minor offenses. But all had been arrested with proper regard for form, and steps had been taken to make certain that "the maximum of guarantees be given to individual freedom." By the end of September 1944 all 2,980 persons arrested in the aftermath of liberation had been interrogated, and 1,000 of them released, and all four administrative districts under Ingrand's control had set up filtering commissions to make sure that no innocent person was still being held.[9]

"The period of massive arrests of suspects seems to be over," the gendarmerie noted in a secret report covering the month running from September 15 to October 15, 1944. Internments were by that time being carried out with due respect for law, "and if some abuses are still being reported, the occasionally serious but inevitable errors committed immediately after the liberation seem to be disappearing." Quoted because the harsher critics were later to stress the serious errors without taking account of the efforts of authorities on all levels to curb them.[10] (It is true that everything official was secret, so it would have been hard to find out what the authorities were thinking or doing.)

We can now find evidence that the liberation government very much wanted the internment camps to be above reproach. Serious attention was being paid to health, for example, and before the end of 1944 the Interior Minister had set up a monthly meeting at the Inspection Générale des Camps with representatives of the police, the Ministries of Food Supply, Public Health, Labor, and Social Welfare, the Quakers, and the Red Cross.[11] Instructions issued beginning in December 1944 demonstrate an effort to adhere to strict legality while reducing the discomfort of inmates—e.g., a directive dated December 28 recommends that the cases of interned minors be examined in priority. A note on February 3, 1945, warned that Commissioners of the Republic and prefects were misinterpreting the October 1944 decree on internment in that they were utilizing it as punishment. "There is, in my opinion, a regrettable confusion between administrative and judicial action," stated Interior Minister Tixier. It was for courts to punish; suspects were being interned for the danger they represented to national defense and public security.[12]

But of course the last word hadn't been said about the abuses. One of the most zealous critics of expeditious liberation justice was an eminent attorney who had taken part in the underground planning of postwar legislation: bar association president Jacques Charpentier. And now he had resumed his role as defender. Under his guidance the bar association attacked "mistakes whose impact ... wounds national feeling as well as that of all civilization," requesting a return to normal procedures with a guaranteed defense.[13]

In truth liberation justice was whatever the local powers wished to make of it. When the Provisional Government moved into liberated Paris its writ barely extended further than the capital itself, and nearby suburbs. (At least one high Justice Ministry official felt that a revolution was in progress, and that Paris had to reconquer the nation region by region.[14]) The very procedure for arrests had a revolutionary flavor; arresting officers might wear police or army uniforms—or none at all. Thus for a single district, the Ain, "because of the urgency of the matter" FFI security officers were authorized by the prefect to make arrests of collaborators, although the perfect requested that "to the extent possible" the arrests should actually be carried out by gendarmes and policemen (this on September 5, 1944). The FFI itself in that district issued a warning against arrests made by individual FFI members or groups; the FFI ordered that persons possessing evidence against suspects should not carry out their own justice, but rather should contact military security headquarters, which office would make the arrests through appropriate officials.[15]

Such documents dating from the immediate postliberation weeks are cited as evidence that from the point of view of the organized resistance, as of the Provisional Government, there was never any doubt about the need to respect legal procedures. Naturally critics of the purge were to stress the abuses, abuses which certainly took place but which can be blamed on inexperience, and on the lack of structure of resistance authority. The fact that anyone, at least at the beginning, could consider himself a resistance fighter and participate in acts of purging (among other things) contributed to the confusion. Without any doubt this made it possible for individuals seeking private vengeance to act in the name of the resistance; occasionally, if we believe the worst stories, it allowed collaborators to assume the protective coloration of resistance veterans.

Thus in the tracts and other polemical writings of those hostile to the purge we read that resistance people (genuine or fake) committed robberies, participated in drug running, betrayed other veterans, committed murder for personal gain. A Gestapo agent is said to have passed himself off as a resistance fighter; a woman wishing to get rid of her husband has him killed by a "partisan" who had earlier served in a German army auxiliary unit.[16] Writers often mention the menacing aspect of heavily armed resistance units, e.g., this from Bordeaux: "Automobiles crisscross the city filled with young men with iron helmets and boots, submachine gun or revolver in hand, wearing an armband showing a V and the [Gaullist] cross of Lorraine." And so disorder is inevitable: "The general staffs multiply, ignore and sometimes contradict each other. Armed groups carry out unauthorized searches. . . ."[17] Another theme: Many of the worst abuses were carried out by Spaniards who had come to France as refugees after Francisco Franco's takeover in 1939. "Their total absence of morality, their practices of cruelty and sadism, their savage customs," were blamed for a reign of terror in southwest France.[18]

It is clear that the new authorities were aware of the excesses, of the likelihood that there were going to be excesses, and that they took early measures to prevent them or to correct them. "Leave it to the Republic's justice to punish traitors," declared the Commissioner of the Republic for Normandy, Henri Bourdeau de Fontenay, in a proclamation dated August 26, 1944. "No one should become involved in individual reprisals."[19] In Paris at the end of August the FFI general staff warned that fake resistance men, wearing FFI armbands and badges, were carrying out acts against "public security and private property."[20]

For their part the Communists didn't try to conceal their conviction that popular justice had to supplement, or to supplant when necessary, official justice with its "exasperating delays." The venerable Communist chieftain Marcel Cachin used this term in a frontage editorial in the Party's daily *L'Humanité* a month after the liberation of Paris. He pointed to the summary executions of collaborators at the moment a village or town was liberated, the shearing of "miserable street women," as "a preliminary purge which was responsive to the needs of the public conscience." These acts were "a guarantee of order for the population, which could not have survived in contact with these rotten elements." Cachin warned that "the interminable procedures which are holding up the well-deserved punishment of traitors . . . stirs the legitimate indignation of all moral persons."[21]

This put the finger on a chief cause of the summary executions in the months following the return to republican government: the fear that a despised collaborator would escape punishment, or that he was being treated too gently. As the judicial purge got under way collaborators were to be abducted from the custody of the authorities to be assassinated, sometimes after sentencing. This was the case of one Gaston Vanucci, a member of the Militia and of the Waffen SS, a French contingent of the German army, sentenced to death on December 7, 1944, by a liberation Court of Justice. A resistance commando broke into the Rodez prison on January 3, 1945, and tried to kill him; he survived, but three other prisoners were killed. Next day the FFI men went to the hospital to finish off Vanucci but were prevented from doing so.[22] The Commissioner of the Republic for the Montpellier region, Jacques Bounin, in reporting events such as this one to Paris, warned how dangerous it was to commute death sentences. Should certain convicted persons be pardoned in one district in his jurisdiction (the Gard), he warned, he would find it difficult to maintain order.[23]

In his own memoirs Charles de Gaulle recalls the local pressures on the purge courts, the demands that defendants receive death sentences, the score of cases in which accused collaborators were abducted and murdered. De Gaulle asked his ministers to deal harshly with local officials unable to maintain order, and to indict persons actually performing such acts. "In the event that the trial of certain defendants, or the commutation of their death sentences, risks furnishing pretexts for local troubles, it is the duty of the Minister of Justice and, below him, of the district prosecutors to take or cause to be taken appropriate preventive measures so that the detention, trial, and execution of sentences occur in places and times which limit the risk of incidents to the minimum." This is a note to his ministers of justice, interior, and war on the next to the last day of 1944.[24]

The situation did not improve in the new year. Between January 1 and 15, 1945, the gendarmeries of France reported eleven summary executions, forty-two armed attacks or robberies, forty-five other attacks by bombing attributable to the liberation.[25] In the following fortnight there were forty-two executions, 122 armed attacks or robberies, 151 bombings. Some notable examples: In Gap twenty masked and armed men wearing uniforms remove twelve prisoners from a local internment camp, kill them, and throw their bodies into the Durance River. In the town of La Garenne-Colombes near Paris, police inspectors and members of the local liberation committee kill a lieutenant in the Waffen SS, a Frenchman who had been parachuted back into France by the Germans. In the Oise a man and his wife suspected of collaboration are killed by a police commissioner and two security police inspectors (they are arrested). In the Cher a woman known to have collaborated is shot and killed while sitting at her window. In the Dordogne a gamekeeper recently released from internment is shot and killed at home. In Grenoble a businessman is shot and killed at home (his killers are arrested).[26] The next monthly report covered 14 summary executions, 121 armed attacks, 213 bombings. An ex-commissioner of police is abducted from jail in Dijon by a mob, and hanged; a prisoner is killed during transfer from a Court of Justice to jail in Pau; a former police inspector is killed by masked men inside a Finistère internment camp; a former police officer is abducted from jail in Annecy, later found in a riverbed.[27]

Attacks against collaborators on the grounds that they had escaped adequate punishment were to continue through that first year of liberated France. In early June 1945 at the Cusset prison near Vichy, a crowd estimated at three to four hundred persons broke in to take custody of a French agent of the Gestapo who had been sentenced to death in absentia; he had been arrested on his return from Germany. The victim was hung by his feet to a telegraph pole until he could be cut down and returned to his cell. The crowd then got hold of the French Gestapo chief for Vichy, beat him up in front of the deputy prefect, who was powerless to intervene (he himself was struck while trying to protect the prisoner). The avengers then went on to the Cusset hospital, took custody of a Militia chief and strung him up by his feet; he was dead before he could be cut down. The rioters then returned to the prison and again removed the French Gestapo agent. By then Commissioner Henry Ingrand was on the scene. He discovered that the police were unwilling to move against the mob, but his own prestige as chief of the regional resistance saved the situation, and the victim. But Ingrand warned the Interior Ministry that the return of French deportees from Germany, with the stories they were telling of ill treatment, had heightened tensions once again.[28]

For the liberation of the previous summer had been followed by a second liberation, that of the prisoners in Nazi concentration camps. Often these French men and women had been taken away by the Germans as a result of denunciations by fellow Frenchmen, and some of the latter remained unpunished. Now with the collapse of Nazi Germany in the spring of 1945 it was going to be possible to track down collaborators who had fled to Germany on the coattails of the occupation army; it was also going to be possible to seize enemy records which identified Germany's French helpers. François Mauriac in a *Le Figaro* editorial regretted that the "promise of appeasement" had evaporated. He had long since become an advocate of playing down the purge in the interests of "French unity." But he understood why new tensions had developed: "The allied advance into Germany has suddenly become a descent into hell." Now one could see and hear witnesses "of the cruelest and most comprehensive attack ever made on human dignity. . . . All resentments have been awakened or aggravated against those Frenchmen who collaborated with the authors and the accomplices of these crimes, and who favored their victory."[29]

FIVE

Attitudes

IN THE FIRST WEEKS OF liberation a poll taken by the French Institute of Public Opinion determined that 42 percent of Frenchmen approved the execution of Vichy Minister Pierre Pucheu in Algiers the previous March. Eighteen percent disapproved; 40 percent had no opinion, which many confessed was due to lack of information. "Should Marshal Pétain be punished?" At the time Pétain was in German hands, in the castle of Sigmaringen. Yes, said 32 percent; no, said 58 percent. Of those replying affirmatively only 3 percent (of all persons interrogated) desired a death sentence for the old man, another 9 percent preferring a moral sanction. But to the question "Was it right to arrest Sacha Guitry?" an overwhelming 56 percent agreed that the actor-dramatist should be detained; only 12 percent said no, and 32 percent had no opinion.[1] Yet only a month later 65 percent of those questioned favored a death sentence for Pierre Laval (then also at Sigmaringen), compared to only 3 percent who asked for death for Pétain. For Jacques Doriot, the well-known accomplice of the Nazis, 75 percent of the sampling desired death; only 2 percent had no particular feelings about his case.[2]

It was certain that the rank and file of resistance veterans, often spoken for by local committees of liberation, wanted to see the rascals punished, and quickly. In a resolution presented by the Communist purge expert Auguste Gillot, and voted at the national assembly of Comités Départementaux de Libération held in Paris in December 1944 under the sponsorship of the Conseil National de la Résistance, the delegates declared themselves "unanimously determined in the name of public opinion to protest the considerable and inacceptable slowness of military and civil justice in punishing the traitors. . . ." The resolution asked the Provisional Government to strike "high, swiftly, and justly." Not against the small farmer who made the mistake of selling a dozen eggs to the Germans but against "the leaders of the trusts . . . chiefs of the army and navy . . . politicians who compromised with the enemy," as well as against leading figures of the press, radio, film industry, publishing, literature.[3]

But there was no anarchy, no popular uprising. Despite the seemingly large number of incidents reported, a relatively small percentage of collaborators fell victim to vigilante justice (considering the large number of real or accused collaborators who might have become targets of such action). The purge became a matter for law courts, governmental commissions. From the instant of liberation, and in region after region as the enemy vanished, Gaullist authority prevailed. Charles de Gaulle himself, supported by his cabinet and a network of "delegates" both civil and military who accompanied Allied troops in their sweep, made sure that Gaullist authority prevailed.[4] "At the moment I arrived in Paris on August 25, 1944, I was handed a communication from a representative of Marshal Pétain," de Gaulle was to reveal to the Consultative Assembly in March 1945. Pétain's man wished to discuss "a way to avoid civil war." De Gaulle told the Assembly: "I showed the representative to the door. Gentlemen, where is the civil war?"[5]

Earlier, during a tour of Normandy in October 1944, the head of the Provisional Government had appealed for some indulgence toward collaborators—in the interests of winning the war. "France needs all its children, even if at times some of them made mistakes," he declared.[6] A few days later in a radio speech de Gaulle spelled out his concern for orderly justice, demanding "that all improvisations of authority cease absolutely." He criticized the uncoordinated activities of resistance groups, and the auxiliary police inspired by the Communists which was operating as a Patriotic Militia: "The right to command armed forces of any kind belongs exclusively to chiefs appointed by the appropriate cabinet officers."[7]

There is evidence that as the Provisional Government became entrenched in the farthest provinces, de Gaulle's concern over abuses of authority grew, and he did not intend to tolerate them. Some of the evidence comes to us in the diary of his private secretary, François Mauriac's son Claude. According to the younger

Mauriac, after the trial of a group of collaborators in Maubeuge, when the FFI sought to influence de Gaulle's decision on commuting the death penalties, de Gaulle responded to the pressure by deciding in favor of commutation. The resistance retaliated: Two of the three convicted collaborators who had escaped the death penalty were lynched. De Gaulle then fired back, by banning the Patriotic Militia.[8]

For its part, the Consultative Assembly early in 1945 refused to vote the budget of the Ministry of Justice, and tried to eliminate Minister de Menthon's salary, on the grounds that the purge was a failure. In the name of the resistance group Mouvement de Libération Nationale, Pascal Copeau asked the Assembly ironically whether François Mauriac, with his doctrine of mercy, was now a government spokesman. Replied François de Menthon: "Tomorrow, when one looks back on the way the purge was carried out in France, we won't have to blush."[9]

Certainly there seemed to be a meeting of minds between de Gaulle and his justice ministers, François de Menthon, later Pierre-Henri Teitgen. De Gaulle had confidence in the judgment of these Christian Democrats new to party politics. Eventually de Gaulle would replace de Menthon with Teitgen, for the former lacked the skills needed to handle the often turbulent parliament, and Teitgen had proved himself under fire as Information Minister. Privately Teitgen felt himself to be the carbon copy of the Minister he was replacing; he had been close to de Menthon for many years. The two men had followed identical careers: they were professors together in Nancy, where together they had founded a law journal; they had served in the same regiment at the outbreak of war, had escaped prisoner-of-war camp almost at the same time; together they created the Liberté resistance movement, and worked together in the underground planning group, the General Committee of Studies. And later they were to be among the founders of the left-of-center Catholic Mouvement Républicain Populaire.[10]

In fact the return to law and order as most people understood it (orders from above, respected below) received considerable help from the French Communist Party. At the liberation, when the Party had its own secret army, there had been concern about what that very effective force would be used for. Would the Communists take advantage of the vacuum created by the departure of the Germans, the collapse of Vichy, the uncertain strength of the Gaullists, to mount an insurrection of their own, the revolutionary coup which was after all central to Leninist ideology? They did not take advantage, and we know now that Communist global strategy as defined by the leaders of the Soviet Union did not intend that they do so. In an episode which deserves fuller treatment than we can give it here, Charles de Gaulle traveled to Moscow to talk to Joseph Stalin, and there accepted the return to France of the French Communist leader Maurice Thorez (whose departure at the beginning of the war was considered desertion). At least while the war against Germany was unfinished, the Communists were betting on Gaullist France. For his part, and as early as Algiers, de Gaulle had brought Communists into his government, convinced that he could control them.[11]

All this helps to explain why Maurice Thorez, at a meeting of the central committee of his party in January 1945, withdrew Communist support of the Patriotic Militia—which rank-and-file Communists had wished to maintain as a people's police force operating against suspected collaborators. Thorez also made it clear that local committees of liberation should assist the government—and not attempt to act in its place.[12] Later Justice Minister de Menthon was to say that if Communists at the base sometimes appeared be "hardliners" of the purge, the Party itself had contributed to "the return to civil peace."[13]

This change in the attitude of the Communists was apparent in Paris, where at the time of the Allied landings in Normandy the Party-controlled Comité Parisien de Libération had ordered its local sections to "do away with notoriously dangerous individuals."[14] But after the liberation the same group made it clear that the right of arrest belonged to the Prefecture of Police; its role was to help out.[15] In the far-off Haute-Vienne district, Jean Chaintron, who was at the same time a member of the Communist Party's Central Committee and the government's prefect, proved in his daily acts that he too was on the side of the Republic. "There is no question, as some political adventurers would like, to undertake fundamental transformations or to carry out party programs," he told his district in a radio broadcast on January 29, 1945 (a week after Thorez spoke to the Central Committee); the present task was "to mobilize all national resources . . . to annihilate Hitler Fascism." In the same radio talk he asked for indulgence for minor collaborators; such people could even be used in the war effort.[16] Nearly a year after the liberation this Communist prefect was still denouncing abusive purging. He attacked "the authors of attacks who, throughout France, operate under the cover of the purge or for other 'good reasons.' ..." They were, he said, "enemies of the people's cause. They tarnish the memory of our heroes who fell in battle and discredit the resistance."[17]

Myths die hard. The one that tells us that Communists can be blamed for most of the excesses of the liberation is one of them. Actually the Communists were the best organized of all resistance fighters, the least willing or able to transgress directives from their leaders.

Indeed, there is ample evidence that the new government was having at least as much trouble with those institutions of its own making, the Regional Commissioners of the Republic, the Comités Départementaux de Libération. At the end of 1944 Adrien Tixier, who replaced Emmanuel d'Astier as Interior Minister, brought this matter into the open. The autonomy of the Commissioners and of the committees with respect to the central government was an abnormal situation which could lead to regional autonomy.[18] It is not unlikely that the government was suffering the consequences of the wide-open language of the decrees and instructions produced by Tixier's predecessor, left-leaning d'Astier. De Gaulle himself wished the district committees to be limited to a consultative role, while as a resistance chief d'Astier wished the mainland to have a real voice. De Gaulle's conviction grew even stronger when it became apparent that many of the district committees were overloaded with Communists.[19] And of course the committees were involved in the purge, often exercising police powers; it was a job which the Conseil National de la Résistance had given them during the "insurrectional period," and which some were reluctant to give up.[20] Thus the CDL in the Alpes-Maritimes not only sponsored a purge commission but a purge police composed of FFI men. The commission met nearly every day over a period of five months, seven hours each day, examining 2,550 cases in all, provoking controversy with demands for the arrest of local dignitaries and confiscation of private companies.[21]

The purge was too slow for some, while others decided very early in the postwar that it was time to put an end to the era of suspicion and vengeance (so the gendarmeries of France reported to headquarters early in 1945).[22] The bishops of France appealed for a reduction of tensions: "Let us do away definitively with the spirit of denunciation, suspicion, and vengeance; they are not our way of doing things," read their declaration of February 28, 1945. "Let us put an end to exaggerated or unjust accusations against our brothers."[23] (The corps of bishops was itself undergoing a discreet purge at the time, as we shall see.)

III

A REGION

"Implacable justice, but justice all the same."

—Yves Farge, speech of
September 23, 1944

ONE

Capital of the Resistance

A PREWAR GUIDEBOOK PROVIDES this capsule description: "Lyon, 570,622 inhabitants, capital of Rhône district, seat of an archdiocese, of a regional military governor, of a court of appeals and a renowned university, major industrial center . . ."[1] Lyon was liberated after Paris. For if the Anglo-American armies established their Normandy beachheads in early June, they landed on France's south coast only in mid-August (by which time the Germans were ready to withdraw). The Mediterranean attacking force had soon taken key cities such as Marseille and Toulon, reaching the Lyon region at the beginning of September. Southeast France had been a center of resistance. With varying degrees of effectiveness, but certainly with courage, poorly armed, insufficiently trained partisans took part in the liberation, just as they had in the harassment of the Germans and their French helpers in the preceding months. German troops in that region were certainly not Hitler's best, but they had to be captured or killed or driven out, and the regional resistance was very much part of this effort.

In the south zone—that nominally controlled by the Vichy regime in the first two years of German occupation—Lyon had become known as the "capital" of the resistance.[2] It was a metropolis, large enough to favor the development of structured resistance movements, an underground press. Lyon was not very far from hilly, even mountainous regions propitious to partisan operations; the city was capital of "R. 1," the resistance theater of operations which included the French Alps. Although the resistance had a cen-

101

tral command it was in fact composed of groups of varying origins and strengths, of clashing political coloration and obedience. The lack of organization, combined with the uncertain battle lines, created conditions of anarchy at some times and places, and they would remain in the collective memory.[3]

A report in the files of the Interior Ministry describes the situation in Lyon after the liberation of that city on September 3. Two rivers flow through the city, and all its bridges were blown up during the German withdrawal. The peninsula on which the city center lies lacked gas and telephones; government offices located there had been moved across the Rhône so as to remain in communication with the rest of the district, and the world beyond. There were conflicts between the central authority and local resistance units, and notably with the committees of liberation which were seeking to impose their own decisions. Searches had in some cases been accompanied by looting, outright theft; in many cases the guilty were fake resistance men wearing FFI armbands, "to satisfy personal vengeance or to carry out acts of depredation."[4] Lyon continued to suffer the consequences of the war still raging through the following winter. Food was scarce; distribution of supplies continued to be slowed by inadequate communications.[5]

What Lyon, and "R. 1"—the Rhône-Alpes region consisting of eight administrative districts—had as its principal asset at that moment was an extraordinary Commissioner of the Republic, Yves Farge. An anonymous inspector for the Interior Ministry described Farge then as "a first-class individual with a deep feeling for the State, a remarkable organizer, and who has the complete confidence of the working class; an excellent speaker besides, he can create contact with mass opinion and get it to accept his point of view."[6] A Socialist before the war, Farge had worked for Lyon's daily *Le Progrès,* which during the occupation had been a center of resistance. He himself had played an active role in the development of the region's resistance to the Germans and Vichy; later, in the postwar decade, he would also play an active role in Communist front activities such as the world peace movement. He died in an accident in the Soviet Union in 1953, at the age of fifty-three.[7]

Farge was a southern Frenchman, born in Salon-de-Provence. One of his Communist resistance contacts described him as "merry, enjoying whimsy and practical jokes ... at times imprudent ... profoundly loyal and honest."[8] A resistance planner who can't be accused of sympathy for left-wingers, Michel Debré, was later to pay singular tribute to Farge. Debré had ratified the choice of Farge as Commissioner of the Republic for the Rhône-Alpes region. He admired Farge's reputed audacity, remembering how Farge had moved about occupied France with false identity papers bearing a Jewish name (Lévy). Although Farge's "romantic enthusiasm" both pleased and worried the austere young jurist Debré was, his courage and generosity won over whatever reticence he may have felt.[9]

It was back in April 1944, in a café near the Place du Trocadéro in German-occupied Paris, that Debré handed Farge a note informing him that he was henceforth Commissioner of the Republic. His jurisdiction consisted of the Rhône district, with 1 million inhabitants, the Loire (650,000), Isère (572,000, with Grenoble), Ain (300,000), Ardèche (272,000), Drôme (267,000), Haute-Savoie (259,000), Savoie (239,000).[10] The mission of this proconsul would commence not at the liberation but right then and there. For he was to shuttle back and forth between Paris and Lyon to organize the post-liberation prefectures, provide assistance to the partisans, plan the economic reorganization of his region; his immediate instruments were the underground Comités Départementaux de Libération.[11] He was to spend much of his time in the field, and from D-Day on he was in a position to govern patches of liberated territory in the name of Free France. (On June 6 part of the Drôme was declared liberated in Farge's presence, and he was prepared to replace Vichy officials on all levels down to local judges, and to supervise the movement of food and other essential supplies to the district.)[12]

Farge was in Lyon for its liberation, observing the German destruction of bridges on September 2, the arrival of the FFI—greeted by flag-decorated facades. A witness who accompanied Farge to the prefecture remembered that he and another resistance man insisted that Farge sit between them in the back of the car for his protection. Inside the prefecture they walked around trying doors, for none of them had been inside the building before; when they found the office of the prefect Farge sat behind the large desk. "What do I do now?" he asked. "You can begin by giving me a pass," one of his escorts replied. Farge signed it with his pseudonym, "Gregoire."[13]

A proclamation was ready. Posted on the walls of Lyon and in towns throughout the eight districts of the Rhône-Alpes jurisdiction, it contained both a warning and an appeal:

Your duty is to act in such a way that History will record that in this hour of deliverance, Law and Justice were inseparable from Freedom.

Military tribunals will deal with traitors. All those who served the enemy; all those who killed, deported, robbed the people of France; all those who, by denunciation, contributed to the martyrdom of the nation, will be called to account for their deeds.

But let us avoid premature judgments, mistakes caused by passion. Let us not forget, for example, that in their great majority France's civil servants carried out their duty, and that they often had to conceal their true feelings in order to serve.

I shall allow no obstacle to interfere with the carrying out of Justice, but I shall also see to it that no individual act troubles its serenity.[14]

In his first press conference Farge declared that he would focus attention on profiteers, on those "who grew scandalously rich in collaborating with the enemy."[15] He announced the arrest of Charles Maurras of Action Française, of the Vichy regime police chief René Cussonac, and of the head of the local industrial dynasty, truck manufacturer Marius Berliet. He closed down the local bar association and the Chamber of Commerce.[16]

In his public statements Farge showed himself to be a moderate. "There is a government," he declared to an interviewer in the daily organ of the Mouvement de Libération Nationale. "It governs through the intermediary of the Commissioners of the Republic and the prefects. It is firmly determined not to allow the development of the slightest ambiguity, the slightest sign of anarchy." He concluded: "The insurrection is over. The Republic begins."[17] In a speech on September 23 he made it clear that from then on only the established authorities could make arrests; only regularly organized courts could render justice. "Implacable justice, but justice all the same." He regretted that "it has become banal ... to kill a man," and objected to the use of brutality in interrogating suspects. Because it was likely that the crowded local prisons held some innocent persons, a law officer had been assigned to review individual cases. Farge appealed to partisans to behave like a disciplined army, to avoid excesses which might alienate them from the people from whom they derived. To the population at large he said: "If you find a Militiaman, turn him over to the regular authorities." "No more anonymous letters [of denunciation]." He attacked the practice of levying fines on profiteers and then not turning the money over to the public treasury. "Justice is rendered by judges."[18]

Addressing a crowd estimated at twenty thousand persons on Lyon's vast Place Bellecour on Sunday, October 15, Farge assured his flock that their Commissioner had the purge in hand. He spoke of the dismissal and arrest of high court officers, the shutting down of newspapers. In a month a thousand policemen had been investigated, four hundred of them dismissed, suspended, or arrested. An auxiliary police force had been disbanded. He stressed the point that court martial judges should use their real names: If the purge was to proceed on the basis of trials which no one could contest, "it is necessary for each of us to assume his identity. . . . When he ordered heads to fall, Robespierre didn't call himself Arthur."

He complained that some people wished to jail anyone connected in any way with the Vichy regime. But the point was to punish real traitors, and there were certainly enough of them among Gestapo agents, Militiamen, journalists and writers, business leaders, without adding innocent persons to the list. There were too many temporary policemen running around, upsetting people. He told how he had been stopped six times in the Haute-Savoie by armed men looking for someone else, a seventh time on the way back from Saint-Etienne. He was using FFI military police to track down persons misusing resistance credentials; he asked his Lyon audience to help put a stop to the activities of the "September resistance" (*les résistants de septembre:* He called them the RDS)—those who had joined up *after* the liberation. And he offered his listeners "some principles of elementary honesty":

> Wrong opinions are never punishable. . . .
> A suspect is not necessarily guilty. . . .
> The purge must have limits, both in time and in its very concept. Otherwise, "a pure man always finds a purer man to purify him."[19]

TWO

Punishment
in Lyon

OPERATING FROM the underground, although utilizing his title and even a letterhead of the Provisional Government, on August 12, 1944, Commissioner of the Republic Yves Farge wrote the presidents of the Comités de Libération of the eight administrative districts within his jurisdiction, relaying directives received from the Conseil National de la Résistance and its liaison officers attached to the Commissariat of the Interior. One of these directives concerned courts martial. Wherever people's tribunals or other extralegal courts had been created they must be disbanded. But "it is absolutely necessary that each district have its own military tribunal or court martial," when possible presided over by a regular judge assisted by two officers from the FFI or another resistance movement. It was also important that each such court include one or more investigative officers.[1]

As soon as he arrived at his desk in liberated Lyon on September 3 Farge signed a decree authorizing courts martial, courts that would respect the code of military justice, although because of circumstances the number of judges would be limited to three—and anyone would be eligible to serve. But only the Commissioner of the Republic was qualified to refer defendants to these courts; sentences were without appeal and enforceable. If the accused party had no lawyer the court could appoint one.[2] A subsequent decree set up a court martial for the Rhône district (whose capital Lyon was), headed by General Paul-André Doyen, a native of the region with impeccable resistance credentials.[3]

In his own memoir of that troubled time Farge remembers the very first session of his court martial, held on September 10 in a small room in Lyon's Saint-Paul prison; he tells us that General Doyen had specifically asked to be allowed to preside. Farge observed that the defendant, Charles Dagostini, "no longer had a recognizable face; the brute had been disfigured by blows." To questions Dagostini admitted having been a member of the Légion Tricolore, a French contingent of the German army. He had then been a leader of the Militia, and had participated in an attack against the Haute-Savoie resistance on the plateau of Glières above Lake Annecy. When Dagostini offered an explanation of his behavior General Doyen replied: "The facts are there. I am from Thônes [on Lake Annecy] and I know that there is a graveyard containing seventy Frenchmen below the plateau." Dagostini confessed to action against other groups of partisans. But when accused of having "tortured Frenchmen" he replied: "I am a Frenchman." "You can't call yourself French," one of the resistance judges replied, "because you wore a German uniform." The prosecution called for the death penalty; after a defense attorney pleaded for Dagostini the court ordered his execution for "high treason." He was shot the following morning.[4]

No official record of these courts martial has been found. If ever they are, the likelihood is that they will provide only the barest of procedural reports. Here, as for so many other purge-era trials, the best source is the daily press—not necessarily always accurate or evenhanded. Furthermore, material shortages often reduced papers to a single sheet; emergency conditions, the probable use of nonprofessionals on some newspapers born of the resistance, resulted in inadequate reporting. But it is still all that we have.

After the first session of Lyon's court martial, proceedings were transferred from Saint-Paul to the fortress prison of Montluc. Alerted by the press, spectators began filling up the courtroom hours in advance of the session on September 15.[5] For this day we have the recollections of a young attorney with no previous experience in criminal law, assigned by the head of the local bar association with two other attorneys to the defense of court martial defendants. After obtaining a pass to allow him to cross the only bridge open across the Rhône—an indication of the difficulties still being faced in the city—attorney Jean Bernard and his colleagues made their way to Montluc and introduced themselves to the chief magistrate, whom they discovered to be a resistance leader with no previous judicial experience. They were told that they were present only for the sake of appearances, because those on trial were going to be convicted and executed in any case. "There are five in the dock," lawyer Bernard remembered the chief magistrate telling them, "and tonight there will be five at the stake." The lawyers protested this way of looking at things, and asked permission to talk to their clients; they were given half an hour with each. When they entered the prison, located near the military tribunal where the court martial was to sit, they noticed five coffins and a group of police troopers whom Bernard assumed would make up the firing squad. He also observed that a number of the prisoners were obvious victims of mistreatment.

Each file on a defendant contained only two or three typed pages, with no supporting evidence. The young lawyer found that one of the prisoners he had been asked to defend had been a simple employee of the Militia, an orderly who did routine errands. (As the daily organ of the Mouvement de Libération Nationale was to describe the man's job: "Orderly in the service of intelligence and interrogation . . . he observed impassively the tortures inflicted by the Militiamen.") The chief magistrate commented that "if we believe the defendants' testimony, the Militia consisted only of orderlies."[6] Lawyer Bernard's other client was a veteran labor organizer who had become district leader of the pro-Fascist Rassemblement National Populaire. The defense attorney was able to show that his collaboration had been nominal, and that back in the 1930s he had been among those responsible for improving the condition of the working class. Bernard's orderly was sentenced to death, with no extenuating circumstances, but the old union man got only five years of prison, which his lawyer felt was a true victory in that time and place.

The room was packed, and some spectators had even climbed to the top of the swinging doors to be able to see. Some members of the public kept their hats on even when the judges entered the chamber; it reminded the young lawyer of the French Revolution and its tribunal. He also observed that the stenographer was taking down the remarks of the lawyers as if planning to utilize them to their prejudice; at the intervention of the bar association president this practice was to be abandoned. (After the trial a group of resistance men actually showed up at the defense attorney's home to arrest him for having defended a Militiaman, but he happened to be away at the time.[7]) Of that day's five cases, three ended with death sentences. One of those sentenced to death was a woman with four previous criminal convictions who associated with Militiamen and Gestapo agents, accused of denouncing a family for alleged resistance activity; the other defendant sent before a firing squad had been in charge of Militia interrogations.[8] Reporting the questioning of the woman defendant, the Communist Party's local daily noted: "The public, which was already hostile, manifested its disgust despite threats of expulsion. The supreme penalty for high treason was greeted with satisfaction."[9]

Since his Militia defendant had been sentenced to death lawyer Bernard sought a means to appeal, and was told that only Commissioner Yves Farge could commute a sentence. Bernard was given a ride to the prefecture, where he remembered Farge telling him: "I can't pardon your client. We must have blood—General de Gaulle said so."[10] In his own memoir Farge describes the pardon process: "We had to make decisions overnight, so fragile was the membrane which protected our judicial embryo." He had never confronted a more challenging responsibility. After obtaining staff advice he paced his office, pondering the files on his desk, at times interrupted by a dawn telephone call from a lawyer. Farge felt that these courts martial preserved order, helping to avoid personal vengeance. "Our sentences proclaimed each evening armed those of us who wished to restore the idea of justice." It was the time when every French town was discovering mass graves of victims of the occupation, when the details of torture and murder were becoming known. Now justice had to be seen to be done.[11]

So there was nothing for attorney Jean Bernard to do but to return to Montluc to hear mass with his client, and then to be present at the execution of this man and of the two other prisoners sentenced to death the previous day. The young police officer told his men to do it cleanly, and he was obeyed.[12]

Meanwhile the Provisional Government was taking the country in hand. In dispatches of September 19 and 21 Justice Minister François de Menthon ordered the immediate suspension of courts martial. But Farge protested to Interior Minister Emmanuel d'Astier (on September 25) that these courts were dealing with odious crimes which required severe punishment. Should the court martial be abolished, warned Farge, not only would public opinion react, but there would be a return to summary executions, abductions from prison—disorders which these courts martial had managed to stop. The new Courts of Justice hadn't begun to operate, and when they did begin they would necessarily move slowly because of the jury system.[13]

On September 20 the court martial held its third session. The star attraction was the young niece of a Third Republic cabinet minister. Tall, slim, elegant (said the press), she had been the mistress of Charles Dagostini (tried and shot, as we have seen, at the first session of Lyon's court martial). She had also been Dagostini's secretary, and was accused of taking part in Militia missions, although at her trial she claimed to have exaggerated the strength of the partisans in her reporting, in order to frighten the Militia. Her attorney, in what the local Communist daily described as a "brilliant plea," argued her youth (she was twenty-two) and her failure to realize what she was involved in. The prosecutor replied: "If she failed to realize it, all members of the Militia failed." She was sentenced to death. Two French interpreters for the Gestapo were tried next. One of them, captured with money and objects of value obtained during raids, received a death sentence, the other ten years of prison. A couple who had given the Gestapo a minor piece of intelligence, out of vengeance, received lighter sentences: five years for the husband, one for the wife. Farge rejected the appeals, and so Dagostini's mistress and the Gestapo agent were shot the following morning at sunrise.[14]

In all, between September 10 and October 5, the Lyon court martial pronounced 44 sentences, 28 to death (of which 26 were executed and 2 commuted), 7 to hard labor, 8 to prison, and there was 1 acquittal.[15] And in a report to Paris, Farge provided statistics on the work of the courts martial in the other districts within his region: Ain, 5; Ardèche, none; Drôme, 64; Isère, 52; Loire, 37; Savoie, 11; Haute-Savoie, 101.[16]

But if the court martial had been closed down, the Court of Justice conceived by the Free French planners as the chief instrument of liberation punishment was not yet ready to function. So on October 6, 1944, the day after the final session of the court martial, the Military Tribunal of Lyon replaced it. It met from that date until October 26, making use of the same Montluc courtroom; the procedure was essentially the same, although now the right to commute death sentences was back in the hands of the chief of state. Again the defendants came from the ranks of the Militia, or they were French agents of the Gestapo accused of torture, murder. At the opening session on October 6 two defendants were sentenced to death.[17] Even after the Court of Justice began to function this military tribunal continued to try crimes within its competence under the traditional interpretation of military law; by the end of the year it had sentenced 159 defendants in the Rhône.[18]

In the view of liberation authorities no citizen would take the law into his own hands if the purge was seen to be effective. But for this to be seen, justice also had to be rapid, and that was going to be less and less possible when ad hoc courts gave way to the more orthodox Courts of Justice. Even during the weeks of courts martial, of military courts, there was public pressure for speedier trials and executions. Yves Farge would be alerted by his prefects that crowds were gathering outside a local prison, demanding that justice be done.[19]

The Court of Justice was at last opened in Farge's capital on October 26, 1944. By November 15, the Commissioner noted with alarm, it had fourteen hundred important cases in front of it. He feared that the bottleneck would lead to grave incidents.[20] By February 1 the Rhône district Court of Justice had heard only forty-two cases (in forty-two sittings); it had issued four death sentences, only one of which had been executed.[21]

Grave incidents of the sort Farge had anticipated did occur. The Lyon court sentenced Vichy's regional prefect Alexandre Angeli to death, and the appeal for commutation had gone up to Paris; meanwhile another prominent prisoner, police chief René Cussonac, had also been sentenced to death. Then the appeals panel overturned Angeli's conviction, and there was a rumor Cussonac would not be executed either. Shouting "Angeli to the stake!" a crowd gathered outside Saint-Paul prison, broke in, and seized both Angeli and Cussonac. When Farge and his men arrived they found the regional prefect bloody-faced. The Commissioner argued with the armed vigilantes for over an hour while one of his men protected Cussonac with his own body, shouting: "He will be executed in the form called for by law." In the fray a number of FFI security police were hurt; before the evening was over Farge found himself astride a bed on which Angeli was lying, as his aides appealed to the mob. The demonstrators agreed to withdraw if they could take another prisoner with them—a convicted Gestapo agent; Farge refused. The

Commissioner won. Cussonac was executed according to law a few days after that, while Angeli was moved to Paris for a new trial.[22]

Commutations of sentence had to be handled as secrets of state from then on. When President de Gaulle commuted the death sentence of another Lyon prisoner the Interior Minister advised Farge: "I beg you to take the necessary measures to avoid any incident." Farge accordingly requested that Lyon's prosecutor provide for the security of the beneficiary of the pardon—and also asked that the very fact that the sentence had been commuted be kept secret until this was achieved. This became a regular procedure in the Rhône-Alpes region.[23]

THREE

Around Annecy

ONE OF THE administrative districts in Yves Farge's jurisdiction, the Haute-Savoie, is a land of forests and mountains, of the Mont Blanc peak and Alpine boundaries with Switzerland and Italy. During the German occupation it was an ideal place for young men to hide. The presence of partisans, whose ranks were inflated by persons seeking to avoid compulsory labor service in Germany, made the district a favorite hunting ground for Vichy's Militia and other occupation police forces. Even before the Allied landings in Normandy set off a signal for increased belligerency on the part of the resistance, the Haute-Savoie was a battlefield. Reports of Vichy's prefect were filled with accounts of partisan action: dozens of incidents in a single month ranging from assassination and abduction to sabotage, robberies, bomb attacks. In one such confidential report destined only for the Vichy leadership, the prefect described his district as "in a perpetual state of agitation."[1]

How many summary executions were carried out by the Haute-Savoie resistance? The best available figure is 316, among which 63 victims were women. There were 71 in 1943, 113 in 1944 before D-Day, another 95 between D-Day and the liberation of the district in August, and 37 after that. The total number of assassinations before the liberation (279) has been compared to the number of enemy dead—237 Germans, 4 Italians—but also to the number of resistance men executed or killed in combat in the same district: 433. According to the local historian who compiled this information, the most notable victims of resistance executions were the district Mili-

113

tia chief, 2 gendarmerie captains, 4 police commissioners, 13 police inspectors.[2]

In a report to "Alban"—Auguste Vistel, regional FFI chief—on the day following the liberation of Annecy, the head of the district's Comité Départemental de Libération described the insurrection which had taken place in the Haute-Savoie on order of General Marie Pierre Koenig, national commander of the FFI. On August 11 and 12 the main roads had been blocked, railroad lines cut off. Starting on the thirteenth, FFI men attacked the smaller German outposts; next day, a general offensive was ordered by "Nizier" (code name for Joseph Lambroschini, FFI chief for the Haute-Savoie) and "Ostier" (Georges Guidollet, president of the Comité Départemental de Libération). On August 17 attacks were launched against Thonon, Evian, Le Fayet, Chamonix; after heavy fighting the Germans in each of these towns surrendered. Cluses, Annemasse, fell on the eighteenth; Annecy was surrounded, its garrison yielding without a fight on August 19. The CDL, through the FFI, took power in the district capital, Annecy; with power came responsibility for maintaining order. "Some violations of legality were committed," reported Ostier, "inevitable in the unleashing of public excitement." But all necessary steps were being taken to restore order.[3]

This district was the first in the region to free itself.[4] The events up on the Glières plateau already mentioned help explain not only the intensity of the liberation fighting but the rigor of the repression to follow. On one of the heights above Lake Annecy which can be seen from the town itself, hundreds of partisans had assembled in January 1944—perhaps imprudently, but with the knowledge and assistance of the resistance command and Allied liaison agents. In February the Vichy police, with German ground and air support, moved to clean them out. The final attack on Glières had the help of an Alpine division of the German army. Of nearly 500 partisans based on the plateau when the assault was launched, perhaps 155 were killed during the fighting, another 30 disappeared, and 160 were taken prisoner (executed almost immediately, or imprisoned after brutal treatment).[5]

When Yves Farge learned that the Germans had been murdering prisoners at Lyon's Montluc fortress prison he warned the German command through the Red Cross that the FFI held 752 German soldiers in the Haute-Savoie, and that henceforth they were hostages. Hearing that the Germans had gone ahead with the execution of 80 additional French prisoners, Farge ordered the Haute-Savoie resistance to shoot 80 Germans. This was done. On August 23 a poster went up in liberated Annecy signed by the FFI commander (Nizier) and the president of the CDL (Ostier), announcing these executions. The same day Vichy's prefect in Lyon made it known that the keys to Montluc prison were Farge's if he wanted them. Lyon, as we know, was still ten days away from its own liberation.[6]

The surrender of Annecy's German garrison to FFI commander Nizier was the signal for flags to fly, as resistance troops marched into the Haute-Savoie capital. Enemy strongholds were occupied one after the other; the remnant of the German garrison, Vichy auxiliaries, were taken into custody. According to plan, the Comité Départemental de Libération took over the prefecture, arresting Vichy Prefect Charles Marion in the process.[7] Photographs have been published showing the partisans wearing berets or military caps (or nothing at all) on their heads, with open shirts, rounds of ammunition around their belts, parading among a joyous population. "Everywhere chanting, laughter, songs, dancing."[8] There are also some grimmer photographs showing women with shaved heads.[9]

In taking charge in Annecy, a lakeside resort with a prewar population of under twenty-five thousand, the FFI obtained not only the surrender of the local German garrison, but that of a Militia unit in the bargain. These were Frenchmen, volunteer members of the despised paramilitary corps whose chief mission was to track down dissidents. They had a reputation for ferocity. Those taken prisoner in Annecy were to be tried in the most spectacular of all postliberation courts martial, and then executed in the largest mass shooting. The event has been recalled in the recollections of those hostile to the purge as a St. Bartholomew's Day massacre, punctuated with the last cries of the young Militiamen: "Long live France!" "Long live the Marshal!" "Long live Christ the King!" The victims have been presented as apprentices of a Militia training school who had not yet participated in combat. We are told, in these hostile accounts, that even the people of the village where the court martial took place were terrorized, and "barely controlled their indignation." Before being shot, it is alleged, the prisoners were "savagely ill treated"; later the Communists were said to have built a bonfire with the wooden crosses put up over the graves by families of the condemned men.[10]

As usual, a tense moment has been described only by those taking the side of the purged (none claiming, however, to have been eyewitnesses). Those responsible for the trial and executions have not been moved to write about it, or even to reply to accusations. At least it is possible today to provide the facts that can be known, and some of the atmosphere of that time and place.

For one thing, we have the testimony of a resistance officer who arranged the surrender of the Militia in Annecy. He himself was a prisoner in their headquarters, had been present when they went off on operations against the partisans. These Militiamen were not cadets as had been alleged, but a regular contingent on active duty. When it became clear that the last days of enemy occupation were approaching, the resistance prisoner served as intermediary to allow the surrender of the Militia garrison and the safety of their families, with the assurance that they would be tried with respect for legality. A convoy was organized to get the 109 Militiamen out of Annecy in the hours preceding the surrender of the Germans. The convoy, under partisan protection, passed through villages whose hostile inhabitants had to be prevented from molesting the prisoners; at least once the partisans had to shoot over the heads of a gathered mob. Since none of the villages through which they passed seemed prepared to provide a place to hold the prisoners, they were taken up the mountain to Grand-Bornand, where they were placed in the village dance hall.[11]

The Militiamen were tried with as much respect for legality as can obtain in a field court martial. It happened that a court officer was available in the person of a regional prosecutor. Jean Comet had gone into hiding when the Germans began rounding up court officials denounced as hostile to collaboration. When he offered his services to the resistance he was told: "When the day of liberation comes, report to the prefecture. We'll need judges then." He did that, and was put to work drafting a decree establishing a court martial. His text began by taking note of the absence of communications with the legal government, and established a procedure which called for the presence of defense lawyers. Another decree indicted ninety-seven Militia members for treason under the penal code, and sent them before the district court martial. They were not all young men. Thirty-four of them were over thirty; nineteen were over forty.[12]

Three of the judges were FFI officers, i.e., mainstream resistance men; the two others were from the Communist-oriented FTP. For the sake of appeasing public opinion court officer Comet suggested that one of the FTP officers preside.[13] (The Communists favored more expeditious punishment, and putting them on the court was a way to associate them with a more legal kind of purging.[14]) Comet himself served as court clerk; a police commissioner took the role of prosecutor. Defense attorneys were appointed by the court. Clerk Comet attended the pretrial interrogations. When he asked a policeman whether there were serious charges against the Militia defendants he was told: "Against three quarters of them." It was agreed that the trial would be held at Grand-Bornand. At this time when fighting was still going on in the region the valley of Thônes, the county seat, was safely in resistance hands, and the village of Grand-Bornand was seven miles farther into the mountains, at an altitude of thirty-three hundred feet.

Comet read through the reports of interrogations the night before the trial, and drew up a scale of responsibilities. The least serious charge was to have been a member of the Militia in name only. Somewhat more serious was to have taken part in operations against the resistance without bearing arms—the case of cooks, drivers, nurses. It was a graver offense to have borne arms, graver still to have been responsible for executions, arson, looting, torture; those in command were considered to be the most responsible. Comet made it plain to the resistance judges that the only possible verdicts in a treason trial were guilty or not guilty, and the penalty for the former was death. He prepared ballots for each defendant, one for each judge.

He also ordered seventy-five coffins from a local carpenter, basing the number on the policeman's estimate that three quarters of the Militiamen were guilty of serious crimes; he got local people starting on digging a pit outside the village.[15]

Had brutalities been committed against the Militia prisoners? Jean Comet had seen none during the pretrial interrogations. Some defendants had been struck not by their captors but by local people who had managed to approach them.[16] For the atmosphere was indeed tense. Proceedings were open; the press from nearby Switzerland had been invited, although reporters were asked not to mention the site of the trial, to avoid reprisal bombings. At the opening of the session at 10 A.M. on August 23, clerk Comet read out the decrees setting up the court martial and enumerating the charges. As each defendant was identified a policeman described the contents of the interrogation report. The Militia prisoners were brought into the converted dance hall in groups of twenty. Inside and outside partisans stood guard, for families of victims of the Militia were close at hand, obviously ready to take personal revenge. Resistance men occupied the entire front row of the packed courtroom as added protection. Indeed, the presence in the courtroom of families of victims of the Militia represented a form of pressure on the judges, who heard threats such as "If anyone gets away free we'll get you."

The two defense lawyers divided the cases between them; one would take the floor after each interrogation. Comet had suggested that each intervention of a lawyer concerning the facts be limited to five minutes, while the lawyers would be given all the time they needed at the end of the trial to plead in more general terms. He had calculated that even with these limits the trial would take all day and all night, and it did.[17]

The defense argued that the Militiamen were youths, misguided by Vichy propaganda—loyalty to Pétain, Laval.[18] The verdict was by majority vote. Many of the defendants were known to the judges—some were even related to them. The resistance men were fully aware that they were judging other Frenchmen, and that the war was over. But they also knew that the public wished to see justice done.[19] Seventy-six Militiamen were found guilty of crimes against "patriots," sometimes in cooperation with the Germans. This constituted the crime of bearing arms against France, of collusion with the enemy in time of war, both acts covered by Article 75 of the penal code. It was noted that "present military circumstances require that these crimes be sanctioned with great energy." Twenty-one defendants were acquitted; they were not released, since some were to be prosecuted for lesser offenses. The official report drawn up by the court clerk, signed with the war names of the judges, carefully avoided mentioning the site of the trial.[20]

Privately Jean Comet felt that even under normal circumstances thirty to forty of the defendants would have been found guilty of a crime punishable by death. No Militia defendant who denied the charges against him was sentenced to death at Grand-Bornand.

Before the Grand-Bornand trial Comet had arranged for absolution for sentenced prisoners by the village priest. He also saw to it that the names of defendants were correctly recorded in the death certificates, and that the coffins were numbered. Convicted Militiamen had an opportunity to write a last letter, and to leave personal possessions for their families. Five stakes were set up at the execution site outside town. Prisoners were brought there in alphabetical order, blindfolded or not as they wished. All of them shouted, "Long live the Marshal!" or "Long live France!" at the moment of execution. The shooting began shortly after dawn and lasted until 11:30 A.M.[21]

IV
LAW AND ORDER

"This court is a veritable court martial in civilian clothing which must find whether the defendant is a traitor, and in that case it must be without pity."

—RAYMOND LINDON, prosecutor

ONE

Justice Before the Railroads

THE CHIEF INSTRUMENT for punishing collaboration was going to be the Court of Justice, that new jurisdiction conceived during underground conferences of resistance jurists in mainland France and polished up by the Free French in Algiers. However unorthodox the new court might appear to traditionalists, however much it was criticized then and later—and it was easy enough to do that—the best minds of anti-Vichy France saw the Court of Justice as an improvement over frontier justice. It signified the taking in hand of liberated administrative districts by a central authority. "Little by little, the reprisals which threatened to dishonor the resistance came to an end," remembered de Gaulle of this period. "There were still some arbitrary imprisonments, looting, or murder, whose authors were duly punished. But these final convulsions were quite exceptional."[1] If later on the outrageous aspects of the Courts of Justice were deplored, one needed to be reminded what they had replaced.

Ex-professor François de Menthon, for example, couldn't be accused of making light of legality. He arrived in Paris from Algiers at the beginning of September 1944 to take over the Ministry of Justice on Place Vendôme. He saw resistance courts martial as a violation of the will of the Provisional Government, and although these temporary tribunals had been favored by the Interior Ministry, at no time did he accept them as *faits accomplis,* or ratify their findings. He was upset when he learned of the court martial of the Annecy Militia at Grand-Bornand, which happened to be close to his family castle on Lake Annecy; if to avoid disorder it was necessary to call expeditious measures into play then he would have preferred military tribunals staffed by genuine military judges.[2]

One problem faced by the new men at Justice was the absence, or the inadequacy, of liaison between Paris and the provinces. Contact between Paris and de Menthon's own Haute-Savoie district was established only in the second week of September.[3] To deal with the virtually revolutionary situation de Menthon turned to Maurice Rolland, head of the resistance jurists' task force which had helped put together the purge legislation. A new job was created for Rolland: inspector general of the magistrature. During the month of September he and three colleagues divided France among them, and then went off to establish the new courts in the provinces. Their first goal was to make sure that the purge was being carried out within the ranks of court personnel, and that capable people were available to replace the judges and prosecutors who had been purged. They also had to see that officials dismissed by Vichy got their jobs back, that persons jailed by Vichy for political offenses were all free.[4]

A more immediate concern of Rolland and his team was to close down ad hoc courts. In accordance with de Menthon's feelings, they accepted military tribunals as a stopgap until Courts of Justice could be set up. Often the Paris inspectors had to negotiate with local resistance chiefs, in some cases with veritable gang leaders, to persuade them to relinquish their courts martial. As Rolland saw it, the liberation government had to reestablish justice before the railroads—i.e., had to set up workable courts even before other essential services were in full operation.[5]

As defined in the June 26, 1944, decree, Courts of Justice were to be set up progressively, as the liberation of the mainland proceeded, at the seat of each regional court of appeals. The presiding judge was to be a professional magistrate, who would sit with four jurors. A convicted collaborator could appeal (concerning procedural matters only), and had a right to seek commutation of sentence.[6] But even before the new courts were ready to function a second decree, this one signed in Paris on September 14, made changes deemed essential to deal with the large number of cases that had to be tried. Instead of having a single Court of Justice in each regional court-of-appeals district, there were be at least one for each administrative district *(département)*. Jury selection was simplified to take account of the difficulty of communications.[7] In another departure from prewar legislation, the decision to go ahead with the trial was given to the prosecutor himself, for it was feared that examining magistrates—who normally had that responsibility—would fail to bring many cases to trial.[8] "The Court of Justice is not an ordinary criminal court which examines both the act and the criminal," warned one of the new prosecutors, Raymond Lindon, during the trial of an officer of the notorious Légion des Volontaires Français contre le Bolchevisme. "This court is a veritable court martial in civilian clothing which must find whether the defendant is a traitor, and in that case it must be without pity."[9]

We can now read a remarkable set of documents which suggest the precariousness of Gaullist authority over liberated areas far from Paris. They are reports of the Justice Ministry representative attached to the Allied landing forces in south France. He went ashore at Saint-Tropez on August 29, 1944, made his way to Marseille, where the Provisional Government's liaison with the armed forces was to be based. In a report to Minister de Menthon he called attention to the absence of military tribunals, whose personnel had been expected to land with the liberation army. Instead, people's tribunals were trying collaborators, sentencing them to death, carrying out executions. Thus in Cannes on September 2 members of the Justice mission found a people's tribunal presided over by a justice of the peace. They suggested that he limit his role to investigations, pending establishment of genuine courts. On September 4 the mission confronted a delicate matter in Marseille itself, where the FFI had submitted a plan for a people's tribunal. Pierre Tissier, a government official who was temporarily standing in for Commissioner of the Republic Raymond Aubrac, persuaded the FFI to give up the idea, promising to set up a Court of Justice immediately. But that was too soon even for the Justice delegate, who explained that Paris wanted temporary military tribunals to allow the Courts of Justice time to be created in an atmosphere of calm. The reply was that "urgent" political reasons made it necessary to go ahead with the Marseille version of a Court of Justice.[10]

Raymond Aubrac, a law graduate who had studied at Harvard and MIT, had only just turned thirty, but he was already a legendary hero of the resistance who had been evacuated from occupied France to assist Interior Commissioner Emmanuel d'Astier in Algiers.[11] Unlike most of the Regional Commissioners, Aubrac had not been tapped for the job long before the liberation. Rather, like François Coulet on the Normandy bridgehead, he had arrived with an Allied landing party; his only baggage was a set of the *Journal*

Officiel containing the decrees of the Free French, and a piece of advice which de Gaulle had offered him: "Watch out for the Americans." In other words, take charge of the situation or the Americans with their military government will do it for you. His writ extended over the six districts of the Marseille region: Bouches-du-Rhône, Var, Alpes-Maritimes, Vaucluse, Basses-Alpes, Hautes-Alpes. He was well aware that the purge would be one of his most difficult challenges, and discovered the Marseille prisons full to bursting. There had been summary executions, bodies were still being found on the streets each morning, and no effective police force existed. The hot spots were the cities—Marseille, Toulon, Nice—for people had suffered most there, and would continue to suffer, through a harsh winter, dramatic problems of food and fuel supplies, complicated by the lack of communications (for example, a vital bridge across the Var River had been destroyed).

Aubrac and his men agreed that there was only one way to deal with the perils of frontier justice, and that was by setting up a system of official justice right away. The Commissioner of the Republic knew that southern Frenchmen were particularly responsive to legal form, a heritage of the Roman law which had prevailed in the region. At the time there was no contact with Free French headquarters in Algiers, and nothing in his instructions indicated the path he should take. Just how broad his mission was is suggested by a remark made to him by de Gaulle in Paris on September 11, when the Marseille Commissioner expressed concern that he would not be able to maintain order. "You distress me, Aubrac. You represent the State. You have a duty to carry out."[12]

On arrival in Marseille Aubrac had set up a legal department, bringing in magistrates from the regional court of appeals in Aix-en-Provence. On September 5 by decree he created a Court of Justice, with sections in Aix and Arles, two sections in Marseille. Jurors were to be selected by magistrates and representatives of the Comités Départementaux de Libération. Aubrac's decree provided a one-week limit on pretrial investigations, suspended the right of appeal, gave the power to commute death sentences to the Regional Commissioner himself.[13] A second decree permitted trials without any pretrial investigation at all, suspending all the delays allowed in the original Algiers decree, and calling for court-appointed defense attorneys.[14]

Still, a Court of Justice working to rule was not what the most militant of resistance men desired. The Comité Départemental de Libération of the Marseille region still wished a people's tribunal to try collaborators.[15] But when the Court of Justice won out over this revolutionary jurisdiction, it turned out to be at least as severe. The first time that Raymond Aubrac commuted a death sentence issued by the Marseille Court of Justice his prosecutor submitted a letter of resignation (which Aubrac tore up). The Commissioner of the Republic later estimated that he had pardoned half of those sentenced to death; he would have commuted even more sentences if he had not feared public reaction. Like other Commissioners of the Republic, he felt that the power of pardon was the most awesome of his responsibilities.[16]

This awesome responsibility was brought home to him in another way during his first weeks in office. It happened in Pertuis, a town in the Vaucluse twelve miles north of Aix-en-Provence, with a population of some fifty-five hundred. A mysterious explosion at a nearby castle serving as an FFI barracks had killed thirty and wounded another forty young resistance volunteers. Townspeople retaliated by rounding up thirty-seven hostages taken from the ranks of suspected collaborators—in fact most were regional dignitaries. The town announced that it would execute its hostages at the time of the funeral of the young resistance martyrs. Aubrac was in Paris for a meeting of Commissioners of the Republic when the news arrived; he was told to rush back to deal with the crisis. He set up a special task force composed of FFI men and loyal police officers, rushed off to Pertuis. Leaving his escort outside the village, he proceeded alone to the town hall, first passing a roadblock guarded by women with submachine guns. The hostages were being held in the cellar of the town hall. Aubrac negotiated with the villagers all night, pleading for the lives of their captives. Finally he offered to let them try a district Militia chief, and promised not to commute his sentence if he received a death penalty. He scribbled out a decree proclaiming martial law, telephoned the Avignon prosecutor to ask him to deliver the jailed Militia chief. A temporary court was set up in haste in Pertuis; it tried the Militia chief, sentenced him to death. He was shot at once. Later when François de Menthon came down from Paris, Aubrac heard him say: "You couldn't have done anything else."[17]

Aubrac took more pride from another of his initiatives. On November 6 he ordered all civil and military authorities who had made arrests to publish a list of those detained in a week's time. These lists were to be posted outside prefectures and town halls, including at the town hall where the arrest had been made and the town hall of the place where the suspect was being detained. Complaints—they had to be signed—were invited to be submitted against the persons on the list; the complainer would be subject to the law on untruthful denunciations. After a two-week deadline for such complaints, local authorities had another four days to release the suspect.[18]

If the Marseille Court of Justice was France's first, the Commissioner of the Republic for the Montpellier region, Jacques Bounin, had soon adopted the Marseille simplifications for his own courts in Montpellier and Nîmes, although the FFI regional commander warned an emissary from the Ministry of Justice that courts martial would continue to function up to the day the Court of Justice was opened.

The problem everywhere, of course, was that something had to be done with collaborators while the relatively cumbersome machinery of the Courts of Justice was being assembled. Even the emissary of Justice, after completing his tour of liberated southern France, felt that courts martial had been indispensable. "Patriots who fought and suffered have seen the traitors punished. . . . It is worth pointing out that in the vast majority of cases, sentences ordered by courts martial concern avowed and evident acts, especially by Militia forces." FTP veterans had beseeched this Justice delegate: "Above all, don't be impartial with collaborators."[19]

When Maurice Rolland dropped in on Yves Farge in Lyon in the middle of September 1944 to request that he proceed to set up a Court of Justice, Farge told him that it could be done in a week, by October 1 at the latest. But Farge asked that the court martial be allowed to function until that time, in order to pacify public opinion; he added that de Gaulle himself during his visit to Lyon had encouraged him in this direction. Commissioner Farge even wished Charles Maurras to be tried by court martial, but here inspector Rolland counseled prudence.[20]

Rolland went on to Marseille, where by now Aubrac's streamlined Court of Justice was in full swing. He endorsed the Commissioner's reasoning that the momentary suspension of the right of appeal was essential, given the difficulty of communication with higher echelons of justice. Still, Rolland objected to doing away with the possibility of commuting death sentences. But, considering the state of communications again, he suggested that when necessary Aubrac delegate his own power to commute to his district prefects.[21]

Rolland visited another hot spot, Limoges, only at the end of October. For his Minister back in Paris he painted a picture of a region where, on one hand, armed resistance units continued to be active, and on the other, the population was ready for peace and quiet. In the middle, the administration lacked the means to enforce its law, and so was obliged to negotiate. But the inspector general was impressed by the "rather strong unity on the moral terrain," for the Communist prefect Jean Chaintron spoke with respect of the archbishop. It would be nice, Rolland told de Methon, if this moral unity could be applied to practical matters.

After a time when justice was meted out by court martial in liberated Limoges, there had been a military tribunal. The latter began by issuing death sentences, but showed more moderation as time went on. Its prosecutor had now transferred all his cases to the Court of Justice. All three districts within the jurisdiction of the Limoges Court of Appeals, the Haute-Vienne, Corrèze, the Creuse, had Courts of Justice by early November, and the Limoges court was already hearing cases. Rolland found himself helping out with material matters such as finding office space for the court, obtaining the release of judges from military duty. He set up a liaison among the prefecture, the Court of Justice, the Comité Départemental de Libération, and the police, and stressed the need for judges to do their job quickly.[22]

As late as January 1945 Charles Zambeaux, de Menthon's staff director, accompanied inspectors on a visit to Bordeaux. En route at Angoulême they discovered that the Charente district Court of Justice hadn't been able to function because the military tribunal refused to close down. Zambeaux contacted the prefect, and with gendarmes simply evicted the FFI officers, installing the court in their place.[23]

These Courts of Justice satisfied no one. For strict legalists, the selection of jurors seemed shocking. Jurors were to be endorsed by resistance groups, so of course they would be resistance veterans who might themselves had suffered at the hands of the collaborators they were trying.[24] To that objection Pierre-Henri Teitgen, who replaced François de Menthon at Justice, replied that in any case collaboration "left none of us indifferent."[25]

Some of the sentences of the Courts of Justice were felt to be unduly severe. There was criticism, for instance, of the penalty of *indignité nationale* handed out to persons who may have done nothing more than join a Vichyite group; and this, despite a growing feeling that the true profiteers of collaboration, financial collaborators, were seldom punished.

For the Communists, debating the issue in the Justice and Purge Committee of the Provisional Consultative Assembly—the temporary parliament which bridged the gap between liberation and the first elections—the inadequacy of the purge created "unimaginable scandals." Even for Socialists justice seemed to be dragging its feet, while the guiltiest offenders weren't being touched. This was at the beginning of December 1944, and Minister de Menthon had to plead the material difficulties of getting the new courts under way.[26] They were dealing with a new kind of crime for which the previous experience of judges had not prepared them. And the number of cases they had to handle—over three hundred thousand were submitted to the liberation courts—was unprecedented. The continuing shortage of qualified personnel exacerbated the difficulties. In the end it would prove impossible to prepare cases against many of those who had been arrested, indicted, and brought into court.[27]

The Courts of Justice were accused of not protecting the rights of the defense. It was said that the local press, provincial populations, exercised intolerable pressure on courtroom proceedings. To that, de Menthon's successor Teitgen pointed out that there had been constant recourse to change of venue, i.e., transferring cases from an overheated environment to a cooler one. The right of appeal lacked? It never existed for criminal cases, in which a new trial is possible only in the event of irregularities in procedure.[28]

But before the new courts had been in operation for more than a few weeks it became obvious that the very rules which had set them up were slowing them down. And dangerously, for the appeals procedure was cumbersome, creating a bottleneck at the top, while in the provinces impatient citizens demanded that justice be done— or (as we have seen) Commissioners of the Republic simply rewrote the decree to meet local demands. Late in November 1944 Minister de Menthon called in his staff director, Zambeaux, who had been working on a revision of the decree to take account of difficulties that had arisen in its early application. Now he was informed that because of persistent agitation in south France the job had to be finished then and there. The earlier decree, as amended on September 14, provided for appeal via a court of procedural appeals; now such recourse was to be directed to a special section of each regional appeals court, and with a strict deadline for each step of the procedure. Appeal would be possible only in case of violations of the rights of the defense, but it could deal with the facts of the case as well as procedures, thus precluding the need for a new trial.[29] Zambeaux, with jurist René Cassin, wrote the new decree late into the night. When they had finished, de Menthon woke up Jules Jeanneney, substituting for de Gaulle, then visiting the Soviet Union, for his signature. The decree was printed at once, rushed to a military airport at dawn for dispatch to the hot spots of the south.[30]

TWO

The Paris Trials

IF THE PARIS COURT OF JUSTICE was not the first, it immediately stole the limelight. For many of accused collaborators brought into court in the early weeks were newspaper columnists whose names everyone knew. They were not the first to come to trial because they had symbolized collaboration by their public professions of faith in it, but for the more banal reason that it had been easy to collect evidence against them: their published articles. These articles became both their indictment and their sentence.[1]

In these trials of men whom a prominent defense attorney was to describe as "the propagandists of collaboration," juries took into account the notoriety of the author (the more famous he was, the more damage he had done), good faith (writers who had already been pro-German before the war might get off more lightly, for they obviously hadn't been opportunists), and the amount of money each collaborator had earned by serving as a spokesman for collaboration.[2] Later critics of the purge regretted that defendants had been punished so severely only for what they had written;[3] in a sense it was a tribute to their influence. In the view of the purgers, propaganda was a serious matter.

Something else can be said as an introduction to the Paris Court of Justice. It was able to function without the intermediary step of courts martial or military tribunals, for from the start the nation's capital was under the eye of Charles de Gaulle and his ministers; no aberration had been possible there.

The first case on the docket, tried during a single day—October 23, 1944—concerned Georges Suarez, "man of letters and journalist." Two weeks short of his fifty-fourth birthday, Suarez had been a popular historian before the war, known for his biographies of Georges Clemenceau and Aristide Briand. But he had also been a supporter of Jacques Doriot's fearsome Parti Populaire Français. When arrested (only three weeks before his trial) at the home of a woman he described as a former mistress, Suarez told police that he knew that he was wanted, but on the advice of his attorney he had decided to wait before turning himself in, aware that abuses were "always possible during a change of regime."[4]

The charge against Georges Suarez identified him as political editor of a Paris occupation daily called *Aujourd'hui.* His attorney protested the accusation of treason, on the grounds that France had signed an armistice with Germany in June 1940, so there had been no "enemy" with whom Suarez could have been in collusion—the principal charge against him under Article 75 of the penal code. The judges withdrew to consider the attorney's objection, returning to declare that "an armistice is a convention under which two belligerent powers agree only to suspend and not to cease hostilities." The trial could begin. The evidence consisted of 103 articles written by the defendant. "I read them with much sadness, infinite sadness," commented the presiding judge, "because in reading them I was thinking that they were written by a Frenchman at the moment that so many other Frenchmen were fighting and dying heroically. . . ." Suarez broke in to say that Vichy's policy of collaboration had been made by another Frenchman (he referred to Pétain). The court proceeded to read—in continuing dialogue with the defendant—articles in which Suarez had promoted collaboration, even praised Hitler's generosity. After the Allied invasion of Normandy Suarez had written: "It's the Germans who are defending our soil." He had favored Germany's policy of choosing hostages to kill among Jews and Communists; he had even suggested that the Germans take Jews as well as American and British residents of France as hostages against British bombings, and against "Gaullist provocateurs." He had approved denunciations, the track-down and killing of resistance fighters. He had even signed a hard-line manifesto which accused the Vichy regime of being insufficiently pro-German.[5]

In his defense Suarez offered witnesses to testify that he had invervened with the Germans to save persons arrested for their opinions. The summing-up stressed Germany's tactic of making use of a collaborationist government, of French propagandists. Suarez's lawyer cited Talleyrand—"Treason is a matter of dates"—and sought to present his client as a well-intentioned if misguided Frenchman of solid literary achievement. Suarez, he said, had followed Pétain's collaboration policy without knowing where it would lead. Wasn't he rather a victim to be pitied? The prosecution sought a death penalty, the defense lawyer suggested, because his client was the first to be tried and an example was required. But he hadn't committed a crime, only a mistake. The jury decided that Suarez was guilty under Article 75—of collusion with Germany, of promoting Germany's interests. He was sentenced to death, confiscation of property, *indignité nationale*.[6] His appeal was rejected; he was executed by rifle fire at Fort de Montrouge, just outside the city, on the morning of November 9.[7]

Indignité nationale: This sentence of "unworthiness," or exclusion, was to accompany all the verdicts of the Courts of Justice. This was the new sanction conceived by the resistance planners in Paris and Algiers. Standing alone, it was a sentence given to minor offenders—persons not indicted for acts of treason, but who had been tempted by collaboration all the same. What the punishment signified was defined in two decrees issued on August 26 and December 26, 1944.

A long preamble to the first of these made it clear why the new penalty was necessary. The criminal behavior of collaborators had not always taken the form of specific acts covered by penal law. Yet "every Frenchman who, even without violating an existing penal law, was guilty of a clear antipatriotic act, has dishonored himself; he is an unworthy citizen whose rights must be restricted to the extent he ignored his duties." Among acts constituting this new crime of *indignité nationale:* belonging to the Vichy government, holding a responsible position in a Vichy propaganda agency or at the Commissariat for Jewish Affairs, membership in a collaborationist unit such as the Militia. *Indignité nationale* brought deprivation of the right to vote or hold public office, exclusion from government employment, military rank, or professions such as law, teaching, trade union activity, the press and other media, even directing or participating in the management of a private company.[8] The December 1944 modifications provided that the new penalty could be ordered by the High Court (which was to try Pétain and his ministers), by Courts of Justice, or by special tribunals, identified here for the first time as Civic Chambers. It was explained that the crime of *indignité nationale* was punished by *dégradation nationale,* the details of which punishment had been defined in the earlier decree.[9]

It was a controversial innovation. Bar president Jacques Charpentier, already defined as both of the resistance and of the tradition of due process, expressed alarm at the notion of crime without proof of intention.[10] But in daily *Combat* one of the postliberation generation's moral guides, Albert Camus, spoke for the resistance: "It is just that a man who showed no concern for his country be excluded from the debates which are deciding the future of this country. It is not less just that his property—either the product of his treason, or aggravating it in the measure that it should have been accompanied by a sense of duty proportionate to the amount of his fortune—returns to the nation he abandoned."[11]

A week after the trial of Suarez, Stéphane Lauzanne, a seventy-year-old journalist, appeared in the same courtroom to answer for his pro-German editorials in another occupation daily, *Le Matin*. His defense was that he had received no direct payment from the Germans, had committed no act of collusion with the enemy—therefore couldn't be guilty of treason. In his final statement he expressed regret for his errors, although insisting that they had been inspired by "deeply French sentiments." He was found guilty on all counts, sentenced to twenty years of solitary confinement, confiscation of property, *indignité nationale*.[12]

The next significant prosecution of a writer took place at the end of December, when Henri Béraud, then fifty-nine, went on trial for his editorials in weekly *Gringoire*. Everything about this case contributed to making it the most sensational to date: the defendant's fame as a between-the-wars novelist, his notoriety as journalist and polemicist. This was also the first case of a dedicated new prosecutor, Raymond Lindon, he who was to describe the Court of Justice as a "court martial in civilian clothing." A prewar Paris attorney, Lindon had offered his services to prosecutor general André Boissarie, who was looking for legal talent not compromised during the occupation, not already serving the government. Boissarie informed Lindon that the Béraud case was the next one on the docket, but that the prosecutor who should have handled it refused to ask for a death penalty because of his Protestant convictions. Remembering Béraud's incendiary articles in the collaboration press, Lindon said he would have no such qualms. (Article 75 automatically called for a death sentence in the absence of extenuating circumstances.)[13]

Béraud was accused of writing regularly in a collaboration periodical from 1940 to 1943. But in the first interrogation of the accused columnist the prosecution was caught in a series of factual errors concerning his career—the titles of the newspapers he worked for, his literary prizes, even the titles of his books.[14] (When he took over the case prosecutor Lindon had been given three days to prepare the indictment.[15]) In his defense Henri Béraud declared: "What was Marshal Pétain in November 1940? He was invested officially and constitutionally with the powers of the chief of state. All French civil servants from the highest tribunal to the humblest town-hall employees had taken an oath to him. Cities fought for the honor of giving his name to their finest boulevards. He only had to appear in the streets to be acclaimed. Archbishops received him solemnly in their cathedrals. Marshal Pétain was uncontested. . . ."

The prosecution read some of Béraud's columns to the jury. "One must be an anti-Semite, with nuances, with honorable exceptions, but one must be one . . . because the salvation of France depends on it." Britain, for Béraud, was "this false ally"; de Gaulle was a name "that History will vomit." In summing up Raymond Lindon declared: "Do not forget, gentlemen, what is happening as you consider your decision. The hazards of war have brought battle lines closer. Already, as François Mauriac wrote in a recent article, already hideous hopes take off their mask; already there are people who are regaining confidence because the Germans have momentarily recaptured the initiative." The prosecutor referred to Germany's apparently successful counteroffensive in the Ardennes, when enemy paratroopers were dropped behind the lines in the direction of Paris. "Think of the harm Béraud did and the harm he can still do."[16] The sentence was death by firing squad, confiscation of property, *indignité nationale.* "The death sentence fell in an atmosphere of stupor," observed a spectator. "All the press was dumbfounded, even the hard-liners."[17]

On page 1 of *Le Figaro,* François Mauriac, armed with the moral authority of his contribution to the intellectual resistance— but already becoming known as a critic of the rigors of the purge— spoke out bluntly: "That he be punished for taking the wrong track, that he pay dearly, very dearly, is quite natural, and in the logic of these frightful days when as we know every gesture counts. . . . But that we dishonor and execute as a traitor a French writer who did not betray, that we denounce him as a friend of the Germans, while there never was the slightest contact between them, for he hated them openly, this is an injustice against which no power on earth will prevent me from protesting."[18] Béraud would later say that Mauriac's article had saved his life.[19]

His appeal rejected, Béraud was packed off to a death cell, placed in chains.[20] But de Gaulle then commuted the sentence to hard labor for life. Two years later this sentence was reduced to twenty years, and in December 1949 it was brought down to ten years, which he was then serving at the prison of Saint-Martin-de-Ré. The reduced sentence soon made him eligible for parole.[21]

Of course the most talked-about trial of a collaboration journalist, the trial usually recalled in reminiscences of that time, is that of Robert Brasillach. He was then two months short of his thirty-sixth birthday, and he was described in the prosecution's opening statement (on January 19, 1945) as an "essayist and literary critic of considerable authority." Part of the impact of his case comes from his promise (promise largely unfulfilled, although Brasillach's literary reputation was inflated by his execution). The Brasillach trial also provided a platform for a young defense attorney of talent, Jacques Isorni, who was to go on from there to join the defense of Philippe Pétain.

Brasillach was accused of having served German propaganda, following his release from a German prisoner-of-war camp. He had served the Germans through his writing, travel in Germany, contacts with German organizations. In his editorials he had advocated sending French workers to Germany, denounced Jews, denigrated France's former allies, praised French soldiers who fought alongside the Germans, called for punishment of de Gaulle and of resistance partisans.[22] Defender Isorni opened his case with a brief which argued that Pétain's government had been legal. Since Brasillach had only followed its policies, Isorni wished the trial to be postponed until Pétain and his ministers were brought to court. Prosecutor Marcel Reboul replied that Brasillach's trial was independent of any other proceedings. The court agreed.[23]

As in all French trials, before, during, after the purge years, the interrogation of the defendant was actually a dialogue, an opportunity for him to argue with the prosecutor. Brasillach took the opportunity to compare his behavior with respect to the Germans to that of establishment writers such as Georges Duhamel and Jean Giraudoux, and of a seemingly untouchable book publisher, Gaston Gallimard.[24] In his summing-up prosecutor Reboul described Brasillach as "Fascist ... with passion," "antidemocratic with frenzy," stressing his support of the Germans, his calls for punishment of prewar French leaders, for the shooting of Communist members of parliament and of those he considered responsible for the war. Reboul quoted Brasillach: "What we want is not collaboration, but alliance."[25] Brasillach had publicly applauded Hitler's invasion of the Vichy zone in November 1942, on the grounds that the Germans would protect France from the Anglo-Americans. In conclusion the prosecutor called attention to an earlier case in which a twenty-year-old Militia member had been spared execution when his lawyer asked the jury: "What will you do when the intellectual instigators of his crime come before you?" Well, Brasillach was one of them.

Brasillach's attorney stressed his client's literary significance, citing François Mauriac, who had called the defendant "one of the most brilliant minds of his generation." Mauriac felt that the execution of this writer would be "a loss for French letters." Isorni characterized the case as a "trial of opinions" and sought to demonstrate the relativity of the notion of treason. He pointed out that the prosecutor himself had collaborated with Vichy, to save what could be saved.[26] Brasillach was found guilty of collusion, sentenced to death. When a spectator protested, "It's a scandal!" Brasillach was heard to reply, "It's an honor."[27]

He was put in chains, given a pair of trousers without a belt which opened along the sides, so they could be removed while he wore the chains. Brasillach wrote his brother-in-law Maurice Bardèche that he had no illusions; he expected few persons to come to his defense. "There's only poor Mauriac, whom nobody pays attention to anymore ... and then he probably won't do much for me—he has no reasons to do anything."[28]

He was wrong about Mauriac, who was becoming the most prominent critic of the harsher aspects of the purge in his forum on the front page of daily *Le Figaro*. Mauriac did try very hard. He led a compaign among writers and artists which produced a petition to de Gaulle asking for commutation of the death sentence. Signers included Paul Valéry, Paul Claudel, Jean-Louis Barrault, Jean Cocteau, Colette. Some of the signers were to face troubles of their own before the purge was over; others were known for their resistance attitudes—Albert Camus, for example.[29] Camus had hesitated before signing, and then made it clear that he was doing so in his personal capacity, not as editor of *Combat*. He despised the writer, the man who had encouraged the brutal treatment of his friends, and on his side Brasillach had never asked for clemency for resistance writers. Camus opposed the execution of Brasillach only because he opposed the death penalty.[30] Although Jean-Paul Sartre didn't sign for Brasillach, we know something about how the Sartrians felt about the case. Simone de Beauvoir attended the trial and was impressed by the dignity with which Brasillach faced his accusers. "We desired the death of the editor of *Je Suis Partout*," she remembered a year later, "not that of this man ready to die well. . . . The more the trial took on the aspect of a ceremony, the more it seemed scandalous that it could lead to an actual spilling of blood."[31]

Today we know more about the campaign of writers in behalf of a member of the flock gone astray. Thanks to the candid memoirs of Mauriac's son we know not only how deeply François Mauriac felt about the case, but how much his son agreed with him. And this son was the secretary of the man who would decide whether or not Brasillach would die. "To chop off the head of a thinking man—the idea is unbearable," François told his son. That night the son drafted a petition including the line: "It is horrid to cut off a thinking head, even if it thinks wrongly." In *Le Figaro* Mauriac *père* used his own phrase again, and added his son's contribution: "even if it thinks wrongly." Meanwhile defense attorney Isorni was preparing a shorter petition for those who might have been unwilling to sign Claude Mauriac's version. At the French Academy, François Mauriac used the longer version to convince fellow academicians to sign the shorter one. (Although Claude sought to influence de Gaulle by stressing the number of letters appealing for a pardon for Brasillach, he did not tell de Gaulle that he himself had drafted the petition.[32])

Brasillach was shot at Fort de Montrouge, an old military installation just outside Paris then being used for executions, on February 6, 1945. His defenders would later allege that the jury, and then de Gaulle when he examined the case, mistook a photograph of Jacques Doriot in German stormtrooper uniform for Brasillach, who was actually standing alongside Doriot in civilian clothing.[33] But there is no evidence that de Gaulle was influenced by such a photograph, or that he was confused about the identity of persons shown in one. His subsequent remarks indicate that in the view of the chief of government, exemplary punishment of those who symbolized collaboration was a national priority.[34] Brasillach's attorney

Isorni has since concurred that de Gaulle had made no mistake about a photograph. He let Brasillach go to his death simply to prove his determination to carry out a thorough purge.[35]

De Gaulle had no trouble letting Paul Chack go before a firing squad. A former naval officer and popular writer on history, Chack had placed his reputation at the service of the enemy in public rallies and front-page editorials. He went before the Court of Justice on December 18, 1944, and received a death sentence. De Gaulle's secretary felt that the General had been influenced by, among other things, an order given to members of an Anti-Bolshevik Action Committee to join the Militia; it was signed by Paul Chack as "Lieutenant Commander."[36] Paul Ferdonnet, who had worked in Berlin during the war and was accused of writing propaganda for the German radio, was tried in July 1945 and shot in August.[37] In September Jean Hérold-Paquis, a leading commentator for Radio Paris during the occupation who had followed the Germans in their retreat to broadcast propaganda from enemy soil, was sentenced to death and executed. In his summing-up prosecutor André Boissarie pointed out that Hérold-Paquis was guilty of more than simply having wrong opinions: He had been an accomplice in war crimes, the spokesman for the enemy.[38]

Jean Luchaire had been a symbol of newspaper collaboration as publisher of daily *Nouveaux Temps* in German Paris, president of the press association (which made him the ideological guide for collaboration journalists). As a friend of German Ambassador Otto Abetz he had been one of the most conspicuous personalities of occupied Paris, one of the most powerful. Prosecutor Raymond Lindon took on this case in January 1946. His summing-up began: "Among those who became traitors by the pen, their treason was often inspired by Fascism; in the case of Luchaire, it was inspired by corruption and rottenness. A year ago in this very room I pleaded against Béraud, moved by the anger of a Frenchman and free man who was silenced for four years and who, for four years, saw his country dishonored. It is the same feeling which moves me today; but now there is also disgust." The jury found Luchaire guilty of collusion, demoralization of the nation with the intention of harming national defense. Death, confiscation, *indignité nationale*.[39]

There was one more notable trial of opinion makers. In November 1946 Robert Brasillach's associates on *Je Suis Partout*, Pierre-Antoine Cousteau, Claude Jeantet, and Lucien Rebatet, appeared before the Paris Court of Justice. A fifth member of the group, Alain Laubreaux, was a fugitive. (Laubreaux was later sentenced to death in absentia; he was in Spain but the Spanish authorities considered his treason a political crime and refused to extradite him.) The *Je Suis Partout* trial was dominated by the personality of Rebatet, author of a book that had shocked even Vichy. In *Les Décombres,* Rebatet indicated that he preferred the German occupation to Pétain's regime, because the latter was insufficiently anti-Semitic and antidemocratic for his taste. Evidence in the trial went beyond opinion—e.g., one witness declared that an article by Rebatet called "Jewish Marseille" had asked for the arrest of the witness; the witness was indeed arrested with forty-three other persons, some of whom were deported by the Germans and never heard from again. Rebatet and Cousteau were sentenced to death, confiscation, *indignité,* Jeantet to hard labor for life, confiscation, *indignité.*[40]

Once again there were people ready to stand up for a convicted writer because of his talent, even if Rebatet's talent had been demonstrated most fully only in the pro-Nazi *Les Décombres.* Free French propagandist Pierre Bourdan wrote to de Gaulle:

> Without excusing Rebatet's criminal behavior, I nevertheless feel, with many other Frenchmen, that the courts are outrageously partial in dealing with collaboration. Writers and journalists who by their signatures accepted responsibility for their acts are subjected to the full force of the law. On the other hand, a remarkable clemency, and sometimes total immunity, applies to other forms of collaboration, even the most serious, the basest, or the most efficacious: lawyers who denounced Frenchmen to the enemy and who are now back arguing cases in court, generals and admirals responsible for the death of hundreds of French and Allied soldiers, businessmen who reinforced the German war machine and who serve minor sentences in comfort; finally and especially publishers of newspapers who inspired collaboration in the press and who financed it, but without signing their names.[41]

Albert Camus, who had pleaded for Brasillach's life, could not do less for Rebatet.[42] But Rebatet attributed his salvation—"alas"—to the execution of Brasillach.[43] For the death sentences of Rebatet and Cousteau were commuted to hard labor for life in April 1947 by the first postwar President of the Republic, the Socialist Vincent Auriol.

THREE

Justice and Charity

AFTER THE RIGHTEOUS ANGER of the first hours of liberation a reflux was not long in coming. There were too many establishment personalities prepared to plead the case for indulgence for it not to take root in the public mind. It will be easier to understand this if it is also remembered that the overwhelming majority of French men and women had played no part in the occupation, neither in collaboration nor in resistance. The first vigorous challenge to purge justice came from an unimpeachable man, François Mauriac, one of the few members of the French Academy who had taken real risks during the German occupation. He had belonged to the underground writers' movement, the Comité National des Ecrivains, and even wrote a book for an underground publisher, Editions de Minuit. At the liberation he had a privileged platform on the front page of *Le Figaro*, whose publication in the Vichy zone until November 1942 had not prevented its return to the newsstands under the liberation government. As early as September 8, 1944, just a fortnight after the liberation of Paris, Mauriac was warning of the dangers of slipshod justice. He did not wish to plead for the guilty, he said, "but only to recall that these men and women are accused of crimes, but that no court has yet convicted them of the offense or crime for which they are indicted." He was not looking for excuses or seeking to block strict justice; how could he, who had seen "Jewish children squeezed like poor lambs into freight trains"?[1]

Le Figaro was a venerable institution. *Combat* was a new Paris daily, a reincarnation of the underground sheet distributed during the occupation, published by a group of resistance writers the best known of whom was Albert Camus. In an unsigned editorial on *Combat*'s front page Camus called for swift and thorough justice. "Let us first say that the purge is necessary. This is not as obvious as it appears. Some French people would like to leave these things as they are. . . ." For Camus, there were situations in which error was possible, and others in which "it is nothing but crime."[2] Next day Mauriac called for "national reconciliation."[3]

"We don't agree with Mr. François Mauriac," announced Camus's unsigned reply to that. He conceded that frontier justice was uncalled for. But punishment was necessary despite whatever misgivings one might have. "Our conviction is that there are times when one must be able to overcome one's feelings and at the same time sacrifice peace of mind."[4]

So it would be a debate. In *Le Figaro* (dated October 22–23) Mauriac replied to "*Combat*'s editorial writer": "And as I have reason to believe that the author of the article is one of my juniors for whom I have much admiration and sympathy . . . I feel embarrassed. . . ." Mauriac had been hurt by Camus's reminder about peace of mind. Did he mean that one should be hardhearted?[5] Camus told his readers that he hesitated to reply, but letters he was receiving convinced him that the matter was of concern to many people. He didn't like killing either. But now that the first death sentence had been pronounced in Paris (that of Georges Suarez on October 23) he had to take a stand. Perhaps a Christian could believe that human justice is always compensated by divine justice. But what about non-Christians? "We have chosen to accept human justice with its tremendous defects, careful only to correct it with a desperately maintained honesty." He wanted France to have clean hands, but that required "justice both prompt and limited in the time it takes to mete it out."[6]

We know from the confidences of his son how affected Mauriac was by the appeals for help he was receiving. "I become dizzy when I realize how important I am—how important they think I am. . . ."[7] A few days later he was pleading for young Militiamen, "adolescent victims" of the collaboration propagandists; instead of punishment, couldn't they be sent off to serve in a distant colony under reliable officers?[8] It was true that Frenchmen who had delivered other Frenchmen to the enemy should be shot, that those who served the enemy and got rich doing it should be punished. "It is true and very true that the blood of those who died cries not for vengeance but for justice." But he decried the abuses of the purge, for example the detention of persons against whom no charges had been filed.[9] In an editorial entitled "The Lottery" he protested the inequality of sentences at the Courts of Justice, where "everything is chance and arbitrary."[10]

Albert Camus replied, agreeing that the courts were coming up with "absurd sentences" and "preposterous indulgences." He suggested that further purge laws were needed.[11] "What a pity," retorted Mauriac, "that our young master, who has ideas about everything, hasn't deigned to offer some on this law. . . ." He blamed Camus for emitting judgments "from on high, from the heights, I imagine, of his future work." It was an attack as personal as any that would come out of this exchange. In the same editorial Mauriac compared the purge to repression during the German occupation "to the extent that we too have forgotten charity."[12] "Mr. Mauriac has just published an article on 'misunderstanding charity' that I find neither just nor charitable," replied Camus, this time in a signed article which concluded: "We shall until the end refuse a divine charity which will deprive men of their justice."[13]

Mauriac pursued his crusade during that first liberation year. During the Pétain trial he was to point out that the old Marshal hadn't been the only one to choose the road he had chosen (but Mauriac did not disapprove the verdict).[14] For his part Camus, in a talk at a Dominican monastery in 1948, conceded that "despite some excesses of language on the part of François Mauriac, I have never stopped meditating about what he said." And he felt now that Mauriac had been right and he had been wrong.[15]

Still, there was little space in the paper-short press of the liberation for a serious critique of the purge. Mauriac himself had complained that "although we have many papers there is really only one, that of the Resistance."[16] Shortly after Henri Béraud was found guilty an opinion poll determined that 49 percent of the French approved the death sentence for this writer, 30 percent opposed it, 21 percent were without an opinion. When de Gaulle commuted Béraud's sentence 34 percent approved the act, 42 percent opposed it; and 52 percent approved (18 percent disapproved) the death sentence for Brasillach in the fortnight preceding the rejection of his appeal.[17]

That it was not simply a debate between believers and nonbelievers is demonstrated by the attitude of the Christian Democrats who published the monthly called *Esprit*. In its lead article in June 1945 a newspaper editor, Roger Secrétain, argued that the purge had not gone far enough. Because of abuses of the purge, there had been a reluctance to punish those who were truly guilty. "Thus we are torn by this contradiction: to support this undignified revolutionary justice, or to take the part of guilty persons on whose punishment the very survival of France depends." He agreed that if one were to "purge truly, deeply, completely," a fourth of the French population would have to be taken to court. Yet the spirit of indulgence was benefiting many truly guilty persons. He quoted Catholic philospher Charles Péguy's warning that "regimes which don't begin with a massacre of the evil shepherds always end by a massacre of the flock itself."[18]

So it had to be, in Camus's words, "human justice with its tremendous defects." But not all the trials concerned writers, journalists. On October 25, 1944, just two days after the Court of Justice in Paris had completed its first case (against Georges Suarez), there was what *Le Figaro* described as a "major case." The defendants were members of the Militia accused of one of the more sensational of the atrocities attributed to that organization, the murder of former Minister Georges Mandel, detested for both his defense of democratic institutions and his Jewish origin. The conquering Germans had interned Mandel, then transferred him to French custody; the Militia had taken him from prison to shoot him down in the forest of Fontainebleau. The man who had actually done the killing wasn't in the dock; apparently he had been killed during the liberation of Paris, but his accomplices had been caught. "Behind these three Militiamen," summed up prosecutor Robert Vassart, "I see the most horrible moments of four years of occupation, and it is in the name of the victims—deportees, the tortured, and the shot—that I ask for justice, that is, the supreme punishment." Two of the defendants were sentenced to death, the third (who had claimed not to know the purpose of the motor ride in the forest with Mandel) to twenty years at hard labor.[19]

Another trial stirred considerable interest, that of Georges Albertini, number two man to Marcel Déat in the Rassemblement National Populaire sponsored by the Germans in occupied Paris. Much of the interest in the case came from the relatively light sen-

tence Albertini was given after his conviction for collusion with
Germany and demoralization of the army and the nation: five years
at hard labor, five years of having to reside outside the Paris region,
confiscation of property, *indignité nationale*. Albert Camus, for one,
felt that it was unjust to let Albertini off so gently.[20] Some opinion
makers, and apparently the jury as well, had been moved by the circumstances of Albertini's arrest. He had hidden under a false name
at the liberation. "How can you blame him for that," one of his attorneys asked the jury, "at a time when justice was not in a position
to protect those to whom justice was to be rendered?" The defense
lawyer, Maurice Paz, told the court that Albertini's young wife had
been abducted and confined, "not by the police, not by court order,
but taken away with her infant by partisans. . . ." She had been
beaten, burned with cigarettes; her seventeen-month-old baby had
been turned over to a public welfare agency where it was still being
held at the time of the trial; the mother was still in detention (the
lawyer knew where she was, and told the court). Even Albertini's
parents had been arrested, his mother released after three months,
the father still interned. (The baby subsequently died, apparently
while in public custody.) On the facts, lawyer Paz argued: "When
one sees Marshal Pétain accepted, one can say, by the whole world,
how resist? And let me add: very few of us did."[21]

The Lafont-Bony case presented fewer moral problems. Henri
Lafont (born Chamberlain), with Pierre Bony, had led a gang which
in their sinister headquarters near the Avenue des Champs-Elysées
arrested, tortured, looted in the name of the German security services. They were in effect mercenaries, well rewarded by what they
took from their victims. Lafont and Bony, with seven accomplices,
were sentenced to death, and two of the gang received hard labor for
life. One death sentence was commuted because the defendant had
subsequently been arrested by the Germans and he had participated
in the resistance. The two leaders and six of their men were executed
on December 27, 1944.[22]

Financial collaboration was a harder nut to crack. Cases
against large companies, and company directors, required extensive
examination of records in order to determine how much income and
profit derived from normal business, how much from serving the
enemy with zeal. Political collaborators, in comparison, were relatively easy to prosecute, as Justice Minister Teitgen was to explain,
for "they wrote and signed the proof of their treason." But indus-

trial, commercial collaboration was carried out behind closed doors. "You have to examine the books and all the correspondence of the corporation under investigation; the deals made with the enemy were generally done through intermediaries; you have to carry out expert examination of a whole series of banking and accounting operations. . . ."[23]

The Paris Court of Justice was divided into political and financial sections. Early in 1945 prosecutor general André Boissarie called in Raymond Lindon, who had by then acquired his reputation as an energetic prosecutor, to tell him that the financial section was dragging its feet; he needed Lindon in there. Under Lindon's direction, and in the absence of legal precedents, the financial section applied its own doctrine: To be proved guilty a defendant had to have helped the enemy wittingly; the extent to which he had been forced to cooperate was taken into consideration. Lindon came to realize that the most useful sanction was a fiscal one. When a company's directors were prosecuted the sentence would take the form of fines, which allowed the firm to continue to function and thus to assure employment for its workers.[24]

There were to be few major cases, few chairmen of the board put in jail. Penalties were usually limited to confiscation of property; public opinion found these financial trials of little interest.[25] A typical one was that of the chairman of a company which manufactured automobile parts. The purge committee of the firm had requested an investigation of its activity during the occupation, when most of its production went directly or indirectly to the Germans. The chairman had claimed that he had refused to manufacture war material, had intentionally limited output; he was nevertheless charged with placing the interests of his company over that of his country. But before the close of his two-day trial the prosecutor admitted that production had been less significant than had originally been estimated, and that the owner of the firm had not personally profited, had not betrayed his country. Had the chairman wished to do so, he could have tripled production. He had shown himself to be anti-German, and so the prosecutor could not ask for a sentence for this man who had already spent over a year in pretrial detention. The defendant was acquitted on all counts.[26]

There were less momentous affairs. A carpenter jilted by his girl joined the Légion des Volontaires Français. He got five years at hard labor. A young woman denounced a worker for insulting her because she associated with German soldiers; the worker she denounced was shipped off to Germany: She too got five years at hard labor.[27] A fish vendor's clerk, jealous of another clerk recently hired, denounced him, and got fifteen years at hard labor.[28] A latheworker belonged to three Fascist movements and supported German propaganda in his factory: three years of prison.[29] A nightclub dancer who had been Jacques Doriot's mistress received a year in prison.[30]

The best available statistics, put together long after the fact from what could be found of Court of Justice files, give the figure of 6,053 sentences handed down by the Paris Court of Justice. Of those crimes that could be identified, 1,862 verdicts sanctioned military collaboration, 2,741 political collaboration, 1,110 financial collaboration. Of the 372 death sentences in Paris, 110 were executed (the others either were pronounced against fugitives, or were subsequently commuted). There were 2,032 sentences of hard labor or solitary confinement, 2,906 to simple prison, 284 to confiscation of property with fines, 87 to *indignité nationale*. (This concerns cases in which a Court of Justice ordered a sentence of *indignité* as the main sanction, but does not include decisions of the Civic Chambers.) Of the 1,110 persons convicted of financial collaboration, 3 were sentenced to death but not executed, 159 to hard labor or solitary, 606 to prison, 255 to confiscation of property with fines, 87 to *indignité*.[31]

We can learn a great deal from the regional press during the purge years; news stories and not official files can tell us much about the atmosphere inside and outside the courts. Reports of the Commissioners of the Republic and their prefects are often limited to bare statistics. But when they do enter into detail they rarely confirm the claims of purge victims of an overheated atmosphere. The public "is hardly excited," noted the Commissioner for the Bordeaux region, reporting on the status of the judicial purge at the beginning of spring 1945.[32] In our own time scholars have begun to look at court records and other local sources for a more objective view of postwar justice than has been available until now. One of them exploded the claim that in southern France it required many months to reestablish orderly justice. In the Pyrénées-Orientales district the Court of Justice opened its doors on September 22, 1944, and sat until August 9, 1945. In 72 sessions it tried 319 accused collaborators, pronounced 310 penalties, of which 12 were death sentences subsequently executed. Another 104 death sentences were not executed—77 of them had been ordered in the absence of the defendants. There were 101 sentences of hard labor, 82 to prison or solitary, 13 to *indignité nationale,* 1 to a fine. Nine defendants were acquitted. The judges were considered proresistance, but despite local pressures—from the press and political groups—sentences were soon appropriate to the crime; e.g., those executed were Militiamen who had participated in combat and German agents, all specifically accused of murder. The district Civic Chamber, which began hearing cases on December 5, 1944, tried 1,303 persons by its final session on July 25 of the following year. It issued 1,144 sanctions (reduced to 956 after appeals); 802 defendants received *indignité nationale* for life or for specific periods, 145 others were sentenced but immediately excused because of resistance activity. In all, only a third of the defendants received *indignité* for life or for terms of ten years or more. In weighing evidence, letters of denunciation were treated with caution—so found this scholar; where the evidence was not convincing the defendant was acquitted. Contrary to claims that have been made, there were no manifestations of class hatred. Most defendants could hardly be described as upper class; they were craftsmen, shopkeepers, small property owners, employees, factory workers, minor civil servants.

The severity of the courts declined, expectedly, as time went by. After March 1945 clemency often won out. In all, only 2.6 percent of all defendants (and this includes a court martial which preceded the opening of the Court of Justice) were executed—hardly, concludes the scholar, a bloodbath. There was simply no people's justice, no anarchy, in the Pyrénées-Orientales.[33] In another reputed center of agitation, the Toulouse region, the Courts of Justice of the five districts handed out 405 death sentences, only 28 of which were executed. They represented 1.74 per 100,000 inhabitants, less than the national average of 1.89. The number of acquittals in the Civic Chambers was 33.72 percent (against the national average of 29.1 percent).[34]

Everywhere it seemed that little people were more likely to be taken to court. The explanation was not always difficult to discover. Thus one prosecutor reported that Militia chiefs, who were better informed than their men about how the war was going to end, had managed to slip away before capture. These chiefs were tried in absentia, while their underlings stayed around to be arrested and tried.[35]

FOUR

The LyonTrials

JUSTICE IN LYON WAS attuned to the ardor of the purgers of southeast France. The Rhône-Alpes region controlled by Commissioner of the Republic Yves Farge had more than its share of notable trials, thanks first of all to the ferocity of the Germans and their French allies during the occupation, and then to the presence of significant resistance forces. The first major case at Lyon's Court of Justice was the treason trial of Alexandre Angeli, the highest-level official of the Rhône-Alpes as Vichy's regional prefect. He was accused of having served Vichy with zeal, and in particular of having obliged Catholic Church officials to reveal where they were hiding one hundred Jewish children (after four hundred non-French Jews were arrested in June 1942 for transfer to German custody).

In the first round of courtroom dialogue Angeli pointed out that he had been prefect in Brittany until the Germans deemed him undesirable (he asked that an effort be made to find the German request for his transfer out of that region). "Given that trials before the Court of Justice must be dealt with rapidly," replied the presiding magistrate, "it is impossible to follow all the usual rules of pretrial examination, for the higher interest requires that we move quickly. So the truth must be found during the trial itself." The court did see some evidence in Angeli's favor, such as an attack against him in the scurrilous collaborationist sheet *Au Pilori*, which on February 10, 1944, blamed the regional prefect for terrorism in his region because he refused to crack down on Jews and Freemasons. As for the pursuit of Jewish children, there was an affidavit from Lyon's Cardinal Pierre Gerlier stating that Angeli had not insisted on finding the children, and that he had issued a very light sanction against the church for not revealing their whereabouts.[1]

In his charge to the jury, prosecutor Alexis Thomas acknowledged that Angeli had been a "tough adversary" during the trial, and had plausible excuses for each charge against him. But he argued that Angeli had been the agent of Vichy and of Vichy's Interior Minister, enjoying full powers. He was one of those responsible for carrying out Laval's policy of helping the Germans win the war. "In consequence, you don't have a modest civil servant before you. . . . You have, and I'm not afraid to say it, a representative of Vichy; you have the government of Vichy itself on trial here." Yes, Angeli had been patriotic, had defended some Frenchmen, but a patriot could become a traitor; Marshal Pétain had been the hero of Verdun in the First World War and yet an arrest warrant was out for him as a collaborator now. The defense attorney called attention to the reticence of the prosecutor to put all the blame on Angeli, and painted the portrait of a patriotic official who had sought to minimize repression. Then Angeli himself took the floor, admitted that he had served Pétain and Laval, but said it was because they had been trying to avoid the worst. All the prefects felt that way, he added; not one of them had resigned during the occupation.[2]

Angeli was sentenced to death. "Assassins! Long live Angeli!" spectators shouted.[3] Staid *Le Progrès,* Yves Farge's old newspaper which was being published again, began its page-1 report: "The death sentence of Mr. Angeli will shock people." It pointed out that the evidence showed that the regional prefect "had sought tenaciously, cleverly, to limit the consequences and the repercussions of the policy directives received from Vichy." There should have been a "balanced sentence," not a "totalitarian decision punishing a public office symbolically."[4] In Paris, Wladimir d'Ormesson on *Le Figaro*'s front page called the verdict "iniquitous." He revealed that a year earlier Angeli had warned him and *Figaro* publisher Pierre Brisson that they were among those "sentenced to death" by the Militia.[5]

Angeli's death sentence was quickly voided, on the grounds that the pretrial preparation had been inadequate, that witnesses were lacking.[6] But in Lyon the Comité Départemental de Libération voted a resolution which regretted that the trial had failed to reveal Angeli's "grave responsibilities."[7] It is now that an angry crowd will march through the streets of Lyon chanting, "Angeli to the stake," forcing the gates of Saint-Paul prison in an attempt to lynch the prefect with police chief René Cussonac; their rescue by Farge has already been described.

So Angeli would go on trial again, but not in Lyon. The prison violence called for a change of venue, a request made not by Angeli but by the Lyon prosecutor.[8] The new trial was not to take place until May 1946, when the Court of Justice in Paris found Angeli not guilty of collusion with the enemy, yet guilty (under Article 83 of the penal code) of "acts harmful to national defense" for the purpose of "furthering the cause . . . of Germany, enemy power." That called for a lesser penalty than the capital one, and in fact Angeli drew four years of prison, a fine, *indignité nationale*.[9]

Although Lyon's Commissoner Yves Farge was able to announce the arrest of Charles Maurras at his first press conference, it was not at all sure that this historic personality would be tried elsewhere than in Paris. We have eyewitness evidence that when de Gaulle realized that Maurras might be taken to court outside of the capital he telephoned Justice Minister de Menthon: "It's important that he not be tried in some hole; the country wouldn't understand that. . . . Lyon doesn't exist!" De Gaulle may also have been worried that far from Paris, Maurras was in danger of being sentenced and executed before a pardon could reach him; at least his aide Claude Mauriac suggested this to him.[10] But Commissioner Farge kept his prisoner. Maurras was spared a court martial, however, and a Court of Justice examining magistrate was assigned to the case. The pretrial investigation dragged on for four months, slowed by the need to examine all of Maurras's articles in *L'Action Française*—and Maurras had been a prolific writer—as well as to establish the connections between his public denunciations of Jews and other political opponents, and the actual arrests of the persons he denounced. Dispatched to Lyon to observe the trial for his Minister de Menthon, Inspector General Maurice Rolland emphasized to the judge and prosecutor that the trial should not turn into an attack on the doctrines of Action Française, since the acts of which Maurras was accused by themselves sufficed to justify the prosecution. The government did not want international opinion to conclude that Maurras was being tried for his ideas.[11]

As Courts of Justice proceedings went in those days, the

Maurras trial was a long one, lasting all of four days. At the opening session on January 24, 1945, every seat in the court was taken, extra protection had been placed around the Palace of Justice. There was the "picturesque" note that because of Maurras's deafness an interpreter communicated questions to him by written notes or by shouting at him at close range.[12] "A bearded little man, nervous, agitated, and seemingly unbalanced, with gestures somewhat choppy like a puppet's . . ." So Inspector Rolland saw him.[13] Three months short of his seventy-seventh birthday, Maurras was tried together with his chief deputy, Maurice Pujo, himself seventy-three.

It was a lively event. First Maurras refused to reply to specific questions unless he was allowed to explain his policies in their ensemble; he finally got his way, and in a long speech described the trial as a "frightful hoax." In the prosecutor's opening statement Maurras was called a writer of considerable talent whose prestige derived from his patriotic attitude during World War I. Thanks to his influence he had been in a position to promote Vichy's policies, while his rabid anti-Semitism, neatly suited to Nazi philosophy, combined with anti-Allies, anti-Gaullist tirades, had served the Germans. Prosecution witnesses sought to link Maurras to specific attacks on persons who were subsequently the targets of the Vichy police or the Germans. Poet and playwright Paul Claudel, in a written affidavit, accused Maurras of having denounced him for resistance activity, and that had led to a Gestapo attempt to arrest him. Claudel's contribution provoked a long ideological statement by Maurras, for the two writers had been lifelong political enemies.

More effective were the direct quotes from Maurras in *L'Action Française,* such as this from the issue of January 15, 1942: "The worst of our defeats has had the good result of getting rid of our democrats," or his call for more punishment of Jews. Far from being consistently anti-German, Maurras (as prosecutor Thomas was able to show) had favored sending French workers to Germany, accepting the German promise that French soldier prisoners would then be released. Thomas summed up: Maurras was old but he was lucid; his responsibility was complete. Certainly he was talented. But this augmented his responsibility. He was old, but when an old man caused young men to die, he deserved no pity. Maurras's lawyer, calling the prosecution statement "abominable," said that he could not understand why Maurras's patriotism, courage, and age didn't constitute extenuating circumstances. If Articles 75 and 76 were used against his client, what charges would be made against a real spy? The lawyer noted that Paris and Lyon had disputed the honor of trying his client; he didn't think that Paris would have been more lenient. "It seems to me that writers are dropping like flies in our capital."

The jury found Maurras guilty of collusion with an enemy power, but it did grant him extenuating circumstances. He was sentenced to solitary confinement for life, and *indignité nationale*. His aide Pujo, guilty of acts compromising national defense, was given a five-year prison sentence.[14] After the verdict Inspector General Rolland confided to his Minister that it had been a surprise, because everyone had expected a death sentence. The jurors apparently felt that they should not be without pity for an illustrious writer who was also a crazy old man for whom death would have been out of proportion. And they had also avoided creating a martyr. "It's Dreyfus's revenge!" Maurras cried out anyway, after hearing the verdict. For the Dreyfus affair had remained for Maurras a current event. "Locked into his deafness and his syllogisms for over fifty years, sure to have discovered the truth, he has gradually moved out of the world . . . without realizing that he was no longer, even for the most respectful of his followers, anything but a hollowed-out idol that one admires without listening to his words of wisdom. . . ." As soon as the verdict was announced the two old men were taken away in a police van, to avoid the likelihood of a demonstration or even an attempted abduction.[15]

Maurras had not been made a martyr, but his case would become a rallying cry all the same. We have a report that copies of the transcript of the trial were circulating under the counter a full two years after the trial.[16] In 1949 the prisoner, confined at Clairvaux, a converted monastery in the Aube district, produced a request for a new trial in the form of a two-hundred-page book.[17] He won a medical pardon in April 1952, on condition that he reside in a private hospital (where he was to die shortly thereafter).[18]

The very first case before Lyon's Court of Justice had been the trial of René Cussonac, then fifty, Vichy's police chief for the Rhône-Alpes. In accordance with the rules, a panel of twenty jurors had been selected for that month, and four of them were chosen to hear the Cussonac case (one was a woman who had been imprisoned at Montluc during the occupation). The trial began on November 3, 1944. The prosecution described Cussonac as zealous in tracking down resistance people, Jews, fugitives from compulsory labor brigades, and charged that he had worked with the Militia in serving German policy. He was appreciated so highly by the enemy, according to a police officer responsible for liaison with the Germans at that time, that when he vanished shortly before the liberation, Gestapo officer Klaus Barbie appeared upset and wished to have nothing to do with any other police official.[19] Cussonac's defense was that he had obeyed orders; he was sentenced to death all the same. Before the execution he was a victim of the near lynching already described.[20]

Lyon's second trial heard the case of a street hawker who on his return from a prisoner-of-war camp enrolled in the Militia: five years of solitary. A railway employee had joined the Militia in April 1944 after his son, then serving in the Militia, was killed by partisans: acquittal. A linotypist had denounced a Jewish family to earn a reward: three years of prison.[21] These were the smallest of small fry, and soon the Lyon court was telling Paris that it lacked cases; the police were taking too long to investigate. There was also a shortage of courtrooms, for most of those in the courthouse had been damaged when the Germans destroyed the nearby bridges.[22]

By the end of 1944 Yves Farge reported to Paris that of 9,988 suspects arrested in the eight districts in his charge, 2,674 had been sent before the Court of Justice.[23] Most defendants were hardly notorious—e.g., an Italian hairdresser came to court accused of denouncing a neighbor to the Gestapo, although his witness claimed that he was an anti-Fascist who had helped the resistance. He received three years in prison. An eighteen-year-old student had been in the Militia but now wished to take part in the war which was continuing against Germany. "He was denied an honor he didn't deserve," reported Lyon's *Le Progrès*. "Fifteen years of hard labor and *indignité nationale* will teach him not to listen to the evil shepherds who, in fleeing to foreign soil, abandoned the sheep that they dreamed of turning into tigers."[24]

By the first weeks of 1945 a second Court of Justice was functioning in Lyon, and that summer a third was made ready because of the decision to close the courts at nearby Bourg and Saint-Etienne.[25] After November 1945 only cases which had been opened before that date could be heard; all new suspects were to be referred to the Military Tribunal. Among notable cases still to be heard by the Court of Justice was that of the Francis André gang. André, known by a sobriquet which can be translated as Twisted Trap, had been the leader of a strong-arm squad of the Parti Populaire Français whose specialty was torture and murder. One of its raids was referred to as the Grenoble St. Bartholomew's Day massacre. The PPF gang was authorized by its German sponsors to keep the cash and goods it found on its victims. Thus one gang member, Antonin (Tony) Saunier, had a license to enter and search the homes of Jews; he turned all money found over to his party and kept 10 to 15 percent. When he raided a home he identified himself as "German police"; sometimes after he tortured a victim he turned the person over to the Germans. The André gang was divided into three groups totaling sixty persons, sometimes working out of Gestapo headquarters. Before the liberation André and some of his cohorts managed to join the Germans in their retreat; they were discovered in Italy in July 1945 by the American and French armies. Nineteen gang members were indicted in Lyon in January 1946, but eight of this group were still fugitives. André, Saunier, and seven accomplices were sentenced to death; four others received, respectively, hard labor for life, fifteen, ten, and five years of hard labor.[26]

Lyon also heard the case of the Militia chief accused of killing Victor Basch, a Jewish philosopher and prewar president of France's League of Human Rights, and his wife, each of whom was eighty years old. The killer got death.[27] So did a curious couple who had tracked down Jews for the Gestapo, receiving a fee for each person found. In one case the couple was able to pick up two Jewish children who were playing on a village street; the person taking care of them innocently admitted that the children were Jewish.[28] Because of the case load the Lyon Court of Justice was expected to remain in activity until 1949. But even after that the court was needed to deal with people already tried in absentia and who after an amnesty decided to give themselves up. For the sentences of fugitives in absentia had included confiscation of property, and these convicts hoped to recover their possessions.[29]

FIVE

Problem Solving

ONLY ONE MAN COULD save a collaborator from the firing squad after a Court of Justice sentenced him to death. That was the chief of state, who until January 20, 1946, was Charles de Gaulle. "Nothing in the world seemed sadder to me than the display of murders, tortures, denunciations, which thus came to my attention," he would confess in his memoirs. "With a clear conscience I declare that except for 100 or so cases, all those convicted deserved execution." Yet he commuted 1,303 death sentences, notably all of the women, most minors, and most defendants who had acted under orders and while risking their own lives. The 768 rejected appeals concerned persons who de Gaulle felt had acted personally, spontaneously, to kill Frenchmen or serve the enemy.[1]

De Gaulle would receive the case files each evening at his residence on the Bois de Boulogne just outside Paris from the hands of Maurice Patin, a reserved, bespectacled fifty-year-old former attorney general of the Paris Court of Appeals. Each file included a draft decree in two parts, one of which called for commutation of the death sentence, the other confirming it, and both had been signed in advance by the Minister of Justice. Sometimes seven or eight cases had to be reviewed in a single evening, and the meeting with Patin would go on until three in the morning.[2] We have the testimony of de Gaulle's private secretary that the General dreaded these sessions. What he looked for in examining the files was evidence of direct collusion with the enemy. Thus he let Paul Chack go to his death in January 1945, for Chack had encouraged enlistments in the

157

German army. But he commuted the sentence of the writer Henri Béraud.[3] Justice Minister Teitgen sometimes recommended commutation of a death sentence but didn't get it; de Gaulle told him that there were two categories of traitor who deserved no pity: talented writers and army officers.[4] Later, when the Fourth Republic received its constitution, its first President, Vincent Auriol, exercised the right of pardon sitting with members of the High Council of the Magistrature.[5]

Although it is not apparent from the testimony of de Gaulle or those closest to him, one function of presidential pardon was to regulate the disparity of sentences between Courts of Justice in Paris and the provinces, and from one province to another. Dealing with this disparity was the chief concern of an officer of Patin's Bureau of Pardons, Adolphe Touffait, a former prosecutor in Normandy. His chief weapon was ministerial pardon. When a sentence was handed down in a particular court the local prosecutor attached his opinion and passed it on to the regional appeals court and to Paris, where it landed on a desk in the Bureau of Pardons. Only death sentences went a step further, to de Gaulle. Lesser sentences were weighed by high-ranking Justice officials sitting as a Commission on Pardons, presided over by Patin.[6]

The disparity was apparent from the beginning. Reporting three executions in Montauban nearly four hundred miles south of Paris following the verdicts of a military tribunal, and a death sentence issued by the Court of Justice in Marseille, the Communist Party's *L'Humanité* commented in mid-October 1944: "In Paris, not a single traitor had been shot until now!"[7] And then one was— Georges Suarez. That brought another headline in *L'Humanité:*

FINALLY A LITTLE JUSTICE

ELSEWHERE THAN IN THE PROVINCES![8]

A Paris prosecutor felt that the disparity in the treatment of collaborators could be explained in part by the fact that in rural areas, and in small towns, people knew who the collaborators were; in Paris it had been easier for them to disappear.[9]

A historian had the patience to study the verdicts of one southern district from day to day, starting with the extreme severity of the courts martial and the inflexibility of the early weeks of the Court of

Justice, going on to a period (from December 1944) when the court rendered verdicts "more appropriate to the accusations," followed by the time (after March 1945) when clemency often won out. For by then, as a juror confessed to him, there was more time for reflection, less tension. Thus an armed Militiaman sentenced to death in absentia in February 1945 was arrested and brought before the court in June of the same year; his youth and lack of judgment got him off with a term of *indignité nationale*. Indeed, those sentenced to death in absentia in the first months of liberation could expect, with the passing of time and the passing of amnesty legislation, to receive a light sentence or even acquittal when finally retried. The chief of the Militia of this district, sentenced to death in absentia in August 1945, turned himself in nine years later. He received only a five-year term of imprisonment, and was immediately freed under the provisions of the amnesty law.[10] "A rather large number of major criminals of collaboration with the enemy escaped their country's justice by hiding, more often by escaping abroad," Minister François de Menthon would later recall, surely with bitterness.[11]

Of course there are statistics concerning the accomplishment of the Courts of Justice district by district. They demonstrate, among other things, that the courts of southern France were most severe: The proportion of death sentences was highest there. Regions with the largest numbers of cases sent to trial included Alsace, the district on the German border which the Nazi Germans had annexed, and whose inhabitants were subjected to considerable pressure. Paris tried more cases than the national average but handed down more acquittals and dismissals, fewer death sentences too: 2.8 percent against the national average of 6.1 percent, representing 3.1 death verdicts per 100,000 inhabitants against 7 per 100,000 nationally.[12] Obviously full understanding of why there were more cases in one region than another, more severity here than there, requires knowledge of a region's topography, among other things, for topography had a lot to do with the implantation of resistance groups and thus with the intensity of antiresistance activity. We also need to know how many collaborators were eliminated before the Courts of Justice opened their doors—by summary execution, say.

It has already been seen how emotions flared up after the collapse of Germany, when the gates of the Nazi camps opened, and their inmates came home with further details of collaboration crimes. As early as March 1945 the gendarmerie had been expecting that. "It is to be hoped that the purge will be terminated before the massive return of [those expelled by the Germans from Alsace] and camp inmates; otherwise violent incidents, even summary executions, are to be feared."[13]

The camp inmates returned, and so did many of the most conspicuous collaborators, including Vichy officials who had participated in the puppet government set up under German sponsorship in Sigmaringen. These collaborators were found and arrested in Germany, in Austria, in Italy (and many others managed to hide out until the end of their lives, as Marcel Déat did). Fernand de Brinon, Vichy's spokesman to the Germans (and vice versa), was found in Germany. He said that he had turned himself over voluntarily to the American army. "You will remark that unlike so many others," he told reporters, "I didn't go to Spain or to Italy."[14] Philippe Pétain returned to France via Switzerland, but the Swiss let it be known that they would deny transit to collaborators, who could always give themselves up to French forces occupying German soil—not far from the Swiss border.[15] Pierre Laval fled to Spain, was expelled to Austria, where American forces took him into custody and turned him over to the Free French.[16] The press regularly reported arrests, extraditions; in a single day, as late as October 1945, 222 suspects found in Germany were brought back to France.[17]

Nearly a year later the chaplain of the Légion des Volontaires Français, Jean Mayol de Luppé, was discovered in Germany living under a false identity.[18] An officer of that German auxiliary corps, Jean Bassompierre, had been captured by Soviet troops in February 1945, escaped during his transfer to France, managed to get to Italy. He was about to sail for South America when arrested in Naples.[19] The problem was that Militiamen and French members of the German army were mixing with returning war prisoners to avoid arrest. Genuine war prisoners and former camp inmates were being asked to assist the purge, and denunciations were flooding the courts. A justice that had become serene, or closer to peacetime normal, suddenly became agitated again, with more passion on the part of the jurors. All this made the Justice Ministry's Inspector Maurice Rolland pessimistic. "The end which we had been able to hope would be relatively close three months ago now seems further away than ever."[20]

Defense lawyers also had strong feelings. In February 1945 the Paris bar, headed by that well-known lawyer—Jacques Charpentier—who had played a part in planning the purge, called for substantial revision of trial procedures, notably concerning jury selection, pretrial investigation, and appeals.[21] But in the climate of the moment nothing was going to be done to satisfy strict legalists. The lawyers returned to the attack that autumn, with a statement stressing the shortcomings of jury selection. Jurors were being recruited by unauthorized groups, while "the power of decision has been taken away from the immense majority of the French." It often seemed during trials, said the lawyers, that jurors considered themselves to be delegates of the groups which had selected them.[22]

And when citizens felt that collaborators were being insufficiently punished, say by sentences to *indignité nationale* in the absence of any other penalty, they sometimes threw bombs to express their displeasure. (It happened in the Landes district in November 1944.[23]) Reporting on the purge in his territory an underprefect of the Lot-et-Garonne noted as late as February 1947 that the public was reacting angrily to the "defaulting" of local purge courts, particularly when time passed between the conviction of a traitor and the day of execution. "This agitation of public opinion might well take the material form of violent acts if certain notorious collaborators, spared by the judges and now living in the shadows, decided to return to the front of the stage."[24]

SIX

Courts and Chambers

IT SHOULD BE CLEAR that from the moment of its inception there were people—and not only accused collaborators—who wished to see an early end to the Court of Justice. The decrees which had set up this special jurisdiction made it clear that it would cease to be competent to take on new cases after a certain deadline, which was eventually announced as November 1945. But the Court of Justice was a long time dying. Taking office in February 1949, a new justice minister, Robert Lecourt, gave the court another three months of life.[1] But it would take another law, voted in July 1949, to close it definitively—and still it didn't die. The work of the Paris Court of Justice was extended until the end of that year, but even courts and Civic Chambers which were officially terminated were maintained in activity to hear cases that were already in the pipeline. (All other cases were to go to a Military Tribunal.)[2]

The press announced, for example, the closing of the Lyon Court of Justice on July 31, 1949.[3] But Lyon's court continued to take cases of collaborators previously sentenced in absentia, and who had since been apprehended or had given themselves up—in order to regain property seized under the original sentence, if for no other reason. What is more, the about-to-be-closed Lyon court became responsible for all cases in the region previously served by twenty-seven other Courts of Justice.[4] By early 1950 the Lyon prosecutor could report that seventy cases were in the investigative phase, twenty-seven accused persons were in detention. Eleven cases had been dealt with; nine were to go to trial; two would be dismissed.

The "new" Court of Justice had held ten sessions, the Civic Chamber one, deciding forty-one and eleven cases respectively.[5] The last Courts of Justice were really to disappear in 1951, with Toulouse, Lyon, Colmar, and then Paris.

Balance sheets of the Courts of Justice were being released almost from their inception, in part to show public opinion that the government was performing its duty to purge, and later to contest exaggerated reports of purge excesses. We know, for example, that in December 1944 when nearly all of the Courts of Justice had been created, 623 of France's 2,200 judges were working in them.[6] In January 1945 there were 18,700 cases in process, of an estimated total of 50,000.[7] In May of that year Justice Minister de Menthon appeared before the Justice and Purge Committee of the Consultative Assembly to announce that already there had been 17,300 trials and 1,598 death sentences. Civic Chambers had issued 17,500 sanctions of *indignité nationale.* Courts and chambers together were issuing sentences at the rate of 5,000 per month.[8]

Since the Courts of Justice could receive no new cases after November 1945, de Menthon's successor at Justice, Pierre-Henri Teitgen, could feel that he was offering some definitive statistics in a speech he made in April 1946. In all, 108,338 cases had been investigated; of that total 36,000 were dropped before trial, another 42,000 referred to the Courts of Justice, the remainder to the Civic Chambers. By March 15, 1946, the Courts of Justice had heard 39,308 cases, the chambers 51,950 (this figure includes cases referred by local Committees of Liberation in addition to the Justice Ministry), so that 19,000 remained to be heard. There had been 3,920 death sentences, 1,508 to hard labor, 8,500 to prison. To those who complained that wartime France had had a lot more than 108,338 collaborators and that the French Revolution had done a better job, Teitgen responded: "The revolutionary tribunals of 1793 limited themselves to a total of 17,500 convictions. So that if you compare the number of sentences pronounced by the tribunals of 1793 and those of today's Courts of Justice, you can't say we didn't do much; you have to say that we did a great deal." And had there really been so many traitors in occupied France? Teitgen quoted a memorandum sent to Vichy by Marcel Déat and other notorious collaborators in late 1943 in which they complained that there were not more than 50,000 collaborators in France.[9] Later that year, speaking to the Consultative Assembly, Teitgen wound up a summary of purge achievements with a similar comparison: "You certainly think that in comparison with Robespierre, Danton, and the others, the Minister of Justice who stands before you is a child. Well, they were the children, if you judge by the figures!"[10]

Final figures, figures published after the very last of the Courts of Justice had closed their doors, indicate that 124,751 cases were investigated (by courts and Civic Chambers together). Of these, 45,017 never went to trial, and 28,484 persons who did face the juries were acquitted. There were 6,763 death sentences, 2,853 of them in the presence of the defendants, 3,910 in absentia; in all, 767 of the death sentences were actually carried out. Penalties of hard labor for life were given to 2,777 defendants, hard labor for limited terms to 10,434 others, while 24,116 were sent to prison, 2,173 to solitary. The Civic Chambers pronounced 48,484 sentences of *indignité*, although 3,184 of them were immediately excused.[11] And this is not to talk about the military tribunal which inherited the purge (but which showed an indulgence suited to its time). Thus when Horace de Carbuccia, publisher of *Gringoire,* a well-known collaboration newspaper, went before the Paris Military Tribunal after years of hiding in France and Switzerland, *L'Humanité* concluded its report of his trial with some irony: ". . . Horace de Carbuccia has finally been acquitted. What else could have been done with him? His editor Henri Béraud was sentenced to death. But that was ten years ago!"[12]

The Civic Chambers were that unique institution invented to deal with a unique crime: *indignité nationale,* a crime that even its sponsors agreed was retroactive, as we have seen, even if this was a benevolent retroactivity designed to save collaborators from the harsher penalties they risked in more conventional courts. In determining guilt or innocence a chamber had to consider the extent to which the defendant had been under pressure, the significance and frequency of his acts; it could excuse or remove a penalty if the defendant had subsequently participated in the war against Germany or had provided assistance to the resistance. Defendants had the same rights of appeal as they had in the Courts of Justice.[13]

Everything that is wrong with the concept of *indignité* has already been mentioned, for even as they invented the crime, and the punishment, resistance jurists worried about it. A legal analysis by one prosecutor takes note of the line of reasoning that *indignité* was a state of fact rather than a crime, that it was punished not by a penalty but by a forfeiture. The decree did emphasize that the accused party must have acted knowingly. Thus social contacts or even intimate relations with German military personnel were not in themselves punishable, unless accompanied by reprehensible acts. Acts of collaboration could not be excused on the grounds that the defendant was only following orders, if he or she had done nothing to avoid being subjected to such orders (so decided the chambers as they developed their jurisprudence).[14]

These things need to be said, for the chambers have had a bad press. On one hand, observed a lawyer, defendants had a clear advantage: They appeared in the dock as free men, and left court as free men regardless of the sentence pronounced. But on the other hand, the charges could be fragile—e.g., sending flowers to the wife of German Ambassador Otto Abetz was the basis for one prosecution. An employee of a funeral parlor was accused of giving a Fascist salute before the coffin of an assassinated collaborator; the chauffeur of Pierre Laval got five years of *indignité* just for being his chauffeur. For no worse crimes, said this lawyer, tens of thousands of persons lost their jobs, often their property, and sometimes at a late stage of their careers had to start over again.[15]

No transcript exists of a Civic Chamber trial. We can re-create the atmosphere thanks to the diligence of the press. But the only complete accounts come to us from defendants who felt themselves victims of injustice and wished the world to know about it. Thus a doctor who in his district was responsible for public-welfare medical aid published his version of the proceedings against him. He had written popular books on health and in one of them, published during the occupation, he had suggested that the French ought to be grateful to Hitler for having spared them; he saw in Hitler's indulgence a sign of the coming of "a new Europe," if the French acted in the right way. In January 1945 he was called in to be heard by an examining magistrate, then went to trial before the Civic Chamber of the Allier district (at Moulins) in early March. He was able to sit in the courtroom to observe the trials preceding his own. A young woman who had done laundry for German officers was accused of having had intimate relations with them. Although she denied the charge (and the doctor himself felt that her explanation was convincing) she got thirty years of *indignité*. Two other women accused of similar offenses seemed to the doctor attractive enough to have had such affairs; one confessed to a liaison and got a life sentence, the other denied the charges and received twenty years. A cook for the Militia against whom no other charge had been made also received twenty years of *indignité*. A radio technician accused of having read Vichy propaganda over the air at least once was acquitted because—our doctor observer says—he was married to the daughter of an American general.

And then it was the doctor's turn. The judge read out an extract from his book in which he blamed the democrat rabble of prewar days for the bad health of the French; and then came his remark about Hitler's indulgent attitude. The doctor declared that he had written these words because he believed them. "So you regret nothing?" "I recognize that this sentence can produce an unhappy reaction today, but I wrote it without a bad intention, and in addition to that I obtained no advantage from it." The first defense witness was another doctor who testified that the defendant had been anti-German, had helped some young men avoid compulsory labor service in Germany. Two other defense witnesses, one of them a Jewish doctor, stated that at the time the controversial book was written it had been possible to be wrong about the occupation. The prosecutor himself recommended acquittal. The defense attorney pleaded not the facts but the well-meaning attitude of his client, "a good Frenchman, a father, a humane and distinguished author. . . ." After ten or fifteen minutes of deliberation the jury returned with a sentence of ten years of *indignité*. Next day a press account of the previous day's fourteen cases—four sentences of *indignité* for life, seven others totaling ninety-five years of that sanction, three acquittals—said that the doctor's book had expressed "admiration" for Hitler. Soon he was called in by the purge committee of the regional doctors' association; he failed to appear, but by decree the Minister of Public Health barred him from practice for two years. But then he had some better news: He won his appeal against the Civic Chamber verdict; he received all his rights except the right to vote or to hold office. It took another five months for the ban on practicing medicine to be lifted.[16]

Clearly there were more small fry than big fish in the dock. At random, scanning a file of cases we find a traveling salesman, a sculptor, an office boy, a secretary in a government office, an electrician, a roadworker, a farmer, a theater director, a nurse, a sales manager, a cleaning woman, a policeman, a chauffeur, a newspaper publisher, a gardener, a stenographer, an insurance clerk, a cook, a medical doctor.[17] A random sampling of cases brought before the Paris Civic Chamber turns up the following: a waitress, aged thirty-four, who in a pretrial hearing admitted having had intimate relations with German soldiers to earn extra money, at least until she caught syphilis. She swore that she had denounced no one, begged indulgence because she had a fifteen-year-old son born out of wedlock who was not aware of her behavior. But she failed to show up for her trial (in June 1945); her sentence of *indignité* was accompanied by a ban on residence in the Paris region.[18]

The same month, a woman of twenty-eight who had worked as cleaning woman for a German air force unit in Dreux was accused of having been the mistress of a German noncommissioned officer. The investigation determined that she had had relations only with one German, and no other accusation against her was on record. She was acquitted.[19] A student of nineteen—his mother as legally responsible for him accompanied him to court—was alleged to have joined the PPF and to have served as a guard at its rallies. His defense was that serious illness and his mother's being out of work had obliged him to accept paid work for the PPF. He too was acquitted.[20] In July the director of a Paris theater was acquitted on the charges of pro-German activity, although in separate actions the Ministry of Education suspended him from his position for a year, and the National Interprofessional Purge Commission also gave him a one-year suspension because of pro-German statements he had made in the press of occupied Paris following return from a trip to Berlin.[21]

In October 1945 a twenty-three-year-old singer, member of a well-known musical family, was acquitted when he said that he had been obliged to join a Fascist movement in order to obtain employment.[22] The next month another singer who was accused of recruiting for the same movement received fifteen years of *indignité*.[23]

The case of Corinne Luchaire made the newspapers in June 1946. By that time her father, Jean Luchaire, the leading newspaper collaborator, had already been sent to death by a Court of Justice. "Corinne Luchaire remains elegant in her very simple tailored suit, with her hat in the style of an English Red Cross nurse. Her large eyes, her pale complexion, reveal a sick woman who hasn't lost her little-girl expression." This from a brief account in Paris's most serious newspaper. Apparently nothing worse than her liaison with a

German officer could be pinned on her. The jury, including a woman with the hat of a churchgoer, and a man with a serious beard (same newspaper), gave her ten years of *indignité*.[24] (She was to die of tuberculosis soon afterward.[25])

The newspapers also ran reports on the Civic Chamber appearance of André Salmon, critic and journalist. He had written not only on art and literature but on the war in Syria, on French soldiers serving in the German army, and on the Freemasons, in the collaboration daily *Le Petit Parisien*. He testified that he had written these articles with his "soldier's feelings," notably after watching the burning of Rouen following Allied air raids. A defense witness said that Salmon had helped rescue paintings by Jewish artists from the Germans. Extenuating circumstances limited the sentence to five years of *indignité*.[26]

It is difficult to find a significant business leader among defendants in Civic Chamber cases. A rare example, in October 1946, dealt with a manufacturer accused of producing metal parts for the Germans; he was also said to have been pro-German in attitude and behavior. His case had been dropped by a Court of Justice, and the Civic Chamber simply acquitted him.[27] A furniture maker accused of offering his services to the Germans in return for release from jail, where he awaited trial for fraud (he had a long record of convictions), was acquitted in 1948 (by which time the chambers were more indulgent anyway).[28] In January 1949 a café owner whose business relations with the Germans had won him an in absentia sentence of *indignité* and seizure of property back in February 1946 (at which time he failed to receive notification of his trial, he said, because of war damage to the house to which it had been mailed), appeared before a chamber to hear his sentence reduced to five years.[29]

V

GOVERNMENT AGAINST GOVERNMENT

"Political justice isn't political
methods and means applied to
justice, it is justice with its principles
and essential rules applied to
political activity."

—PIERRE-HENRI TEITGEN

ONE

The High Court

EVEN BEFORE THE WAR and Vichy a High Court existed in France. Sitting as a tribunal, the upper chamber of the French parliament, the Senate, could try the chief of state or his ministers. But after the liberation the Provisional Government of Charles de Gaulle possessed only a provisional legislature, handpicked from the ranks of resistance movements and parties, excluding prewar legislators who had been compromised during the occupation. Yet punishment of the Vichy leadership could not wait for a new constitution and an elected parliament. In the words of de Gaulle, "domestic order and the foreign status of France" required immediate action.[1] The decree he signed in Paris on November 18, 1944, set up a High Court of Justice whose composition suited this temporary state of affairs. It would be headed by a chief justice of the appeals court assisted by two other magistrates. The twenty-four jurors were to be selected by lot from two lists drawn up by the Provisonal Consultative Assembly. One of them was a roster of fifty members of each house elected to the last prewar parliament. The other was composed of personalities nominated by the Assembly. All would be noncollaborationist, proresistance. The decree spelled out the jurisdiction of the new court: to try the Vichy chief of state, Pétain; his chief of government, Laval; ministers and other high officials of the "governments or pseudogovernments" which had ruled France under German occupation, with their accomplices.[2]

The decision to bring Pétain and his men to justice had been made in Algiers a year before the liberation. The ways and means had been the subject of difficult negotiations between de Gaulle and his Justice Minister François de Menthon. De Gaulle wished to see Pétain and his ministers go to court together, the unique charge to be their responsibility in signing an armistice with Germany in June 1940. De Menthon refused to accept collective responsibility; he felt that it was not possible under French law, and he was prepared to resign over the issue. For him, some Vichy ministers were 100 percent responsible and some only 10 percent responsible; and the armistice itself was a grave error but not a crime. The debate between the two Free French leaders was pursued in the months following the liberation.[3] De Gaulle lost that fight, but in any event the men of Vichy were to be charged with the worst crimes of which a public official could be accused. Many of these Vichy leaders were still in Germany, or in hiding, at the moment of liberation of French territory. "They will lose nothing by waiting," declared Communist daily *L'Humanité*. "Soon a large public will gather to applaud their hanging."[4]

Already in September 1944 the Paris Military Tribunal had drawn up indictments against Pétain and his ministers.[5] Those of the ministers who could be apprehended were turned over to military justice.[6] But the November decree setting up a High Court changed that plan, and before Christmas the Consultative Assembly had worked out a procedure for the selection of jurors. The list of parliamentary candidates was to be compiled by the Parliamentary Resistance Group, which was to give priority to members of the prewar parliament who in July 1940 had refused to grant constituent power to Pétain, while nonparliamentary jurors were to be chosen by the Justice and Purge Committee of the Assembly.[7] One jurist involved in drafting purge legislation, bar leader Jacques Charpentier, was later to say that the "essential vice" of the High Court was jury selection. "Where judges were needed—and judges of exceptional impartiality—they gave the power to judge to partisans."[8] Another particularity of the High Court was the absence of appeal: The only recourse was to de Gaulle, who could commute death penalties.[9]

The High Court was ready to try its first case in March 1945, at a time when Pétain, Laval, and other leading figures of Vichy were not yet in custody. So it began with what it had. The first person to be brought to trial under presiding judge Paul Mongibeaux was Vichy's resident general in Tunisia, Admiral Jean-Pierre Esteva.

The site was a courtroom in Paris's Palace of Justice; de Gaulle felt that this location would offer more serenity than the Palais Bourbon, seat of the prewar lower chamber of parliament.[10] The indictment had overtones of historical narrative: "On November 8, 1942, an immense hope filled the hearts of Frenchmen at the news that the Americans had just landed in North Africa, although in Vichy, Marshal Pétain ordered French troops to fight against those who had come as allies. . . ."

Admiral Esteva, who was then aged sixty-four, was accused of willful collaboration with Germany, recruiting troops for the Axis and workers for enemy fortifications. He described himself as devoted to the Marshal, insisted that he had sought to minimize the support he gave the Axis. He had always hated the Germans; he had allowed Robert Murphy and other American officials to move about in Tunisia although he knew that they were doing more than just supervising food distribution (actually they were planning the Allied landing). Then why had not Esteva used his powers to help the Allies? For the evidence was that he had obeyed Vichy's request that he cooperate with the Germans. Esteva argued that the collaborationist messages he sent Vichy were lies which enabled him to continue "to carry the French flag." In his summing-up prosecutor André Mornet (a veteran magistrate who had taken part in clandestine planning of the purge laws) said that in forty-three years of service he had rarely asked for a death sentence, but he had to do it against Esteva. "With his trial, the Pétain-Laval trial begins today."

Speaking in defense of Esteva, attorney Georges Chresteil accused the prosecution of giving the impression that the chief defendant was Pétain, that Esteva was his accomplice, and that since Pétain was surely guilty the jury could only convict a person "devoted to him body and soul." Then why, asked Chresteil, wasn't Pétain tried, even in absentia, before Esteva? On March 15, 1944, the jury found the admiral guilty of treason under Article 75 of the penal code, but noted that on the eve of the arrival of Axis troops in Tunisia he had released arrested "patriots" and facilitated the departure of Allied officials. So he escaped execution, with a sentence of life imprisonment and loss of rank, together with *indignité natio-nale* and confiscation of property.[11]

De Gaulle saw Esteva as "led astray" by a false discipline; it had made him "accomplice, then victim, of an evil entreprise."[12] Was the second trial before the High Court to be more of the same?

For General Henri Dentz, sixty-three, Vichy's high commissioner in Syria and Lebanon, was charged with similar acts under similar circumstances. He was specifically accused of giving air bases to the Germans, facilitating enemy arms shipments, and then joining the Germans in war against Free French and British forces in May 1941. Dentz, who was now ill, declared in court at the opening of his trial on April 18, 1945, that this would be the first time since his return from Syria that he could speak openly before the French public about what had happened. His policy, he argued, had been to put a brake on German demands, while doing what he had to do for the Germans to avoid a pretext for a permanent enemy occupation. The court—Mongibeaux again presiding, Mornet prosecuting—pointed out that the "double game" of General Dentz had actually worked to the advantage of the Germans, just as it had in mainland France. He quoted Dentz's speech to his troops denouncing "democrato-Masonic politics and Judeo-Saxon finance," and calling the British "age-old enemies." In other words, declared the prosecutor, Dentz had betrayed through conviction. He deserved death.

Dentz's attorney René Vésinne-Larüe referred to prosecutor Mornet's own four years of service under Vichy; Mornet protested this "infamous" remark, for he had served those who were persecuted, had publicly protested the absence of Vichy justice. Vésinne-Larüe persisted: There was a difference between a court official's obedience, for he made his own decisions, and a soldier's, for soldiers were instruments and owed blind obedience. And Dentz's defender repeated what Esteva's defender had argued: Pétain must be convicted before his followers could be. Nevertheless Dentz was found guilty of assisting the enemy, willingly and even secretly, in fighting the Free French and the British, causing the death of fifteen hundred Frenchmen and perhaps as many British troops. The sentence was death, demotion, confiscation.[13] De Gaulle commuted it and the general died in a prison hospital.[14]

Of course the High Court should have tried Pétain first, but Pétain was not on French soil when the court was ready to hear its first case. The Pétain trial could have been held in absentia, for de Gaulle himself wished it that way, and ordered that if the French army found Pétain's ministers in Germany they should be arrested, but if possible Pétain himself should not be returned to France.[15] Late in December 1944 in the Provisional Consultative Assembly, resistance delegate Jacques Debû-Bridel called for an in absentia proceeding. "What matters to us is not the carcass of that old man, it's what he was, what he represents."[16] The November 1944 decree provided that an in absentia trial would be considered definitive unless the defendant could later prove that he had not been able to present. The indictment of Pétain was read to the examining board on April 23, 1945.[17] On April 26 Pétain and his suite crossed the Swiss border into France to give themselves up.

After refusing for long months to let himself be used by the Germans as head of a puppet government, Pétain had resisted efforts by the Germans to evacuate him from his Sigmaringen castle to a mountain redoubt as the Allies advanced through Germany. In the end his captors had allowed the old man to enter Switzerland, and the Swiss were ready to let him stay. But Pétain insisted on returning to France to face his country's justice. He was arrested as he stepped onto French soil, transferred to Paris by special train, suitably protected, but not against occasional crowds which shouted hostile threats along the way.[18]

The High Court trials of Admiral Esteva and General Dentz had been treated as hardly more important than a Court of Justice trial of an outspoken collaboration propagandist. But Pétain's trial had to be a national event. There would be the legal case against him, based to the extent possible on documents and eyewitness accounts, tied to the extent possible to the principles of law and the terms of the decree which set up the High Court. But there was also to be the political trial—or debate—between Pétain and his supporters on one side, and on the other a militant jury which included members of parliament who had themselves been victims of Vichy, together with resistance activists. The jurors could intervene, and often they did. All this in an atmosphere of violence, for the judges and jurors had themselves received threats. The prefect of police offered pistols to the jurors, who also had a police escort at the end of each day's session.[19]

When the trial opened, on July 23, 1945, the defense attacked the legal competence of the court. Only the Senate could try a president of the Republic. Prosecutor Mornet objected that Pétain had not been legally elected, and after deliberation the court rejected the defense motion, declaring that the High Court had been set up according to law. In an early statement defense lawyer Jacques Isorni, who had represented Robert Brasillach before the Court of Justice, objected to the haste with which the case had come to trial. Important witnesses had not been heard in pretrial interrogation, crates of evidence essential to the defense hadn't even been opened, and many vital documents had not been turned over to Pétain's lawyers. Furthermore, the defense charged that the prosecutor, the chairman of the examining board, and presiding judge Mongibeaux had made public statements indicating that they were already convinced of Pétain's guilt.

But the trial went on. Before it was over many of the leading figures of the prewar Republic appeared in court: Premiers Paul Reynaud, Edouard Daladier, Léon Blum, even President Albert Lebrun. General Maxime Weygand and leading members of the Vichy regime contributed to the atmosphere of political debate.[20] In his summing-up on August 11 the prosecutor enumerated the principal complaints against Pétain: "the definitive acceptance of the defeat, the humiliation of France, the underhanded war against our allies, the furnishing to Germany of men to work and to fight . . ."[21] He called for a death sentence. "These are the gravest charges I have made during the course of a too long career—as I too arrive at the close of my life—not without deep emotion but in the consciousness of accomplishing a strict duty here. . . ."[22] Isorni's defense—his description of the forthcoming execution of the old hero—brought tears.[23] After deliberating for seven hours in the night of August 14 to 15 the jury sentenced Marshal Pétain to death, *indignité*, confiscation, but with the proviso: "Taking into account the age of the defendant, the High Court of Justice expresses the wish that the death sentence not be executed."[24] De Gaulle had soon commuted the sentence to detention for life, and the Marshal was to spend the rest of his days in a citadel on the Ile d'Yeu off the Brittany coast.[25]

In another era the emotional event we call the Pétain trial might not have taken place, or not in that form. But for the liberation and its government to be legitimate, Pétain and his suite had to be guilty; it was just that all the evidence of their guilt was difficult to produce at that time. And so there was the paradox: Even if Pétain's guilt in the eyes of liberated Frenchmen was certain, the trial itself, like so many other purge trials, failed to resolve all the issues. In the United States or Britain, which had the good fortune not to have been defeated and occupied, it is likely that the psychodrama of a Pétain trial, of a Béraud or a Brasillach trial, could not be duplicated. But this does not mean that Pétain, Béraud, Brasillach, tried under Anglo-American rules of evidence, would not have been found guilty.

Whatever was wrong with the Pétain trial was repeated in the Laval trial. There simple wasn't enough time to compile a case against four years of Vichy. Laval had been a fugitive as late as August 1, 1945, when he was brought back to Paris in time to testify at the Pétain trial. An indictment had been ready since June, and the High Court was prepared to try him in absentia. On his return he was submitted to a round of interrogation, but pretrial examination was considered insufficient by Laval and his lawyers.[26] For, as Laval wrote Minister Teitgen on September 22, he was being accused of "the gravest or most abominable crimes that a man can be accused of," and yet in pretrial examination he had been questioned only about isolated acts and statements, "while it would be necessary, in order to try me fairly, to examine the totality and the essence of my statements and my acts." His defense was in fact summed up in this protest letter: "I contributed to the survival of our unfortunate country during a period of four years while others courageously led another struggle for its liberation. I saved the country, in taking a personal risk, from worse misfortunes than it suffered. . . . When the truth becomes known neither my patriotism nor my courage will be contested."[27]

The Laval trial opened on October 4, 1945. He was present without his attorneys. In a letter read in open court by presiding judge Mongibeaux, Laval's attorneys Albert Naud and Jacques Baraduc explained their failure to appear by the lack of pretrial examination, which they attributed to the government's haste to finish the trial before the elections.[28] The lawyers felt that the government wished to prove, by rapid sentencing of Laval, that it was pursuing the purge with energy.[29] The presiding judge admitted that he had wished to expedite the case, but only so that the jurors who were running for office had time to campaign in their respective constituencies.[30] And prosecutor Mornet had earlier made the point that the Laval case needed no investigation, for everything had been on display for all to see since June 1940.[31]

Nothing about this trial went according to form, not even the form adopted by liberation justice. In Pierre Laval the resistance jurors had before them the most despised symbol of Vichy's subservience to, connivance with Hitler; it was hard for them to sit still. The first outburst came from a parliamentary juror: "A little more modesty, rascal," he shouted, at a moment when Laval was describing himself as a patriot.[32] When a young man in the courtroom applauded Laval a juror exclaimed: "He deserves twelve bullets, just as Laval does."[33] The tension was heightened by Laval's behavior: Ardent in his own defense, he expressed himself with anger at times, often with defiance. After one such outburst—"Convict me right away; things will be clearer"—he was ordered evicted from the courtroom.[34] The defense lawyers' boycott of proceedings also contributed to the drama. When he finally appeared in court, lawyer Naud asked for "a really major trial" as would have taken place in the United States or Britain.[35] The prosecution insisted: The evidence consisted of Laval's broadcasts, his acts, the laws he had signed.[36]

On the third day Laval protested the tone of judge Mongibeaux's questions. "The insulting way you posed your questions a while ago and the behavior of certain jurors show that I might become the victim of a judicial crime. I don't wish to be an accomplice to it." He refused to speak again.[37] He did not appear at the next session, nor did his witnesses; would the court dare to proceed with the trial without him? "I dare," replied prosecutor Mornet, "as I should have applauded the act of people's justice," had liberated Paris been able to seize Laval in August 1944. "Justice would then have been done."[38] The sentence, as expected, was death, *indignité*, confiscation. But in a meeting with de Gaulle on October 12 the defense requested a new trial. Naud argued that a real trial would "situate and limit the responsibilities for collaboration," and he pointed to the "scandals" which had occurred during the trial. De Gaulle refused the request, and rejected the application for commutation of the death sentence.[39]

The execution itself has entered into legend. When the official party, accompanied by Laval's lawyers, arrived at the death cell at Fresnes prison on the morning of the execution—October 15, 1945—they discovered that the prisoner had poisoned himself with a small tube of cyanide. A doctor called for a stomach pump. When the prisoner showed signs of life those present proceeded to dress him, and managed to get him on his feet. It was decided to carry out the execution on the prison grounds, so a stake was set up in haste. Laval asked not to be tied to the stake but his request was refused. He died shouting, "Long live France!"[40] No one seemed proud of the trial and its aftermath, and a fortnight later the Communist Auguste Gillot, speaking as president of the Justice Commission of the Counseil National de la Résistance, alleged that the trials both of Pétain and Laval had been "sabotaged." He criticized the decision not to honor Laval's request for further pretrial examination.[41]

Shortly before the Laval trial the High Court had prosecuted another symbol of collaboration: Joseph Darnand, founder of the Militia, sponsor of a French contingent of the German army; the indictment claimed that he had been the first Frenchman to take an oath of allegiance to Hitler. "Darnand betrayed for four years, without any remorse, without any hesitation," the prosecutor summed up his case. "Darnand betrayed with such harmfulness, Darnand, I repeat, has so much French blood on his hands that as far as I am concerned I cannot find the slightest extenuating circumstances in his favor." The defense tried, nevertheless, even going so far as to suggest that the execution stake be set up on the Champagne battlefield where the prisoner had displayed exceptional courage in 1918. He was sentenced to death and executed.[42] In its first year of operation the High Court also ordered in absentia death sentences for Marcel Déat, and French Academy member Abel Bonnard, both of whom had been Vichy ministers.[43]

But now France was moving toward normalcy. A Constituent National Assembly was elected on October 21, 1945, holding a first session on November 6, and it had soon elected Charles de Gaulle—unanimously—President of the government. One of the first acts of his Minister of Justice Teitgen was to submit to a vote a revision of the High Court rules. Now jurors would all be members of parliament, chosen from a roster based on the proportionate strength of each party. Judges were to be elected by the Assembly from its own ranks.[44] There were eighty-five accused Vichy officials ready for trial, twenty-five of them in detention, six hospitalized, twenty-seven fugitive, thirty-two on parole.[45]

A notable trial in 1946—the first to take place in the Congress Hall of the Versailles Palace—was that of an eminent Third Republic politician who had served, briefly, as Foreign Minister in Vichy. This trial allowed a review of Pétain's foreign policy, for Pierre-Etienne Flandin presented himself as the Marshal's intermediary with the former British ally as well as with the Americans, and one of his witnesses was Winston Churchill's son Randolph. But the prosecution reminded the jury that for a Vichy minister the sentence

of *indignité nationale* was automatic; nothing more nor less was requested for Flandin. One of the defense attorneys objected that this
would mean applying the rules "like a lower-court judge giving a
seven-franc fine to a housewife who shook her rug out of the window after seven in the morning." In its decision the court insisted on
its statutory right to judge the ministers of Vichy, although
acknowledging that the defendant had done some positive things.
So he was sentenced (on July 26, 1946) to five years of *indignité*,
which sentence was immediately excused.[46]

When the court reconvened a few days later to hear the next
case the associate judge delegated by the Communists, and the
Communist Party jurors, were absent—in protest against Flandin's
sentence. Today we can see the boycott in the context of the growing
schism between France's Communists, then entering into a new
hard-line phase, and their onetime resistance partners—Socialists,
democratic Catholics, and others of the moderate left and center.[47]
Faced with a formal request to replace the defecting Communist
jurors with new ones, Jacques Duclos, chairman of the Party's
caucus in the Assembly, replied that his group approved the boycott,
which represented a refusal of the Communists "to associate themselves with the work of a court which too often saves from their just
punishment the chief persons responsible for Vichyite treason and
collaboration with the enemy."[48] In the parliamentary debate which
followed, Justice Minister Teitgen declared for the government:
"Political justice isn't political methods and means applied to justice, it is justice with its principles and essential rules applied to political activity." He asked the Assembly not to apply the rules of
electoral battle to the courtroom.[49]

The court met all the same, but with a fortnight's delay, to hear
the "case of the admirals." Actually only two of the officers who
should have been there were present: Jean Abrial, once Vichy's secretary for the navy (he got ten years at hard labor), and André Mar-
quis, who had negotiated with Axis military authorities on Vichy's
behalf, notably concerning the disposition of the French fleet at
Toulon (five years in prison). A third admiral, Gabriel Auphan, also
a secretary for the navy and a confidant of Pétain, was a fugitive, so
he was given an in absentia sentence of life at hard labor. Admiral
Jean de Laborde, who had commanded the French fleet at Toulon,
was excused because of his health. He went to trial in March 1947,
accused of collaboration without hesitation, notably by favoring a

joint French-German attack on Chad. He was found guilty of treason, sentenced to death, *indignité*, confiscation.[50] His sentence was later commuted to life in prison, but in fact he was released some years later.[51]

Over two years had passed since the liberation of Paris, and of Vichy, but the trials of Pétain's government were far from over. Some of the most blatant collaborators were yet to be brought to justice. The year 1947 began with the High Court trial of Fernand de Brinon, who had seemed to symbolize collaboration as Vichy's liaison with the Germans in occupied Paris. Even a severe critic of the High Court was to say: "For the first time, the High Court is trying a defendant directly involved in the Vichy government policy of collaboration with a substantial if not complete file of evidence."[52] But Brinon declared that he would not appear in his own defense, and neither he nor his lawyer made a final statement. The prosecutor summed up Brinon as a "total traitor" with no saving graces; the verdict was death.[53]

Xavier Vallat, Vichy's first Commissioner for Jewish Affairs, challenged the right of one of the judges to sit on his case because he had called collaborationist defendants cowards. Vallat explained: "I won't allow Mr. Benjamin Kriegel, son of Isaac, a Frenchman for less than twenty years, to judge the former infantry officer I am." (A Socialist member of parliament, Louis Noguères, was chief justice, assisted by Kriegel-Valrimont, a young resistance leader and member of parliament, and Maurice Guérin of the Christian Democratic MRP.) The jury found Vallat guilty of collaborating with the Germans in his anti-Jewish work, and of favoring the enemy and harming the Allies in his radio broadcasts. But because of World War I wounds—he had lost his left leg—he received the benefit of "considerable extenuating circumstances," with a sentence of ten years of prison, *indignité* for life.[54]

Then in this court of political justice where professional politicians meted out justice, there was another crisis. The court was hearing the case against Vichy Minister Adrien Marquet, a longtime mayor of Bordeaux. There had been evidence of his benevolence along with evidence of collaboration. The jury was asked to decide, in the words of the prosecutor, whether "the evil and harmful attitude of a man ... can always be 'laundered' by individual services, even very fine individual services." But the majority of the jury refused guilty verdicts on the most serious charges, at which point the nine Communist jurors simply walked out. The presiding judge sought in vain to postpone the case, leaving Marquet free in the interim, but the eighteen remaining jurors, representing a majority of the panel, preferred to sanction the defendant only for his participation in a Vichy cabinet, and voted ten years of *indignité nationale*.[55] Like other High Court defendants before him, Marquet had already spent long months in detention. He had been confined in his Bordeaux region for five months before being transferred to Fresnes prison in January 1945, allowed a single visit and a single package each week; the formal pretrial examination began only in December 1946. The case was originally scheduled for July 1947 but was postponed during the reorganization of the court; it opened in December of that year only to be postponed again to allow further investigation of certain facts. Marquet won his freedom on January 29, 1948, after forty-one months of detention.[56]

Marcel Peyrouton, who had opposed Laval when he was Vichy's Interior Minister, and who had finished the war in the service of the Free French, was found guilty of "grave errors" as a member of the Vichy cabinet. Yet his active opposition to Laval was taken into account, with his subsequent services in North Africa. He had committed no crime; he was acquitted (on December 18, 1948). He had been in detention ever since his arrest in Algiers in November 1943.[57]

One of the last cases heard was that of René Bousquet, Laval's secretary-general for the police. The prosecution agreed with the defendant that he deserved ample extenuating circumstances, for if he had helpd the Germans locate resistance radio transmitters and had participated in Vichy's repressive police, other facts spoke in his favor. He got a minimum sentence of five years of *indignité*, immediately excused.[58] But more will be heard of Bousquet and his case.

The court seemed to have done its job, putting to rest its last case on July 1, 1949 (that of a Vichy official who received another suspended five-year sentence of *indignité*).[59] But a new and slimmed-down court—three judges, seven jurors—was to sit in the mid-1950s to deal with collaborators already sentenced in absentia, and who were now willing to give themselves up. One predictable result was that, considering the time that had elapsed since the occupation, Vichy officials were now to receive lighter sentences or even acquittal on charges of the same level of seriousness as those which had carried a death sentence for Pierre Pucheu in Algeria in 1944.[60] One of the first cases heard in the new court was that of a Laval man, René Bonnefoy, whose activities had earned him an in absentia death sentence in July 1946. Now, in January 1955, his attorney Pierre Véron revealed that Bonnefoy had never left France. "He thought—you will decide, gentlemen, if he was right—that in the wake of the liberation justice had not acquired the serenity that it has attained since that time." So he remained in hiding, doing badly paid translations, giving private lessons, all under a false identity. Although the prosecution now demanded prison the jury limited the sentence to five years of *indignité*.[61] Next day the court heard Charles Rochat, secretary-general of Vichy's Foreign Affairs Ministry, who had followed the Germans to Sigmaringen—taken by force, he argued. Why hadn't he returned to face justice? "I don't have to tell you the reasons . . . you guess them. . . ." Prominent resistance people, including postwar Foreign Minister Georges Bidault, testified in his favor. The 1946 death sentence became five years of *indignité*, immediately lifted.[62]

That became a habit. Admiral Auphan's life at hard labor of 1946 became five years of prison—suspended—and five years of *indignité*, immediately lifted.[63] In 1956 the retrial of General Charles Noguès, orignally sentenced to twenty years at hard labor in absentia for resisting the American landing in 1942 and assisting the Axis as resident general in Morocco, brought many witnesses. Noguès himself explained that he hadn't given himself up earlier because no proper court had then existed to try him; to this, High Court Justice Vincent de Moro-Gafferri replied that there had indeed been a High Court capable of trying him, but that he had had the right to wait. The prosecutor pointed out that under the law, when a defendant convicted in absentia was tried again and found guilty of a lesser offense, he was exempted from the penalty if more than five years had transpired between the original conviction and his appearance. This was Noguès's case, so the prosecution asked only for a moral conviction. The jury agreed, sentencing him to *indignité*, immediately relieved.[64] In 1958 Laval's secretary, Jacques Guérard, originally sentenced to death in absentia in 1947, received a suspended sentence of *indignité*. It was hoped that this "symbolic" sentence would incite other Vichy personalities to return from exile.[65]

Clearly time had passed.

TWO

The Politicians

THE LAST CHAMBER OF DEPUTIES before the war had been elected in
1936. That was the Chamber of Deputies of Léon Blum's Popular
Front. Sitting with the Senate, it had voted constituent power to
Marshal Pétain in Vichy in July 1940, and then Pétain had sent it
home. Charles de Gaulle's Provisional Government had no intention of allowing the men who had voted for Pétain to return to public life as if nothing had happened. Even Vichy legislation had to be
purged, a truly immense job, for the Pétainists had been filling up a
Journal Officiel with decrees over a period of four years. "One must
realize, indeed, that the daily life of a country rests for a large part
on its legal structure," a special committee of the Free French Consultative Assembly sitting in Algiers had pointed out in June 1944.
"One cannot, without risking impossible situations, change brutally,
from one day to the next, a collection of laws and decrees which already fill four fat volumes each containing close to one thousand
pages."[1] The report was heeded. Many Vichy laws, Vichy institutions, survived in the Fourth, even in the Fifth Republic.

As for the men who made the laws, when the Free French set
up the Provisional Consultative Assembly in Algiers in September
1943, the form to be taken by the purge of the old parliament was
already clear. For the new Assembly excluded from its ranks any
member of the old parliament who had voted for Pétain in July
1940, at which time there had been 569 affirmative votes, to 80 nays.
Nor would the Free French accept any member of a Vichy cabinet,
anyone who had acted, written, spoken in favor of collaboration,

184

who had accepted a position of authority, an advisory post, under Vichy. Those who had voted for Pétain in 1940 could purge themselves, however, if they had participated in the resistance and could get the Conseil National de la Résistance to say that they had.[2] And then came that comprehensive decree of April 21, 1944, with the ambitious title: "On the Organization of Public Powers in France After the Liberation," the decree which was to serve as a book of rules for reestabishing democratic institutions on the municipal and district levels as well as in Paris. In practice resistance groups in the provinces were to yield power only reluctantly to the old municipal and district councils even when these bodies had been purged of collaborators; temporary assemblies were to hold local power in many regions until true elections could be held.[3]

After the liberation of Paris in August 1944 the politicians, and the CNR, urged the Provisional Government to call the Consultative Assembly into session. This temporary parliament convened for the first time on French soil on November 7, 1944. Its membership was considerably different from that of the Assembly in Algiers, for now the mainland resistance had 148 seats, with 28 seats for the resistance outside France, 12 for representatives of French territorial possessions, 60 for former members of parliament proportionate to the size of the political groupings at the outbreak of war.[4] Only one appointed member—the candidate of a small center party—was refused by the new Assembly, after extensive debate in which he defended himself: Yes, he had voted for Pétain in July 1940, but had been against collaboration ever since. But the Assembly barred him, 171 to 6.[5]

And then, when it came time to prepare elections for the municipal and district councils, the question of eligibility became a prime consideration again. After debate in the Consultative Assembly, and with that Assembly's approval, the Provisional Government issued a decree on April 6, 1945, listing new criteria—banning candidates who had been sanctioned by administrative or professional purge commissions, or who had been fined for earning illicit profits during the occupation, for example. A jury of honor was created, composed of the vice-chairman of the Council of State, René Cassin; an officer of the Order of Liberation, André Postel-Vinay; a delegate from the CNR, Maxime Blocq-Mascart; this jury was empowered to reverse decisions of ineligibility.[6] Its first findings were announced on April 26, 1945: Three members of the prewar lower house, one then still in detention in Germany, three members of the prewar Senate, were relieved of ineligibility, and thus could be candidates in local elections.[7]

With logic the jury-of-honor procedure was applied to candidates for national elections when the time came to hold them. Examples of the jury's decisions as they appear in the *Journal Officiel:* A senator from the Cher district had voted constituent power to Pétain, thus was automatically barred from election, and his case was automatically subject to review by the jury. "Considering that the subject manifested no opposition to the usurper ... and that on the other hand he accomplished no acts implying direct and active participation in the resistance," he remained subject to the ban. But another senator, from the Saône-et-Loire, who had voted for Pétain but since that time had indeed participated in the resistance, had publicly urged young men not to go to work in Germany, had even been stripped of office by Vichy before being arrested and detained by the Germans, was relieved of the interdiction.[8] Among those whose ineligibility was reconfirmed was Jean-Louis Tixier-Vignancour, a minor Vichy cabinet officer.[9] This did not prevent him from facing a national television audience as a candidate for President of the Republic a generation later.

The October 1945 legislative elections produced a new electoral map. The 152 Communists and allied groups, 142 Socialists and UDSR (the Union Démocratique et Socialiste de la Résistance), 141 MRP, represented 80 percent of the seats in the new body, which was qualified to write a new constitution.[10] The new Assembly was also to sit in judgment on recently elected members against whom charges had been filed. Thus on the basis of information sent in by the Comité Départemental de Libération of the Cantal district, it scrutinized the record of a new member of parliament from that district, and in his presence. The man had already been excluded from his profession for his collaboration record; could he represent a constituency in the liberation Assembly? That body voted, 252 to 4, that he could not.[11] Although the Assembly was only supposed to determine whether new members had been properly elected, as a matter of fact a number of conservative politicians were challenged on the floor as alleged collaborators.[12]

This became a precedent for challenges to other eminent personalities to whom the Communists were hostile, even to the wartime Premier Paul Reynaud. Reynaud had been an opponent of

Vichy and its prisoner, but this didn't stop his prewar political opponents from accusing him of having opened the door to Vichy in June 1940 (by stepping down as premier on the issue of whether or not to ask Germany for an armistice). He pointed out that under purge criteria he was not ineligible, and he had been elected according to rule. "We must validate an election and not approve policies here," a spokesman for the MRP argued. After debate Reynaud was accepted, by a 298–132 vote.[13] Edouard Daladier was subjected to the same procedure, and the turbulent debate became an attack by the Communists on Daladier's policies before the armistice; it was he who had cracked down on the Communists when the Soviet Union signed a nonaggression pact with Nazi Germany on the eve of the war. Daladier's election was finally validated in a 311–132 vote.[14] The best available statistics indicate that of 416 assemblymen and senators investigated by the jury of honor, 114 were relieved of ineligibility. Of 639 final decisions, a third (193) were favorable to the candidate.[15]

Political parties purged their own black sheep; it has been observed since that the Socialists did the most thorough job of it.[16] In a remarkable front-page editorial that party's organ *Le Populaire* explained "Our Purge," and this within a week of the liberation of Paris. Socialist members of parliament, the newspaper said, had been systematically eliminated if they voted for Pétain in July 1940; the Socialists had furnished the largest group of opponents of Vichy in that parliament. "It remains true," admitted the paper, "that the Party had its fainthearted, its cowards, its traitors."[17]

Just as the new parliament had, the Socialists lifted the ban on members who had voted for Pétain, provided that they had joined the resistance immediately after that "weakness." The rule was applied severely, and even a former Socialist member of parliament who had subsequently served as a British agent organizing parachute drops into occupied France wasn't accepted as part of the resistance. Of the 168 prewar Socialist members of parliament, only 53 were maintained in the party without conditions (of this group 32 had voted "no" to Pétain in July 1940, and the others were reintegrated on the basis of "unquestionable" resistance records). But no fewer than 84 Socialist parliamentarians were excluded definitively, and that was precisely half the Socialist contingent of the 1936 legislature. Among the rejected were 12 of the 17 Socialist cabinet ministers still alive. The purge was called a "Socialist St. Bartholomew's

Day massacre" and it was also said that if he had had his way, Léon Blum himself would have been more conciliatory.[18]

Prewar Fascist movements such as Jacques Doriot's Parti Populaire Français disappeared with their leaders, who were in jail, in hiding, or dead. But one prewar movement which had *rejected* Fascism yet stood apart from the traditional right and center seemed to have no place in postliberation France, at least in the minds of the Gaullists and their allies who controlled the government. And indeed the purge of the Parti Social Français through its controversial leader, Colonel de La Rocque, was an act of government rather than of law. It is one of the most curious episodes of the purge, one of the most mysterious until this writing.

Lieutenant Colonel François de La Rocque, severely wounded and decorated in the First World War, became famous (or notorious) in the troubled 1930s as leader of the Croix de Feu (Crosses of Fire), whose mass demonstrations made it a formidable opponent of the Popular Front, which saw it as a potential danger as great as the more extremist and pro-Fascist movements; on coming to power the Popular Front banned it as it banned the Fascists. The Croix de Feu transformed itself into a Parti Social Français, which accepted the Republic and its parliament, offering a non-Marxist alternative to the traditional left. Before the end of that decade the PSF had become the largest organized political group in France, with some eight hundred thousand members.[19] This membership was fiercely patriotic, fervently loyal to its leader. Indeed, the movement frightened the extreme right as well as the left, and although it might have seemed compatible in its announced goals to Pétain's own program for Vichy, La Rocque soon fell out with the Marshal's entourage. La Rocque had thought, perhaps naïvely, that he could serve as a bridge between the Allies and Pétain. After a meeting with Pétain in March 1943 during which La Rocque outlined such a plan he was arrested, and spent the rest of the war in a German camp.[20]

At the liberation his followers began making plans for postwar activity, intending to participate in the forthcoming elections. Their first public statements after the war announced clear opposition to the "forces of subversion"—the extreme left (which happened now to be sharing power with the Gaullists). After an attack on the La Rocque movement by Communist delegate Jacques Duclos in the Consultative Assembly, the Provisional Government announced that "the Parti Social Français was and remains banned." The PSF protested that the government statement was erroneous: It was true that the Croix de Feu had been banned in 1936, but its successor, the PSF, had operated quite legally in the years before the war, electing members to parliament and a multitude of local officials. Its deputy Jean Ybarnégaray had been taken into Reynaud's war cabinet in May 1940. Indeed, the PSF declared, the only time the party had been banned was in German-occupied Paris, by Nazi police chief Karl Albrecht Oberg.[21]

And then, with the victory over Germany, the camps were liberated, their inmates released and repatriated to France. La Rocque, who was then fifty-nine years old, arrived in Paris by air on May 8, 1945, the day the Nazis capitulated in Berlin. He was immediately apprehended and placed in police custody, confronted with an order from the prefect of police of Paris which assigned him to "residence" in Versailles under the October 4, 1944, decree on "administrative internment of individuals dangerous for National Defense or Public Security." According to this decree La Rocque was to call each week at the neighborhood police station.[22]

All quite proper, on paper. But in reality La Rocque was not placed in forced residence. He was locked up in the attic of a police barracks.[23] This type of confinement was not authorized by the October 1944 decree, which provided that suspects could be dealt with in one of three ways: banned from their normal place of residence, obliged to reside in a designated area, or interned in a camp, in which case the suspect was to be examined within a given period by an inspection commission.

The La Rocque affair was handled at the highest possible level, by Interior Minister Adrien Tixier himself. Tixier personally telephoned his colleague at Justice, François de Menthon; in de Menthon's absence he spoke to his staff director, who told him that Justice had no case against the PSF leader.[24] Interior Ministry files now available reveal a stubborn insistence on Tixier's part to hold on to La Rocque even after one of his deputies warned him of the "contestable" legality of the detention. Tixier wanted to hold on to La Rocque, and wanted him tried.[25]

La Rocque himself had been informed that his arrest was intended to protect him, because his life was in danger owing to the hostility of the Communists. But he himself was convinced that he had been confined to prevent him from reviving his political movement, which would have represented a challenge not only to the left but to the Gaullists.[26] On May 13, 1945, just five days after his arrest, he wrote the local prefecture that "my best security would be to return to my home as early as possible," for he lived in a small private house on a quiet street in Paris; by chance there was an office of the national security police across the way. It would be more dangerous, he added, for him to be forced to reside in a strange neighborhood. Furthermore, he was suffering from an aggravation of wounds received in the First World War because of the ill treatment he had been given in Germany (he had been operated on for tears in internal scar tissue caused by emaciation). Were he released, he assured his captors, he would stay home, would not engage in political activity for the time being.[27]

We can now read an extraordinary communication from the Seine-et-Oise district prefect Roger Léonard, directed to the attention of Interior Minister Tixier, which pointed out the contradiction between the order for forced residence and the actual state of affairs. Léonard suggested that a new order be drawn up to legalize this situation.[28] It took six weeks for something to happen—i.e., La Rocque was ordered into residence at the Versailles barracks where he was already.[29] The prisoner protested, demanding to be interrogated by the inspection commission according to law.[30] The prefect informed Paris, but nothing happened. La Rocque renewed the request in August, three months after his arrest, and the prefect duly sent it on. "I believe," the prefect told his Minister, "that you will agree with me that the present situation, that in any case had been seen as a very temporary solution for a delicate case, cannot be prolonged without abuse." He pointed out that La Rocque's so-called forced residence was "purely and simply" imprisonment, and this for a man suffering from war wounds and who had just spent two years in captivity in Germany.[31]

Did Charles de Gaulle know what was going on? La Rocque did try to tell him. His first letter to the President of the Provisional Government, dated May 13, explained that he had been told that he was being held "out of concern for my security." He was skeptical about this excuse; he would be safer in Paris, and there he could be treated for his wounds, "aggravated in captivity." On July 14 he wrote de Gaulle again, addressing him as a fellow officer and Christian, calling attention to the status of his political organization. He reminded de Gaulle that the extreme right had ostracized him ever since he had refused to join violent demonstrations against parliament on February 6, 1934, and now he was being called a Fascist in the bargain. His family was receiving only half of his retirement annuity "under the badly defined pretext of sanctions." In fact he had been in charge of one of the principal British intelligence networks in occupied France before the Germans arrested him, and he assured de Gaulle that he was loyal to the liberation government. Was it because of his anti-Communism that he was being treated in this fashion? Some were trying to lure his members into other parties, and even suggesting that de Gaulle approved this. But if the PSF was barred from the forthcoming elections, warned La Rocque, the electorate would not have the opportunity to express itself freely.

He wrote de Gaulle once more in mid-August. He was writing, he explained, "from the attic where, without explanation, without investigation, without trial, without motives, you have kept me locked up for over three months after twenty-six months of detention in Nazi prisons." (This time he was writing to plead for mercy for Pétain, who had just been sentenced to death.) De Gaulle never replied to La Rocque.[32]

In early October 1945, less than a fortnight before the elections for the constituent assembly, the prefect of the Seine-et-Oise again wrote Interior. His prisoner hoped to be released after the elections, but in the meantime his detention made it impossible for him to receive medical care he obviously required. La Rocque was visibly losing weight, a doctor had ordered daily walks. . . . The prefect asked for La Rocque's release by the end of that month.[33] La Rocque informed the unhappy prefect: "Today I discover that even concerning short walks the authorities responsible for my detention maintain an inhumane attitude in every way similar to that of the Gestapo, leaving me to suffer cruel attacks of sciatica and not even answering my request for purchase of a banal sedative."[34] Prefect Léonard was trying to help. On October 23 he told Interior that the situation could not go on like that; the Court of Justice had had all the time it needed to decide whether La Rocque should be prosecuted. His message crossed with one from Interior asking Léonard for a file on La Rocque which could be submitted to the inspection commission. Léonard replied that he couldn't submit a file because there was none; La Rocque had been replaced in detention "on your direct request" without charges.[35]

The day came when La Rocque was heard by the Inspection

Commission on Administrative Internments. Its questions focused on La Rocque's support of Pétain and of Vichy's collaboration policies in his *Le Petit Journal*.[36] On his side, the prisoner was able to produce a certificate from the Allies attesting to his service as chief of an intelligence network from June 1942 until his arrest by the Germans; he had regularly supplied the British with military and political information concerning occupied France.[37] Did La Rocque tell the commission that he had continued to write and publish during the occupation because his British contacts had asked him not to modify his activities, so as not to draw the attention of Vichy and the Germans? He could have, for police files contained a report of interrogation of a French intelligence officer who testified to this effect.[38]

As its session of November 19, 1945, the three-member inspection commission agreed at last that La Rocque's detention was a violation of the decree; furthermore, there was no evidence against him and the deadline for filing charges had expired. Nothing justified further detention; there was no danger that his return would create serious disorder. Even if the file contained articles published by La Rocque during the occupation which were anti-Gaullist and favorable to collaboration, their author had subsequently been arrested and interned by the Germans, had worked for British intelligence (twice receiving congratulations from Allied headquarters). So that "there is no reason . . . not to terminate the measure taken against him, purely and simply."[39]

But nothing would be that pure or simple. La Rocque was not released. At the end of the year he was authorized to reside in an out-of-the-way locality in the same district until a definitive decision was taken on where he could reside; the Interior Minister's decision took note of the prisoner's promise not to take part in politics.[40] A friend had made room for La Rocque in his home in the village of Croissy, where he was at last able to receive a serious medical examination. He needed an operation to deal with his stomach wounds. (It turned out that after his operation in German detention in March 1945 he had leaped over the hospital wall to meet American army scouts parachuted into the region ahead of the Allied advance.)[41] The operation finally took place late in January; in April he was rushed to Paris for a second operation, this time for an ulcer of the esophagus, and he died immediately after that, on April 28, 1946.[42]

La Rocque had appealed to the Council of State, the highest

administrative appeals court, against his arbitrary detention, and in July 1947 the council decided not to issue a finding in view of the plaintiff's decease.[43] There was a certain form of rehabilitation, however, when de Gaulle, then President of the Fifth Republic, approved the posthumous awarding of the Medal of Resistance Deportees to François de La Rocque. Even before that, in 1957, de Gaulle as a private citizen had received La Rocque's son Gilles. When the latter made the point that the detention of his father had been an arbitrary measure without due process of law, de Gaulle replied that the intention had been to protect La Rocque from his enemies.[44]

THREE

Administrations: At the Top

THE PURGING OF public servants had begun, we have seen, in North Africa, as soon as the Free French had secured it from Vichy in November 1942. But it took over a year for the promulgation of a decree which called for the removal from the higher ranks of government of persons who had belonged to hard-line collaborationist groups such as the Militia, paramilitary and military units which had joined the Germans, members of Fascist movements such as Marcel Déat's Rassemblement National Populaire.[1] The most comprehensive decree covering what was to become known as the administrative purge was signed only after the Normandy landings. It called for disciplinary sanctions against civil servants whatever their rank who had collaborated with the enemy, defining collaboration as "favoring the enterprises ... of the enemy ... opposing the war effort of France and its allies ... damaging constitutional institutions or fundamental freedoms ... having willingly obtained or sought to obtain material benefits" from Vichy laws.

Punishment could take a number of forms: dismissal with or without pension, transfer, demotion, suspension or retirement, temporary suspension. It could also mean temporary or permanent barring from a profession (employees of organizations receiving government support were included in the decree). For military personnel a sanction might call for a discharge with or without pension. The only appeal was to the Council of State on the grounds that a decision went beyond the powers granted in the decree.[2]

If there was a priority, it was the purge of the police and judi-

194

cial system, for these were the corps which had to arrest and punish everyone else. As early as 1943 in Algiers the Interior Ministry was compiling lists. One was titled "Civil Servants to Arrest at the Liberation," another "Civil Servants to Eliminate from the Administration at Once."[3] By the end of 1944 there had been five thousand decisions to discharge, suspend, or arrest police officials, and commissioners and most of their deputies had been replaced. All police chiefs were dismissed. Most of them were arrested, and five were even sentenced to death.[4] The job of carrying out the cleansing of the court system fell to resistance jurist Maurice Rolland. He drew up his own guidelines: (1) The chiefs were responsible and had to be replaced unless they could prove that they had been active in the resistance; (2) their subordinates could remain on duty unless charges of collaboration were proved against them. In the court system the "chiefs" were, in each region, the presiding justice of the court of appeals and his prosecutor general. There were two thousand to three thousand other magistrates (the higher figure included justices of the peace). In uncertain cases, judges would be asked to take leave or to retire instead of being dismissed. When a prosecutor had not collaborated but through poor judgment had applied Vichy laws harshly, he was to be transferred. Indeed, the purgers were dealing with a whole corps of court officers who had gone about their normal business during the occupation, applying the law of the moment—Vichy's law—to deal with cases on their dockets. But some of these judges had nevertheless managed to sabotage Vichy's law by slowing down the judicial process, dragging out trials so that the defendant would never reach a sentencing stage. In some cases anti-Vichy judges had managed to keep custody of defendants so that they would not be picked up by the Germans—this was done for Jews, for example. Sometimes the most patriotic act had been to try a Jew or a resistance fighter and to send him to jail to keep him out of German hands. Maurice Rolland himself, as a magistrate during the occupation, had been involved in such acts.[5]

In a final report on the purge of the courts, made to the Consultative Assembly on May 24, 1945, Justice Minister François de Menthon said that his ministry had examined 403 cases, heard 363 of them, and that represented 17 percent of all court officers on the rolls; there had been 237 suspensions. In additon to that, 97 magistrates who had served in special Vichy jurisdictions went before the purge commission of the Justice Ministry. It was found that many of the suspects had actually carried out their jobs in liaison with resistance groups—and such judges were of course exonerated. At the highest appeals court, 11 magistrates out of 61 were heard, and 6 of them were dismissed. Of 48 presiding judges and prosecutors of lower appeals courts serving in mainland France at the liberation, 34 had been brought up on charges; 15 in each category were sanctioned by various penalties. In the Paris Court of Appeals and city court system 32 magistrates were accused of collaboration; 9 were dismissed and 13 received lesser sanctions. There had been 203 sanctions in provincial courts, of which 64 were outright dismissals and 65 forced retirements. Within the ministry itself, all divisional directors and the inspector general of judiciary services had been dismissed with pension or forced to retire.[6]

The purge of the diplomatic corps also began in North Africa, although in those days few French ambassadors came under Gaullist authority. But before the liberation of the mainland the Provisional Government had sanctioned eleven ambassadors (by voiding their nominations), had dismissed sixteen embassy ministers, fourteen councillors and consuls general, twenty-five embassy secretaries, attachés, consuls and vice-consuls.[7] In liberated Paris in September 1944 de Gaulle appointed the president of the Conseil National de la Résistance, Georges Bidault, as Foreign Minister. And Bidault lost no time in setting up a purge commission within his ministry, presided over by an ambassador, Paul-Emile Naggiar; its members represented the Consultative Assembly, the CNR, and personnel of the ministry itself who had not collaborated.[8] It was decided that all personnel decisions made by Vichy would be considered null and void, notably early retirements, dismissals, suspensions—this to bring back the patriots who had refused Vichy, or who had been refused by Vichy. Vichy's recruitment examinations would also be voided, although candidates would have an opportunity to take new examinations. The only exceptional promotions would be for diplomats who had joined the Gaullists early, or who had performed significant acts of resistance.[9]

Just before the arrival of Bidault at the Foreign Ministry and the creation of its purge commission, the first liberation Foreign Minister, René Massigli, announced that he had voided all Vichy appointments of ambassadors; it was made clear that this included Gaston Henry-Haye, Pétain's ambassador to Washington, Léon

Bérard in Rome, Paul Morand (better known as an author) in Berne.[10] The purge commission under Naggiar met from October to December 1944, taking testimony from accused personnel and from witnesses. Bidault personally dealt with higher-level officers who wished to explain their behavior during the occupation. The commission called for eighty-three serious sanctions ranging from demotion to dismissal without pension; in some cases it was simply ratifying a decision already made in Algiers.[11] When de Gaulle wrote to each of his ministers on January 13, 1945, to ask that the administratative purge be completed rapidly, Minister Bidault was able to reply (a fortnight later) that his job was done, except for diplomats still in enemy territory, in Germany or the Far East. These envoys, he said, had been carrying out their duties under difficult circumstances, but they would still be subject to the same screening to which their colleagues had been.[12]

In all, the Foreign Ministry purge commission was to examine 506 cases, recommending sanctions for about one person in six. Two thirds of all ambassadors heard were sanctioned, two fifths of embassy ministers, but only a fourth of councillors, a fifth of the consuls general. At the end of 1945 the status of the purge was as follows:[13]

Grades	Number of cases	Released from functions	Appointments voided	Dismissals	Forced retirements
Ambassadors	15		9	1	
Embassy ministers	46			18	2
Embassy councillors	35		2	4	3
Consuls general	70		3	4	4
Embassy secretaries	50	1		1	2
Consuls	126	2	10	1	

The files of the Foreign Ministry contain numerous references to appeals against purge decisions. The case of Paul Morand is not typical. The end of the war had found this well-known essayist and novelist in Switzerland, where he had been sent as Vichy's ambassador. He simply stayed on. But after his discharge without pay by the liberation government he appealed to the Council of State on the grounds that he hadn't been summoned to a hearing or allowed to present his defense. He argued that he could not be considered as defaulting—the only case in which a sanction could be taken in the absence of the accused party—since his Swiss address was well known. He also contested the ministry's claim that his career had consisted of assignments chosen so that he could obtain material for his books, for (so he said) considerable time had separated his service in any particular foreign post and the book he subsequently wrote about the place. In 1953 the Council of State voided his dismissal, agreeing that his Swiss address had been known. He was later reintegrated, retired with five years' pay and five years' pension.[14]

In October 1940 young diplomat Roger Peyrefitte had been arrested in Vichy while walking into a pastry shop with a teenage boy. Next day he was summoned to the Foreign Ministry housed at Vichy's Hôtel du Parc (which was also the headquarters of Marshal Pétain), to be confronted with the policeman who had arrested him. The ministry already had a file on Peyrefitte's *petites histoires* with teenage lads in Athens, where he had served in the French Embassy for five years. He was offered the choice: resign or be discharged. As it was not healthy to be known as a dismissed functionary in those days, Peyrefitte chose resignation. But he did want to return to duty, and was finally offered a post few would have considered attractive, at Fernand de Brinon's mission in Paris (Brinon was Vichy's liaison with German occupation authorities). For that assignment Peyrefitte needed German approval, so he wrote an old friend, Ernst Achenbach, head of the political section of the German Embassy in Paris, for a recommendation. He was put in charge of an office responsible for handing over German refugees to the Nazis, but he discovered that there were none left to hand over, so the job became a sinecure. And when the liberation arrived and Brinon and other high officials disappeared Peyrefitte stayed on, feeling he had done no wrong.[15] Indeed, he later said that he had managed to help some victims of the Nazis thanks to his "brotherhood of mores" with Achenbach's successor at the German Embassy, Rudolf Rahn.[16]

Peyrefitte himself described the next episode, but he did it in fictional form in the caustic *La Fin des ambassades,* in which real names coexist with invented ones. He called Suzanne Borel, a high official of the ministry who was to marry Georges Bidault, Mademoiselle Crapote. In the novel Peyrefitte calls on Mademoiselle Crapote to show her the memorandum he has written to justify his behavior during the occupation. He finds distinguished senior diplomats waiting their turn to be received by her, for she has become a national heroine. When she finally sees Peyrefitte she shows herself without pity for former colleagues, without pity for the visitor. The author mocks this purge supervised by "the least French of French ambassadors," for purge commission chairman Naggiar was born on the *"île de Levant."* "Wasn't the secret of the purge," Peyrefitte's hero asks himself, "that there had to be victims so that there could be heroes?"[17] Peyrefitte in real life was dismissed without pension or indemnity, but this had little effect on his budding literary career. At a time when the Goncourt Academy was giving its coveted literary prize to a Communist resistance heroine, Elsa Triolet—it was even said that the academy did this to save one of its members from the authors' blacklist[18]—Peyrefitte was runner-up in the voting for his novel *Special Friendships.* On the same day he received the almost-as-prestigious Renaudot Prize for this book which a newspaper called *Résistance* had praised.[19] Peyrefitte attributed this indulgent attitude on the part of the literary community to his friendship with the influential Communist cultural spokesman Louis Aragon, and with a younger Communist writer, Francis Crémieux, whose father Peyrefitte had sought to protect during the occupation. (This was Benjamin Crémieux, who as a literary adviser at a publishing house had read and admired *Special Friendships;* he was Jewish and died in the Buchenwald concentration camp in 1944.[20])

Beginning in 1953, when an amnesty law voided all such administrative sanctions (although without calling for automatic reintegration into the civil service), Roger Peyrefitte appealed the decision to discharge him without pension; it was a case he and his attorneys were to fight for the next twenty-five years. In 1960 the Paris Administrative Tribunal voided the dismissal on the grounds that Peyrefitte had not been informed of specific charges against him, nor had he been given an opportunity to defend himself before the purge commission issued its first decision; furthermore, the commission in its final decision had failed to take account of Peyrefitte's memorandum of justification, nor had it stated a motive for its decision.[21] On the same day, the tribunal ruled on Peyrefitte's claim for damages against allegedly defamatory statements made by the Foreign Ministry after publication of *La Fin des ambassades,* for the ministry had referred to acts committed by Peyrefitte which had been amnestied. Ministry counsel argued that in his novel Peyrefitte himself had referred to these acts, and that in any case such acts "contrary to honor and morality" were not covered by the amnesty. The tribunal decided that both the government—with its attack on Peyrefitte—and Peyrefitte—by disclosing information about the behavior of diplomats in his novel—were at fault. But the attack by the government hadn't hurt the sales of Peyrefitte's books; on the contrary. And he had provided plenty of details about his private life in his writings. Thus he received only one franc as "total and definitive reparation of the prejudice."[22] The decision was appealed by the Foreign Ministry to the Council of State, which two years later rejected it on the grounds that the ministry's responsibility wasn't reduced just because its statement had been designed to defend diplomatic personnel, nor because Peyrefitte's own behavior had been "reprehensible."[23]

But that was still not the end of the case. Peyrefitte also wanted his back pay, and had every expectation of being reintegrated at an appropriate rank. That meant an ambassadorship, which he had decided he would resign at once. He also expected an indemnity which he estimated at 3 million francs, but when it came (by decision of the Paris Administrative Tribunal in 1976) it was only twenty thousand francs. Peyrefitte appealed again to the Council of State, which decided that his appointment to the Brinon mission had been exceptional, and that—even if Bidault had not dismissed him—all such exceptional appointments made by Vichy had been voided by decree. Thus the twenty thousand francs was considered to be sufficient compensation.[24] In retrospect, Peyrefitte decided that he had not lost everything: Thanks to being purged he was able to become a famous writer instead of an obscure diplomat.[25]

In the desire to rid France of every trace of Vichy the new authorities took a dramatic and perhaps an unprecedented step. They not only purged the French diplomatic corps, but tried to purge the foreign diplomatic corps too. The Gaullists were determined to reject the credentials of ambassadors who had been accredited to Vichy. In fact only a handful of diplomats had remained in Pétain's capital after the liberation. They made the journey up to Paris in late September, but Foreign Minister Bidault refused to receive them. One of the blackballed envoys happened to be the papal nuncio, Valerio Valeri, dean of Vichy's diplomatic corps. De Gaulle had apparently been persuaded to refuse to recognize Valeri's status by the argument that traditionally each January 1 the nuncio presented New Year's greetings to the head of state, and it would be shocking for this man who had presented greetings to Pétain in January 1944 to do the same for de Gaulle in January 1945.[26]

And so papal nuncio Valeri was replaced by Monsignor Angelo Roncalli, then apostolic delegate in Turkey, later to become one of the most popular popes of modern times as John XXIII. In sending Roncalli to Paris (after indicating considerable displeasure at the rejection of Valeri), reigning Pope Pius XII let it be known that in return for this favor he expected the Gaullists to refrain from requesting changes in France's own Church hierarchy. We know a good deal about the liberation government's efforts in this area thanks to the revelations of a history professor, André Latreille, who in November 1944 was put in charge of church-state relations at the Interior Ministry. His Minister, Adrien Tixier, explained that the Provisional Government hoped to obtain the removal of several bishops who were felt to have collaborated. Latreille for his part feared that the Vatican could find it hard to accept this after the removal of nuncio Valeri.[27]

Already there had been indications of official attitudes concerning the church's role during the occupation. Cardinal Emmanuel Suhard of Paris, who in April 1944 had received Marshal Pétain at the gates of Notre Dame Cathedral, was informed by emissaries of the Provisional Government that his presence would be inopportune, even dangerous, when de Gaulle, with Georges Bidault, François de Menthon, and Pierre-Henri Teitgen attended their first mass after the liberation of Paris on August 26.[28]

As for public opinion: A poll in November 1944 (when André Latreille was taking up his job at Interior) discovered that 82 percent of the French felt that bishops who had collaborated should be punished. Ten percent disagreed; 8 percent had no opinion. Of those favoring sanctions, 57 percent felt that the government should take them, 32 percent thought it was a church responsibility, 11 percent said that both government *and* church should act.[29] During the liberation several bishops had been obliged to leave their dioceses; apparently there had been threats to other bishops, kept within limits not without difficulty by local authorities.[30] Latreille reveals that Interior Minister Tixier, a doctrinaire Socialist, showed sensitivity to the demands from his party's rank and file for action against the clergy. A memorandum dated July 26, 1944, which Latreille believes was written by Georges Bidault, then head of the CNR (and a Catholic layman), stresses "the silence of the bishops of France concerning the attacks by occupation authorities and Vichy on the most sacred rights of the human conscience"; the same memorandum identifies the bishops whose removal was recommended. Cardinal Suhard was at the top of the list. There was also a list of churchmen whose promotion to bishop *would* be desirable.[31]

One legitimate reason for removing a bishop was *odium plebis:* public objection. Nuncio Roncalli for his part felt that it would be difficult for him as papal representative to undertake an inquisition. Finally it was decided to appoint Thomist philosopher Jacques Maritain, who had spent the occupation years in the United States, as France's ambassador to the Vatican charged with negotiating the purge of the hierarchy. Latreille drafted a note suggesting the removal of twelve churchmen, three of them archbishops.[32]

By the middle of April 1945 André Latreille discovered that de Gaulle's own presidential office had assumed responsibility for purging the church, and by the end of May seven bishops had been removed, including two (the bishops of Arras and Aix-en-Provence) who had taken the initiative of bowing out. Replacements were chosen for them, and for other bishoprics previously vacated, with no public reference made to the forced retirement of the purged ecclesiastics.[33]

Indeed, we now have a document Latreille certainly did not see. It is a telegram sent to Foreign Minister Bidault, then visiting Washington, from de Gaulle himself, who describes a discussion with nuncio Roncalli in the middle of May 1945. Roncalli wanted to know the government's "definitive demands" and de Gaulle told him what they were: Five bishops had to go. Archbishop Maurice Feltin was "not desirable" in Bordeaux. Neither Feltin nor the archbishop of Reims should become a cardinal. Roncalli reminded de Gaulle that the church had already shown goodwill by removing the bishop of Aix-en-Provence. He promised to look into the other cases, with one exception, the bishop of Saint-Brieuc (although he agreed to keep the bishop out of his diocese for a year). As for Feltin, Roncalli did not wish his removal. De Gaulle commented to Bidault that the archbishop seemed to have won Roncalli's sympathy. But in any case, the nuncio had assured de Gaulle, Feltin would not receive his hat.[34] Feltin became archbishop of Paris in 1949, cardinal in 1953.

FOUR

Administrations: At the Base

ONE OF THE BIGGEST CHALLENGES to the purgers was France's educational system, which from Paris controlled 185,000 women and men in every French city and town, and in that most sensitive of areas: the young mind. Pétain had understood the importance of controlling that channel to French families, and an effective purge of Vichy required that professors, simple schoolteachers, and—importantly—their supervisors be above suspicion. As early as August 1943 a decree promulgated in Algiers called for a purge commission within the Education Ministry, and an investigation committee was set up that same December to deal with the volume of affairs that was expected. Each sector of the educational system was to get its own purge unit (a Conseil Académique d'Enquête), and then a higher body (Conseil Supérieur d'Enquête) would supervise procedures and deal with higher-ranking officers.[1]

For Paris, a Conseil Académique d'Enquête had begun to function informally even before the liberation; with the arrival of the Provisional Government it became the Purge Commission of the Academy of Paris.[2] We know something about the atmosphere of those first days thanks to a candid report in the Communist Party's Paris daily. Committees of the Communist-dominated Front National had set up temporary courts in each of Paris's high schools, ordering the reinstatement of those teachers who had been removed by Vichy, but also rendering justice "to the traitors and cowards." There were immediate suspensions, as well as transfers, forced retirements, the opening of investigations—arrests too. Decisions taken during these unofficial proceedings were apparently accepted by the ministry's secretary-general, himself a Communist and respected educator, although the final disposition of each case was left to an inquiry committee.[3]

And it was the Conseil Supérieur d'Enquête which had the final word on the six thousand cases submitted to it. An objective examination of its case load suggests the difficulties it had to face. On one hand, complaints against teachers and professors often betrayed traces of personal or professional animosity. On the other, the purgers had to weigh errors of judgment, such as that of a teacher who had joined a collaborationist movement in order to obtain the performance of his verse play, the work of his life. Talented artists had accepted invitations to visit Germany, young women had associated with members of the occupation army (who occasionally claimed to be not German but Austrian, and anti-Nazi at that). Or during a ceremony a headmaster might pay homage to Pétain as victor of Verdun.[4] As of June 1945, 2,362 persons within the educational system had been subjected to inquiry; of this number 370 received reprimands, 359 were transferred, 110 demoted, 69 released for duties, 90 retired, 17 suspended definitively or for a given period from pension rights, 194 banned temporarily or permanently from teaching (this was often combined with other penalties), 18 stripped of the right to wear medals; finally, 59 were dismissed with pension, 259 without. Seven cases were turned over to the War Ministry, 114 to the Interior or Justice Ministry. In addition, 357 higher-ranking educational officers were punished, 18 of them banned from their profession.[5]

A critic of this purge in education—anonymous, perhaps because he was one of the victims—blames the *"résistantialiste"* fury for the "ruin of all our university traditions," which he defines as "the freedom of the mind and the brotherhood or solidarity of people." This critic offers a view of the operations of the purge at the grass roots. In each high school or faculty, a committee "composed of porters, attendants, sweepers, dishwashers, students, monitors, teachers," was responsible for the initial investigation of a suspect. It was empowered to suspend teaching personnel and reduce wages by half pending a decision by the higher purge bodies. These inquiry boards, the anonymous writer assures us, were weighted in favor of the extreme left. He offers what he calls picturesque examples of their findings: A history professor in a colonial high school was discharged and replaced by a woman circus rider, since no one else could be found. A professor of modern languages was replaced by a tutor who had never passed a test in that language (the suspended professor refused to give private lessons although parents concerned about their children's final exams beseeched him). We are told that a Communist teacher denounced a colleague for having given a Fascist salute (the accused teacher said that he had only been waving), and of having spoken badly of liberal fellow teachers. The accusation sent the man to an internment camp and a Civic Chamber before he was finally acquitted.[6]

A more objective account of the purge of education concedes that early sanctions were harsh, as they were harsh in the courts. But the utilization of pardons and amnesties, especially after 1948, helped redress the balance. When the Council of State voided a sanction the case was reconsidered; after the 1953 amnesty, which extended the deadline for appeals, five hundred cases were reexamined. Even after the deadline the Education Ministry accepted appeals, and there were many cases of reintegration, reestablishment of pensions, voiding of demotions. This was more difficult in corps containing smaller numbers of persons, such as inspectors and university professors, easier for high school teachers, grade school instructors.[7]

With the teaching corps, the army represented another vast and sensitive institution calling for careful screening. Of course the purge of the armed forces had begun in Algeria, where the Free French war ministry had set up its own purge commission.[8] The December 1943 decree barring collaborators from public office also called for the suspension or forced retirement of officers and noncoms who had belonged to any such group. The military establishment had split not into two but many pieces in the aftermath of war and defeat. There were the soldiers and sailors who stayed in France and with Vichy, those who joined the Free French, and many others, particularly on the mainland, who served neither Pétain nor de Gaulle. In this last group some had joined the resistance, others collaborationist military or paramilitary units; many did nothing at all.

One of the first things the liberating forces did was to neutralize the neutrals. By an order whose number was to become familiar to the postwar army, Number 10010, the Gaullist War Commissariat advised commanding generals how to deal with military personnel found on the mainland. All officers who were not connected with the Provisional Government or the resistance army (the FFI) were to be considered detached from service; they could not wear uniforms or be called up except by individual decision based on evidence that they had served the resistance, or if their command skills were urgently needed. Officers had to fill out a declaration on their honor concerning their attitudes from June 25, 1940, to the present.[9]

What kinds of numbers were involved? The best authority on the subject says that there had been thirty-five thousand officers on active duty at the start of the war; of this number twelve hundred had died, eight hundred were reported missing, and there had been ten thousand prisoners at the time of the armistice. About one thousand officers had joined the Free French, either individually or with their units. On mainland France, the remaining eleven thousand were divided among the armistice army which Vichy had been allowed to maintain until November 1942 (forty-two hundred men), those assigned to civil corps (twenty-five hundred), those given armistice leave (forty-eight hundred). Outside France, eleven thousand officers had served Vichy in North Africa, West and East Africa, and Madagascar. After the Germans took over France's south zone in November 1942 some four thousand officers (out of eleven thousand) joined the resistance, either in combat or in intelligence functions, another eleven hundred found their way to North Africa, and one thousand more were able to retire because of age. This apparently left nearly five thousand who did nothing.[10]

Once estabished in liberated Paris, the Provisional Government's War Ministry took two expected decisions. One simply voided all nominations and promotions made by the "so-called" government of Vichy, although officers could keep the extra wages they had received. This measure would not apply to officers who after the Normandy landings on June 6, 1944, served in Free French forces or the resistance army.[11] The second decree, signed by de Gaulle and his War Minister André Diethelm on the same day, September 22, 1944, created a Commission for the Purging and Reintegration of Military Personnel, composed of a general as chairman, with three other generals to sit with him when the cases of officers of similar rank were heard, or five officers to deal with lower-ranking personnel.[12] The commission got a tough chairman in Major General Philippe-Paul Matter, a veteran of Verdun, director of the infantry after the First World War. With the arrival of Vichy he was forced into retirement because he was a Freemason.[13] The no-nonsense attitude of the Matter Commission can be discerned in its memorandum of October 26, 1944, which expressed concern that "officers about whom there would be much to say haven't hesitated in an effort to whitewash themselves to join [the liberation armies]." The commission requested that the names of such latecomers be sent in.[14] (Resistance people referred to these latecomers as *naphtilards,* literally, moth-ballers.[15]

And heads began to roll. We have an indirect indication of the dimensions of this purge in a remark by de Gaulle in October 1944, on a day when half a dozen officers had appealed directly to him. He exclaimed to his secretary, referring to his former military classmates: "They're all in the can!"[16]

A register recording the investigations of 253 general officers and quartermaster generals by the Matter Commission indicates the range of sanctions. A few cases were simplified by the fact that the officers concerned had been sentenced to prison and *indignité nationale,* and this latter penalty included loss of rank, suspension of pensions, withdrawal of medals. Other officers were dismissed without pension, still others with pension, forced to retire, or retired at the rank held before November 1942. Some were maintained in service but without assignment, while the totally innocent were recalled to active duty.[17] Only 40 general officers were kept on duty, and 1 of them was demoted to colonel. By the end of 1946, 10,270 officers of all ranks had been subject to examination. The Matter Commission returned 6,630 officers to duty, retired 650, dismissed 2,570.[18] It also examined 6,160 files of former prisoners of war, issuing 173 sanctions. Of the 99 general officers investigated in connection with their activity as POWs, only 7 were kept on duty; on the other hand some former prisoners of war or camp inmates were promoted to compensate for their involuntary absence from activity. This step was apparently taken to "lessen the bitterness of the majority," in the language of their historian.[19]

The severity of the Matter Commission, of the liberation government's War Ministry, still failed to satisfy hard-liners. A debate in the Consultative Assembly opposed Communist resistance veterans to the War and Justice ministries. Thus Maurice Kriegel accused the government of casting aside officers of the FFI, and objected to the policy of sending interned collaborators to serve in Indochina; in other words, he charged, patriotic officers were being eliminated while collaborators were encouraged to serve.[20] Indeed, a different kind of problem now faced the armed forces. On one hand the ranks had been filled to overflowing by a policy of integrating irregulars (the FFI resistance) into the armed forces. On the other, the postwar strength of the army was to require a severe reduction in the officer corps. Over eleven thousand officers were thus removed from the rolls in the course of 1946, as gently as possible, by another commission chaired by General Matter.[21]

Not only the central administration was concerned by the purge, of course. Outside of Paris responsibility was in the hands of the Comités Départementaux de Libération, whose recommendations (based on the findings of local purge committees or tribunals of honor) went to the Regional Commissioners of the Republic, who in turn forwarded the cases, with recommended punishment, to the appropriate ministries. It is estimated that between forty thousand and fifty thousand local officials were the targets of investigation, and that over eleven thousand cases went from the Regional Commissioners to Paris.[22]

Archives allow us a closer look at how the purge was handled on the ground. Here is an autumn 1944 decision of the Comité Départemental de Libération of the Ain district sitting in Bourg-en-Bresse: On the advice of its education commission, the CDL asked the rector of the local school system and the Commissioner of the Republic to remove the inspector of primary schools in a neighboring town, and to send him out of the district—but not with a promotion. The motive: In 1940 and 1941 the inspector had shown himself to be "an ardent auxiliary of the repressive policy of Vichy with respect to teachers." His attitude in those years actually called for a harsher sanction, declared the CDL, but his attitude in the last year made it possible to recommend this lighter punishment.

A village teacher was cited for immediate dismissal. The motive: He had been a propagandist and recruiter for the paramilitary Service d'Ordre Légionnaire, and acted as the representative in the Ain district of Vichy's information and propaganda department.[23]

In November 1944 the Commissioner of the Republic Gaston Cusin reported from Bordeaux that he had carried out "a severe purge of all administrative personnel." It had been done gradually in the financial services so as not to disrupt essential functions, rapidly in the political and administrative services. This, he told Paris, had not put an end to criticism of civil servants "whose precise activity during the occupation could not be known and who are thus judged on external appearances or as a result of the vengeance of their subordinates." Such criticism, Commissioner Cusin felt, paralyzed the work of the civil service; he wished to see a deadline for receiving complaints.[24] As late as November 1945 Cusin reported that although the work of the purge commissions had been completed, the press continued to publish reports that alleged collaborators remained in public service.[25] Read in the light of more recent charges against Cusin's Prefect Maurice Papon (at this writing accused by resistance veterans of facilitating the Nazi transfer of Jews to German camps and death), these comments take on unintended significance. On the national level, in 1945 a public opinion poll asked whether the administrative purge seemed sufficient, insufficient, or too severe. Fourteen percent of the sample replied "sufficient," 65 percent "insufficient," 6 percent "too severe." Qualified replies accounted for another 3 percent, while 12 percent had no opinion.[26]

How many civil servants were affected by the purge, in all? Just as was true for the number of deaths, for other sanctions, exaggeration has confused the issue. To the charge that there had been 120,000 such sanctions, the government pointed out that if all government departments were included, as well as public corporations such as the railroads, the total was in fact 16,113.[27] In the national administration alone the purge as called for in the June 1944 decree had affected 11,343 persons:[28]

Dismissal without pension	4,052
Dismissal with pension	521
Forced retirement	841
Temporary or permanent suspension of pension	215
Temporary suspension of duties	1,024
Demotion in rank	367
Demotion in category	608
Automatic transfer	1,516
Warning	347
Reprimand	965
Delay in promotion	36
Ban on exercising profession	822
Withdrawal of medal	29

Those purged could appeal. First, through normal recourse to the Council of State, the final arbiter of administrative acts; later, thanks to parliamentary amnesty. Even a rapid review of decisions of the Council of State allows us to see how various governmental departments dealt with their black sheep, and to what extent their decisions stood up to scrutiny by more fastidious legal minds. The Council of State refused, for example, to accept sanctions against relatives of collaborators—e.g., it did not allow a son's participation in the paramilitary Service d'Ordre Légionnaire to be held against a senior judge even if the latter had not disavowed his son.[29] It did not accept punishment of the wife of an officer of the compulsory labor service for Germany, whatever material benefits she had derived from her husband's position.[30] Nor could a civil servant be held to account because he had not manifested feelings contrary to those of a son who had enlisted in the Militia.[31]

The council distinguished between cases of government officers whose duties had required regular contact with the Germans, and others who in the course of their work had not had to deal with the enemy. The accused had to be shown to have willingly and intentionally committed an act. And a distinction was made between participation in a group with the unambiguous name Collaboration, and simply joining the Pétainist veterans' group, Légion Française des Combattants, which could have seemed the patriotic thing to do.[32]

For a commander of municipal policemen in Paris to have repeated Radio Paris's collaborationist propaganda in talking to colleagues and subordinates justified a sanction, while simply going to hear a lecture by a collaborationist did not.[33] But the Council of State rejected punishment for a group of government officers on the vague charge that they had "served with zeal and admiration the Vichy government and thus can be considered to have favored the efforts of the enemy."[34]

Starting with an amnesty voted in 1947, administrative sanctions were softened. At this time, punishment by transfer (a minor sanction on the scale) was simply amnestied, although this did not give the official the right to return to his job, which often left the person in limbo. But it was the law of August 6, 1953 (to be discussed in its place), which finally wiped out all administrative sanctions.[35] It did not provide for automatic reintegration, but made that more possible. In fact its most immediate effect was to restore pensions. All sanctions previously ordered were stricken from the books, so that a "dismissed civil servant" became, simply, a "former civil servant."[36]

VI

PEOPLE AGAINST PEOPLE

"The engineers, contractors, and masons who built the Atlantic fortifications [for the Germans] walk among us without fear.... They are building walls for new prisons for journalists who made the mistake of writing that the Atlantic fortifications were well made."

—JEAN PAULHAN, 1947

ONE

Engineers and Contractors

Young Raymond Aubrac, Commissioner of the Republic in Marseille, was a revolutionary at heart. And everything about his last-minute assignment as Charles de Gaulle's proconsul for six southern French administrative districts told him that his powers were boundless. In his view he had been put in place to change things; that was what the resistance had been all about. He felt that his determination was shared by Justice Minister de Menthon, as well as by his friend Emmanuel d'Astier, Interior Minister, who was to move ever closer to the Communists in the aftermath of liberation.[1] Like Yves Farge in Lyon, who took over the Berliet family truck-manufacturng empire, and de Gaulle in Paris, who was to nationalize the Renault automobile works, Aubrac acted against big business. And perhaps the Marseille experiment was the most radical of all, in that it was more systematic in its attack on industrial collaboration, and at least as socially oriented as the others. It also contributed to Aubrac's early departure from the Commissariat of the Republic.[2]

What Aubrac did was to take over fifteen large Marseille companies, three of them concerned with shipbuilding, two in heavy manufacturing (including locomotives), five involved in harbor facilities, two in electrical equipment, one each in public works, distribution of electricity, carpentry—companies employing a total of eighteen thousand persons. In Aubrac's view, the purpose was both to purge and to reform, while at the same time maintaining industrial activity for the war effort. The decrees signed by Aubrac to requisition these plants referred both to the January 10, 1944, decree which had created the Regional Commissioners of the Republic, and to a 1938 law which authorized the seizure of installations required in the war effort. Aubrac and his men selected managers from the ranks of the companies taken over, managers who were assisted by consultative committees composed of workers, management staff, shareholders.

It was an ad hoc reform obviously not destined to survive the return to traditional ways. But Aubrac himself would later say that he had never received precise government instructions to revoke these decisions—decisions which were "in their substance as in their form of a temporary character."[3] The requisitions were nevertheless voided by the Council of State, one after the other, starting in December 1946.[4]

What the national government really hoped to achieve is indicated by the October 16, 1944, decree on the purge of business and industry. The preamble provides a rationale: The economic recovery of the nation would be compromised by the presence of owners, managers, foremen, even workers or white-collar personnel who had collaborated with the enemy. But their prosecution in the courts was likely to take a long time. So it was essential to take immediate measures to purge this business community. Collaborators could be transferred to another job, or be suspended with or without salary, could be dismissed with or without indemnity, could even be banned from holding a position of responsibility in the company or profession involved. And none of these sanctions prevented the courts from sentencing the subject for collaboration crimes.

Each region was to establish a Comité Régional Interprofessionnel d'Epuration, composed of court officers, representatives of Comités Départementaux de Libération, of labor and employee associations, middle-level staff, with a representative of employers too. These regional committees could set up separate sections in iron and steel, chemicals, transportation, banking, and other areas. The committees could recommend punishment, but the decision belonged to the Regional Commissioner of the Republic or, in the Paris region, to the prefect; appeal was possible to the Council of State. Finally, a National Interprofessional Purge Commission (CNIE) was established by the same decree. It was headed by a superior-court justice, sitting with two representatives of the CNR, representatives of the government, and the same mix of workers and management already provided for. The CNIE could take up a case on its own initiative or when the government or a regional committee sent it in. It could issue sanctions, subject only to Council of State review.[5]

There was another way to get at business profiteers, and where it would hurt most: taking back the money earned through collaboration. On October 18, 1944, the government issued detailed instructions for calculating the amount of profit made from trading with the enemy, and for getting the money back. "Independently of the penal action which must be applied to bad citizens," read the preamble, "the most elementary fiscal justice requires that the Treasury recover illicit proceeds earned over a period of four years of war and occupation." This measure covered two kinds of profiteering: dealing with the enemy and speculation (for example, profits made by violation of price regulations and rationing, or by taking advantage of enemy rules or requisitions). The confiscation of such profits was to be considered a fiscal measure, and did not rule out the possibility of later prosecution of the same offender for acts of collaboration.[6] In January 1945 the decree was modified to include, among other things, profits earned in connection with seized Jewish property. The same decree speeded up procedures in order to cope with the large number of cases to be dealt with—there were 12,906 on the docket.[7]

How the system could affect a particular company can be observed in records now available to us. The Ateliers de Construction de la Seine, a public works company, had been accused of working for the Germans, and no one denied that it had. Total proceeds for this activity amounted to 129,307,600 francs, of which 10 percent was deemed to be profit. The sum of 8.5 million francs was confiscated, with a 4-million-franc fine added. On appeal, it was agreed to deduct from the total illicit profit moneys owed by the Germans but never actually paid (some 5 million francs), and a sum (6 million francs) which the company could prove it had given secretly to a local resistance group. That left 1,800,700 francs, which after taxes represented a fine of 1,654,800 francs. But the case was also before the CNIE, which had been alerted by Bordeaux, where a bill was discovered in the files of a German military-construction agency for services rendered by the Ateliers. Since a Court of Justice had already acquitted the director of the company on collaboration charges and the Comité de Confiscation had done *its* job, the CNIE decided to drop the case.[8]

It was never simple. The archives contain reams of complicated bookkeeping. They had to find out how much an accused company had earned before the war in order to determine how much of its work during the occupation was to be considered profiteering. Individuals who had made money in illicit ways were clever enough to conceal their earnings, say by the purchase of paintings and other objects. Companies could doctor their books. Many owners and managers had worked both sides of the street, building up records of help to the resistance while dealing with the Germans.[9]

Nevertheless, this particular form of punishment could begin immediately, and could be seen. Minister of Finance René Pleven called a press conference in December 1944 to show how it was done. He described a typical case: One André Marquer had married his cook, a German. Marquer's father manufactured clothing. His German daughter-in-law established contact with the German purchasing agency. Under the arrangement, the Marquers acquired material, blankets, sheets, on the black market, without receipts, and resold these goods to the Germans. Thanks to patient investigation by tax officials, who had begun the job even before the liberation, it was determined that the Marquer family had sold 700 million francs' worth of fabrics to the Luftwaffe, and did 30 million francs' worth of work for the same organization; profits alone amounted to 250 million francs. The family had moved into a luxurious apartment, had acquired rare furniture, tapestries, paintings, three castles, buildings in Paris, property in Monaco, a stud farm with thirty horses, automobiles and trucks, expensive jewelry, gold (found in one of their castles by the FFI). It was estimated that they would have to pay back 500 million francs in confiscations and fines.[10] When all their affairs had been sorted out the levy came to 247,169,465 francs in confiscated illicit profits, 900 million francs in fines.[11]

Soon the press was publishing lists of profiteers, as announced by Comités de Confiscation. Certainly whole books could be written about some of these cases, for example about a speculator involved in dozens of real estate ventures, who faced a 1.9-billion-franc confiscation and a 2-billion-franc fine.[12] In October 1945 the Paris auction house staged what was announced as the first in a series of sales of seized property. It happened to be the Marquer estate; the younger Marquer and his German wife were then in jail and the government sought to collect its fine by sale of the castles and other property; among objects which brought the highest bids were art objects in jade, a gold cigarette lighter and case.[13]

Outside of Paris the harvest was usually less spectacular. In the Haute-Savoie 628 individuals were investigated, and by March 1946, 313 cases had been heard, resulting in confiscations totaling some 70 million francs, and fines of 18.9 million.[14] In the Toulouse region, 2,322 cases were opened by the end of July 1945, and 348 settled, for a total of 527 million francs in confiscations, 592 million in fines; by the end of that year the total was up to 1.85 million francs. The Commissioner of the Republic for that region, Pierre Berteaux, described one particularly difficult case. In September 1944 the Comité Départemental de Libération of the Gers district had decided to levy a voluntary contribution from dealers in armagnac brandy. But it was feared that by a relatively small contribution (100 million francs) these dealers would avoid further sanctions. For it turned out that they had sold considerable quantities of their brandy to the Germans at eight or nine times the market price. After the liberation the dealers were to say that such sales had been a form of resistance, for they had made the Germans pay dearly. The authorities were not going to let the dealers get away with their occupation trading that easily.[15]

Today it is possible to examine the long-secret files of the National Interprofessional Purge Commission. A first reaction may be surprise. For many very large corporations are cited in the CNIE files, yet the individuals called up for sanctions are not often owners or directors of these corporations. They are lower-level management, shop foremen, simple workers on the floor. Some of the major companies which supplied goods and services to the Germans were never punished except through lower-echelon personnel.

The first session of the CNIE took place on December 20, 1944, at which time Paul Mongibeaux, who was to be the High Court's presiding justice in the trial of Philippe Pétain, served as prosecutor. His opening remarks described the intent of the October 16 decree which authorized the purge of business. It was essential, he explained, to prove the intention to help the enemy. He pointed out how difficult it was to punish those most responsible for a financial crime. How remove the top man without hurting his innocent personnel? As for members of a board, how could removing them from operational responsibility represent punishment, when they had no such responsibility to begin with?[16] On January 3, 1945, the CNIE held its first working session. It was hardly a momentous one. Despite the fact that the liberation government had been in power for over four months, the first two cases before the commission were insignificant. An officer of a corporation was accused of denouncing fellow officers; he was ordered to be dismissed without indemnity, banned from his profession, and the case was forwarded to the courts. The director of another company was accused of increasing production for the Germans, favoring the dispatching of French workers to Germany. In the face of his denials the panel held the case for further investigation. It was finally heard on January 24, with witnesses for and against the defendant. Workers stressed his hostility to the resistance, his bias in favor of collaboration. Finally the panel decided to punish two other officers of that company for their activity and attitudes (three months of suspension without pay for each) while the director himself received no sanction—the investigation had discovered that he had participated in resistance activity.[17]

Case after case concerned small fry. Thus at the giant Citroën automobile plant the factory purge committee had drawn up a batch of cases, forwarding recommendations to the CNIE—e.g., for a night watchman accused of having made pro-German, anti-Gaullist, and anti-Allied remarks, they asked for prison and a permanent discharge. Dealing with twelve such cases on February 7, 1945, the CNIE dismissed all but two as insufficiently proved. In one of those two, a worker had been found to have denounced fellow workers; he was to be dismissed without indemnity, his file forwarded to the courts for possible prosecution. In the other, a worker had expressed antipatriotic attitudes and had encouraged fellow workers to go to Germany; he got a three-month suspension without pay.[18]

On March 12, 1946, the panel heard the case against Armand Galliot, managing director of the Nobel Corporation, and of his deputy Maurice Belloc. They were accused of supplying material to the Germans for offensive missiles; the deputy was also charged with having provided the Germans with information, and of facilitating the delivery of explosives to the enemy at the time of the Allied landings in Normandy. The managing director was banned from all activity as a company director, his deputy from management responsibilities.[19] But in June 1948 the Council of State voided the decision concerning the managing director for technical reasons (his deputy had since died). The case was heard again that December, at which time the CNIE determined that the defendant had done all he could have done to delay delivery of material to the

Germans; it noted that a Court of Justice had heard the same charges but dismissed the case. So Armand Galliot was acquitted.[20] The director of the Nobel factory in Normandy was accused of associating with the Germans beyond the requirements of his job; he was ordered to be transferred to another post in the same company.[21]

The range of cases heard by the CNIE provides a broad view of economic activity, and of life in general, during the occupation. But did the commission, despite the conscientious pursuit of complaints connected with industry, from executive office to shop floors, miss the bigger picture—the mentality of collaboration, the intrigues that couldn't be found in the books? It sometimes seems so, for as much energy went into cases against artists, circus owners, theater directors, as against contractors and bank presidents.

But there were some notable affairs. The president and leading officers of the Banque de Paris et des Pays-Bas were accused of collaboration in a weighty file to which Finance Minister Pleven and a Committee of Liberation of the Banks had contributed. The CNIE paid particular attention to the role of Paribas, as it was known, in setting up Franco-German companies with joint capital, and facilitating German participation in French oil companies; it also arranged payment for delivery of French goods to the Germans. The bank's president, André Laurent-Atthalin, was banned from running a bank in future, while several of his subordinates were also sanctioned, with the option of returning before the commission should they receive a dismissal or acquittal from a Court of Justice.[22]

Officers of the Banque Nationale pour le Commerce et l'Industrie, of the Worms Bank, were accused, heard, absolved.[23] Directors of a large plant in the Als-Thom group were accused of supplying war material to the Germans. The evidence consisted of testimony by workers, some of whom were hostile to management because of its labor policies. But the defense was able to argue that these directors had actually slowed down production. It could also be said in the directors' behalf that the company had operated under close German scrutiny.[24]

The commission held twenty-six hearings in its first full year of activity, 1945; next year there were sixty.[25] The mix of cases, the need to deal with factory-floor grumbling as well as with the manipulations of high finance, continued to keep the investigators busy. In

1947, when there were a total of sixty-six hearings, one case involved a worker at the Simca automobile factory against whom another worker testified: "From the beginning of 1942 when I began to work at Simca he had a collaborationist attitude. What is worse, when the Germans captured Sevastopol, this man applauded in the locker room in front of all the others, saying, 'I'm glad that Sevastopol was taken.' . . . In 1943, when we all laid down our tools to commemorate Armistice Day on November 11, he continued to work." But in his summing-up the prosecutor allowed for doubt since some witnesses had been favorable to the defendant, and he had served in the First World War. He was nevertheless discharged without pay.[26]

In the summer of 1947 the delegate of workers and the deputy delegate for technicians on the CNIE panel resigned to protest a decision concerning the Francolor chemical works. Both protestors were delegates of the Confédération Générale du Travail (CGT), the Communist-dominated union, and the CGT approved the move, informing the government that it would no longer send delegates to the panel. What had gone wrong? The CNIE was considering the cases of the president and other top management of Francolor, which company had been founded during the occupation by three French chemical companies and Germany's giant I. G. Farben (which held 51 percent). According to the charge this arrangement represented a German takeover of a significant branch (dyes) of the chemical industry. Francolor's president was blamed not only for running the company but for encouraging the sending of workers to Germany, yet his sanction was limited to his being barred from further responsibilities in the chemical industry. Three of his associates were exonerated, two others to be heard at a later date.[27]

The panel sought in vain to lure the union delegates back. Many cases were still to be heard, and several company directors had been suspended pending the outcome of their cases; the delay was harmful to production. But the CNIE's work was held up for months, and at the time 425 cases were on the docket (454 had been disposed of). Then in May 1948 the government announced that it simply would not accept the resignations of the CGT men. Hearings began again the next month, although neither the union delegates nor those representing the CNR showed up.[28]

Some of the most colorful cases were still to come. The commission had a fat file on antique dealers, for example—some with shops, others working from home. Usually the charge was selling precious French art to the Germans. Thus in 1949 the CNIE heard the case of two dealers who had sold Nazi Marshal Hermann Göring a collection of seventeenth-century tapastries showing the coronation of Hapsburg Emperor Charles V. Each dealer received a one-month reprimand, the decision to be posted at the entrance of his shop.[29] An art dealer and two accomplices were accused of conspiracy to acquire and ship to Germany, fraudulently, four Beauvais tapestries of considerable value. The art dealer was felt to be the least responsible, and received a reprimand limited to two weeks, but one of his accomplices, an advertising salesman, was banned from his profession for two years, while the other, a Russian who claimed to have been curator of the pre-Revolution Petersburg museum in Russia, was found to have been the chief artisan of the deal, and he was given a two-year ban on work in his profession or in any managerial post.[30]

The purge of the nation's business class could never have been thorough, if only to keep the factories humming in the interests of economic recovery.[31] Jurists contested it; its most decisive sanction, confiscation, was seen by bar leader Jacques Charpentier as a return to "the worst traditions of tyranny." He called the purge committees "caricatures of courts," less concerned with justice than with politics; the punishment of a manufacturer could become "a factory revolution organized by discontented personnel against a boss on whom they were taking revenge."[32] Actually, the government was not using the purge to reform the economic and social system; such a tactic was rejected out of hand by Justice Minister Teitgen, who said that to do that would represent "an abominable abuse of power."[33]

So that if the economic purge was less earthshaking than the political one it was at least in part because the government wanted it that way. As a progressive Catholic, Justice Minister Teitgen himself was far from sympathetic to capitalism in its crudest form. But he felt that if a company president had to be indicted because his factory had produced for the Germans, then his top managers, his engineers, would also have to be indicted—and why not the firemen, and then the workers who had actually painted the swastikas on the tanks? If the answer was that the worker had only been trying to earn a living, then wasn't this also true for the company president? When Teitgen took over as Justice Minister he told de Gaulle that he did not look forward to the assignment, yet if duty required that he serve he would do so. But he added that he would not allow forty thousand resistance veterans to judge 40 million other Frenchmen. He'd bring the murderers, denouncers, and other true criminals before the courts—not the others. He made it a point not to prosecute leaders of business or industry, although he did favor the confiscation of profits earned in trade with the enemy. But if a company president had done nothing more than run his plant he was not to be sanctioned. This attitude obviously led to sharp clashes with the Communists.[34]

TWO

The Renault Affair

WHAT RAYMOND AUBRAC had done in Marseille, Charles de Gaulle could do in Paris, and better. If Aubrac had acted against the builders and movers of the Mediterranean, his decisions would not last much longer than the authority of the Commissioners of the Republic. De Gaulle could punish by confiscation and make the punishment stick by nationalization. The companies selected were leaders of their industries, and their owners and managers had been accused of collaboration. Shareholders were awarded compensation (to the protest of the Communists: "We know that the trusts betrayed France," declared Party Secretary Jacques Duclos in October 1944; "their property must therefore be taken away from them").[1]

But in December 1944, when the coal mines of northern France were nationalized by decree, the government made it clear that the purpose was a "desire to found a new economic policy" and not punishment, for mine owners had generally been above reproach during the occupation. Here the idea was rather to facilitate the return to normal operation of these installations, which were brought together in a public corporation. As de Gaulle himself later explained it, this nationalization was aimed at both social reform and economic recovery. Furthermore, de Gaulle hoped to seize the initiative from the Communists. And so one after the other the chief sources of energy—electricity, gas, oil—came under the wing of government, followed by major institutions of credit—the Banque de France at the top of the list.[2]

But punishment was the motive for the takeover of the Société

223

des Moteurs Gnome et Rhône, manufacturers of aircraft engines.[3] Air Minister Charles Tillon, a resistance veteran and not incidentally a representative of the Communist Party in the liberation government, had prepared the ground by declaring; "It's not an arbitrary decision by the state against an important sector of private industry, but a patriotic act made necessary by the attitude of the former directors of this company." True, its chairman was then waiting trial in Fresnes prison.[4] A month later, air transportation became a virtual government monopoly with the nationalization of Air France; Minister Tillon, revealing that Air France had turned over a fleet of aircraft to Germany in 1943, described the activity of the company as "clear treason."[5]

But most large companies were impersonal; except to ideologists who saw the end of the war as an opportunity for changing the form of the economy, their takeover could only seem an abstract, disembodied sanction. It took the Renault affair to make the purge of big business dramatic. Renault was first of all a person, a character suitable for the stage or a novel. He was a crotchety old man, and he had been crotchety as a young man too. Louis Renault lived for his work. A biographer saw him as "always in bad humor, irritable, tense, even more aggressive because of his natural shyness."[6] That writer (no man of the left) described Renault's philosophy in between-the-wars France succinctly: "Henceforth, in this France devoted to orgies, the eight-hour day, with a growing population of stateless persons and Africans, where quality gave way to mediocrity and the work spirit to having a good time, Louis Renault was to behave as a foreigner."[7] An autocrat convinced that he could run his own company in his own way (without interference by unions), he happened to lack the paternalistic instinct which often accompanies such rugged individualism.[8] He was the frog in La Fontaine's fable, so author Pierre Drieu La Rochelle told Renault's wife, Christine. (The fascist Drieu La Rochelle happened to be Christine's lover, and placed her at the center of his novel *Beloukia*.[9])

Not surprisingly, when the Second World War arrived Louis Renault was unwilling to adapt himself or his factories to it. The government was obliged to move in to augment production, and the patriarch was considered inadequate to the task.[10] (He was then only sixty-two, but an old sixty-two.) Instead of remaining far from his sprawling plant on the edge of Paris, safe in southern France when the Germans marched into Paris, Renault returned, and was available when the occupying forces sought his help; the owner's chief concern seemed to be to preserve both plant and workers for the postwar. We have stories of the sparring between the German delegate assigned to the factory and Louis Renault, increasingly handicapped, notably in speech. (It is worth mentioning his health during the occupation, because of subsequent allegations that his later physical condition was a result of brutal treatment by his resistance jailers.) London radio denounced the collaboration of the Renault company, and in March 1942 the RAF bombed the Paris facilities.[11]

The biographer most sympathetic to Renault shows us the *patron* at sixty-seven, pedaling on his bicycle at full speed to reopen his Paris plant on August 20, 1944. But soon the Communist daily *L'Humanité* was accusing the Renault company of having failed to provide tanks and planes for France's war in 1939, and then offering itself to the Germans just a year later. Despite the growing offensive, Louis Renault continued to go to the plant on each of the following days. But eventually he too got the message. He began living away from home (he spent one evening, we now know, with Lucien Combelle, publisher of a collaborationist newspaper who was to be tried and convicted by a Court of Justice).[12] Under the headline PURGE! PURGE!, *L'Humanité* reported ominously on September 19 that Renault had still not been arrested. In fact a warrant had been issued as early as September 4.[13] But Renault was not ready to give himself up. He was willing to talk to an examining magistrate, if he could do so as a free man.[14] In a reply to the examining magistrate's questions Renault declared: "After the armistice I was forced to work for the Germans, but I always sought to limit production. . . ."[15] On September 23, in what the magistrate described as a "painful" session, Renault expressed himself with difficulty. He denied having had direct contact with the Germans: "I never took meals or drank with enemy subjects."[16] Renault was placed under arrest and taken to Fresnes. There he was examined by three doctors who found him "senile, barely conscious of the situation, amnesic, and speaking with great difficulty." He could not give his age or the name of his brother, denied that he was ill or that he had had syphillis. The diagnosis was: "early stage of senile dementia . . ." This and the subject's arterial condition called for transfer to a psychiatric hospital; meanwhile he was placed in the prison infirmary. There he was examined again and it was noted that as early as 1940 he had shown signs of dementia; his condition had worsened progressively; he was considered a danger to himself and to others.[17] Once again, these details are important, showing that contrary to what his partisans were later to claim, Renault's condition was far from ideal when he entered prison.

"With the arrest of Louis Renault, the trial of France's heavy industry begins," declared Albert Camus in an unsigned editorial on page 1 of *Combat*. For French manufacturers, Renault among them, had worked for the enemy. Camus's argument, he admitted, was a moral one. "To say it all in a word, the problem is in the responsibility. An industrial leader who lived with all the privileges of his rank cannot be judged like a minor official who obeyed Vichy because he was used to obedience." Camus dismissed the argument that if Renault had not collaborated the Germans would simply have taken over his factories. "That happened elsewhere and the result was pitiful." He compared Renault to resistance fighters "without stock or cash. . . . What was for them the simple duty they discovered in their hearts should have been for Louis Renault an urgent and ineluctable obligation."[18]

The Renault plants were taken over. Renault and his chief deputy, René de Peyrecave, were indicted.[19] And in January 1945 a decree signed by de Gaulle as President of the Provisional Government liquidated the Renault corporation and transferred its property to the state. The preamble to the decree described the economic importance of these factories, their utility to the enemy, repeating the charge that Renault's production for the French army had been "notoriously inadequate" before the war, while it worked efficiently for the Germans after the defeat. Louis Renault's share of the company was simply confiscated, although other shareholders were to be compensated.[20]

But it was the old man who provided the drama. Later the Renault family and their friends were to make grave charges concerning mistreatment of the prisoner, alleging that he died not of the causes given in his death certificate but of what happened to him during his confinement at the Fresnes prison infirmary, particularly during the night of October 3, 1944, when he received blows causing a brain hemorrhage. It was revealed that Renault's widow had managed to have the corpse X-rayed through the closed coffin, and received the results with a note calling attention to a fracture of the first cervical vertebra.[21]

The night of October 3? What we can learn from heretofore confidential documents is that Renault was transferred to the psychiatric hospital of Ville-Evrard in Neuilly-sur-Marne on October 5; then on October 14 one of his attorneys urged—on the basis of a medical examination—that he be transferred to a surgical hospital. A new examination on October 17 determined that his life was in danger; this time the diagnosis highlighted a pyelonephritis (a kidney disease) at its "final stage," and a chronic prostate condition. The patient was transferred to a surgical facility in Paris, where he died on October 24, "the result and consequence of cerebral complications of vascular origin," so read the official autopsy on October 28. Renault's deputy René de Peyrecave was released on parole on January 4, 1945, and his case was dropped in 1949, for he was found to have taken no personal initiative. By remaining in contact with the Germans when he could have avoided it Louis Renault himself was found to have made it easier for the Germans, but since he was dead the case against him was also dropped.[22]

But the controversy remained alive. Perhaps the company was now and forever the Régie Nationale des Usines Renault—the National Renault Administration. Still, the partisans of the patriarch, his family, his apologists, continued to put forth the charge that his death had been caused or hastened by brutal treatment.[23] As late as 1956, a dozen years after the fact, widow Christine Renault and her attorney Jacques Isorni (now a familiar figure in the defense of accused collaborators) filed a complaint alleging that Louis Renault had died as a result of rough treatment. Isorni was convinced that resistance prison guards had actually removed Renault from the infirmary to beat him up in a section of the prison under control of the FTP (the pro-Communist resistance army).[24] The body was exhumed, but court officers failed to find evidence of the damage which the plaintiffs thought had been demonstrated in the X-ray taken through the coffin earlier. A year later the Renault complaint was dismissed.[25] But a book about Renault published as late as 1969 continued to express doubts concerning the cause of death, suggesting not only that he may have been murdered, but that the murderer might not have been a prison guard but the government itself.[26]

Apart from a few spectacular nationalizations it could not be said that the maximum demands of the resistance for moral reparation were being met. In the following years the industrial map of

France changed less than any resistance ideologist could have imagined would be the case (during the harsh occupation years); few entries in *Who's Who* had to be changed, or omitted. Purge procedures were slow, often focused on minor offenders. Appeals taken to the Council of State modified, mitigated decisions announced in the immediate wake of liberation. The Council of State stressed the limits of the purge of business and industry. It held, for example, that stockholders who had helped set up a business during the occupation could be sanctioned, as could a partner even if he himself had not participated in collaboration although approving it. But a partner who had taken no part in management and received no share of the profits could not be punished.[27] An employee of a film company which had made movies for the Germans could not be punished for that fact alone. But the head of a company who had encouraged his employees to work for the Germans deserved the punishment he received—so ruled the council.[28] Or a factory owner who had fired workers who refused to come in on Sundays or who displayed insufficient productivity, was acting in a way "to favor the enemy's plans," for this company produced goods of use to the Germans.[29]

Labor unions were covered in the same July 1944 decree which dealt with employer associations: The leaderships of both were to be purged according to identical criteria.[30] But nothing was said in this decree about rank-and-file workers.[31] Then a National Commission of Reconstitution of Labor Organizations was established in October 1944 by the Minister of Labor, with the participation of the major trade-union federations. In its first announced decision it banned fifty-six persons from union activity as well as union membership for life.[32] Operating on the basis of directives approved by the unions, the commission thus punished not only union leaders but individual members who had participated in Vichy-sponsored labor activities. Later the Council of State was to set things to rights, pointing out that no law authorized the commission to exclude simple members from a union.[33]

THREE

Ideas in Print

ONLY IN ONE AREA OF economic activity did the purge really work, and conspicuously. It was a clean sweep; here everything had to go. Newspapers confronted every French citizen every day. During the German years every line of every paper had been monitored by the occupation authorities or by Vichy and often by both; it was not only a matter of what should not be printed but what had to be. No daily, no weekly or monthly with political or social content could be free of propaganda. From the point of view of the Free French there were no good mainland newspapers in those years, not even in the southern half of France after November 1942 when the Germans took over what had been Vichy's zone.

There was another side to the purge of the press. For resistance ideologists, the prewar press had been dominated by occult interests: Influential dailies were in the hands of big industry, the banks. Planners for the postwar often stressed the need for cleaning up the financial situation of this press.[1] They called for simple suspension of newspapers which had continued to appear during the occupation, the seizure of their plants—plants to be utilized by the resistance press or by newspapers which had voluntarily suspended publication in the Vichy zone in November 1942.[2] Soon after setting foot on liberated territory in Normandy, de Gaulle's battlefield Commissioner of the Republic François Coulet issued a decree suspending all newspapers and periodicals, placing their presses and other property under government control; the Commissioner would authorize the appearance of new papers as this became feasible.[3] As the liberating armies moved in, the people of France were informed by London radio: "We are sending you press officers who have nothing military about them save their uniforms. They will perhaps arrive with the first Allied troops to outline our ideas and plans. If they don't arrive at once, don't lose any time: Apply the essential principles yourselves. ... Remember, representatives of the resistance, resistance journalists, that you have the duty to see to the confiscation of any press enterprise which operated under the Vichy regime."[4]

Indeed, as a historan of that dramatic month tells us, it is possible to follow the progress of the Allied advance across Normandy through the dates of appearance of the first issues of the new newspapers. Those which had been published during the occupation prudently shut down in the hours preceding D-Day, so that the new Commissioner of the Republic found himself without a daily paper which could publish his announcements. Hence Coulet's launching of the paper newly baptized *La Renaissance du Bessin,* published on the presses of the *Journal de Bayeux,* which paper had been taken over. Bayeux's new paper was able to proclaim on its masthead: "The first newspaper published in liberated France." In nearby Caen, the first issue of *Liberté de Normandie* appeared "under the bombs," printed by hand in a few thousand copies per issue.[5]

Although the Free French planners had supplied the clandestine Commissioners of the Republic and their prefects with instructions concerning the postliberation press, the first significant decree setting forth the policy of the liberators with respect to the press was signed by de Gaulle on June 22, 1944. It called for suspension of all newspapers and periodicals which had served Vichy, the takeover of their property. Regional committees composed of representatives of the Gaullist government, of Comités Départementaux de Libération, and of anti-Vichy newspaper personnel were empowered to approve the publication of new dailies and other periodicals "as it becomes materially possible to do so."[6] The final decision was of course in the hands of the proconsuls of the liberation government—the Commissioners of the Republic. In his memoirs one of these proconsuls, Michel Debré, tells how as Commissioner for the region of Angers he encouraged the birth of new papers, handpicked their publishers; in a sense he had to redraw the map of the press in the districts within his jurisdiction.[7]

But the principal directive was yet to come. It was the decree of

September 30, 1944, issued in liberated Paris, which codified the dreams as well as the practical solutions of the Gaullists and their mainland resistance allies. First of all the new decree confirmed the ban on all newspapers which had seen the light of day during the occupation, and on all papers existing before the June 1940 armistice which continued to appear a fortnight after that armistice in German-controlled French territory, or more than a fortnight after the Germans moved into the Vichy zone on November 11, 1942. Further, newspapers and periodicals which had been published by individuals under prosecution by the purge courts were also suspended until their cases were decided. Papers exclusively devoted to religious, literary, sports, scientific, or professional concerns which had published no collaboration propaganda could be authorized to reappear. The ban on a newspaper was to end if its owners or editors were not put on trial six months after the present decree took effect.[8] This cutoff proved too short, for the courts couldn't move that quickly; in February 1945 the ban was extended for a second six-month period.[9] Another decree ordered a permanent ban on the use of the titles of collaboration newspapers; the preamble explained why: "Whatever the guilt of the publishers of these newspapers, the titles bear the memory of shame, of treason. They cannot be placed at the service of the nation after having been instruments of its servitude."[10]

The September 30 ban on collaborating newspapers was eventually to affect 900 different dailies, weeklies, and other periodicals, while 649 press companies were subjected to judicial seizure.[11] And a wholly new press was ready to take over—new titles, many born of the resistance such as *Combat, Libération, Franc-Tireur, Défense de la France,* or prewar papers which were felt to have gone through the war uncompromised, like *Le Progrès* in Lyon, *Le Figaro,* Socialist *Le Populaire,* Communist *L'Humanité.* New editors and reporters, many of whom arrived in a straight line from the underground, dominated the postwar scene, and in fact the law saw to the strict screening of the older generation. The September 30 decree excluded from the press not only those found guilty of treason but writers who had displayed "a weak patriotism or who had not maintained a sufficiently independent attitude with respect to the enemy."[12] The purification was to be carried out via a system of official press cards without which one couldn't get near a typewriter. This screening, more strict than that for any other profession, allowed one of the new journalists—Camus—to declare in *Combat* that "journalism is the only field in which the purge is total, because we carried out, in the insurrection, a total renewal of its personnel."[13] Perhaps today's press had its faults, he added, but at least it depended on no one. "France now has a press liberated from money. This hasn't been the case for a hundred years."[14]

In his own memoirs de Gaulle tells us how he bent the law, when necessary, to grant authorizations to appear, or to reappear. In the case of *Le Figaro* the authorization was given to an editor who didn't even own the paper; in the case of Catholic *La Croix,* which according to resistance criteria should have been banned, he accorded his personal *nihil obstat.*[15]

By the end of 1944 the profile of the new press—Parisian, provincial—was clear. If most prewar papers had been ostensibly nonpartisan, such publications now represented a small percentage of total daily circulation; the majority of papers were henceforth affiliated to political movements, resistance groups.[16] One of the few significant unattached general newspapers of the postwar was to be *Le Monde,* which used the presses and even some of the staff (as well as the typography and the sober style) of the preoccupation journal of record, *Le Temps.* This conservative daily had been one of the targets of the press reformers, and it did happen that *Le Temps* continued to appear for seventeen days after the Germans marched into the Vichy zone in 1942. It therefore fell under the ban, and of course directors of this paper felt that the deadline had been set at fifteen days to make sure that *Le Temps* would disappear.[17]

Not surprisingly, the articulate people who were excluded from the liberation press, and their apologists, would describe the purge as plundering.[18] "From one day to the next," wrote one defender of the despoiled, "families were cast into misery. How many fine people, printers from father to son, were thus robbed of their property, deprived of their living!" That writer added that the takeover "was accompanied by scenes of violence which were often horrid."[19]

And the press purge got additional punch through a May 1945 decree calling for court prosecution of newspapers—and not only of their owners. It was "inadmissible," declared the decree's preamble, that the company which had published a paper serving enemy propaganda for four years could escape any form of sanction. To punish publishers, editors, didn't always prevent the newspaper company itself from pursuing its activity, with the accrued capital earned through its treason. Owners who had objected to the collaboration of their paper would be protected: In the event of confiscation, their shares would be indemnified. For in the event a newspaper was found guilty in court the penalty would be liquidation of the company, confiscation of its property. The same punishment applied to publishing houses, news and advertising agencies.[20] Paradoxically, the new procedure opened a breach in the September 1944 decree banning collaborationist newspapers, for now if a paper was acquitted in court it could recover its property and publish again; only its original title remained banned.

At the beginning of 1946 the Paris Court of Justice found itself with ninety-four of these cases on the docket—book publishers as well as newspapers. Twenty-four cases were turned over to the court's financial section, for they concerned illicit profits; the other seventy were deemed to concern political collaboration. The subjects of judicial action included notorious collaboration sheets such as *Je Suis Partout,* famous names of the prewar which had become German mouthpieces, like *Le Matin* and *Le Petit Parisien,* even a once-prestigious magazine, *L'Illustration.*[21] One notable case, heard in 1948, concerned *L'Oeuvre,* a daily which had moved out of the Vichy zone in September 1940 to return to its traditional headquarters in Paris, where it served as the organ of collaborationist Marcel Déat. Although the newspaper's owners protested that they had personally opposed Déat, and they pointed out that the Germans had even set up a separate company to run the paper without them, the company was banned, with total confiscation.[22] The case of *Le Petit Journal,* the organ of hapless Colonel de La Rocque, was less clear-cut. La Rocque's successors had been able to demonstrate that their leader had cooperated with the Allies, who had asked him to continue to publish as before, so as not to draw the attention of Vichy and the Germans. Attorneys for *Le Petit Journal* argued that the twenty-five articles from the paper cited as favoring collaboration had been the "ransom" paid by La Rocque to be able to pursue his patriotic efforts. But the prosecutor felt that the paper had been more collaborationist than necessary all the same. The court didn't agree with him; the newspaper was acquitted.[23]

By the end of 1948, of 538 press and publishing enterprises brought to trial under the May 1945 decree, 115 had been convicted. Sixty-four were subjected to total confiscation, 51 to partial confiscation. Thirty were acquitted. Another 393 cases had been dismissed, and 35 remained on the docket in Paris. The right to pardon applied to corporations, often reducing the percentage of property seized, even allowing former owners to recover their papers. Indeed, the old press reborn soon became a threat to the new resistance press.[24] "Can we ... watch without horror the resurgence of these papers with their old leadership more or less camouflaged?" asked resistance writer Rémy Roure in an editorial in *Le Monde* in mid-1948. At the time there was a fear that some of the prewar papers which had served the enemy would survive the purge intact, a prospect which *Le Monde*'s man thought would be demoralizing for the country.[25] And then time would do its work. The longer it took to prosecute, the less urgent it seemed to ban a paper, to dissolve a company. The case of *L'Illustration* came to trial only in December 1949. Even then the magazine was dissolved, and 10 percent of its property was seized. But the dissolution was rescinded in June 1954, along with the ban on publication.[26]

Dealing with book publishers was no less of a problem; in a sense it was more of a problem. For a daily newspaper could be defined by its editorials. But often the same publisher who turned out collaboration propaganda and racist tracts did fine books by prestigious authors. Following the liberation these houses had not been shut down, and some were busily engaged in publishing the work of resistance veterans. How draw the line? Resistance writers themselves were confused. Could you put a big publisher out of business because he had collaborated if he was also your own publisher? Two of the most prominent imprints of occupied Paris, Gallimard and Denoël, happened to be the houses of prominent Communist resistance writers, Louis Aragon and Elsa Triolet; indeed, Aragon and Triolet were published by them during the German occupation.

In the underground resistance authors had worked within the framework of a Comité National des Ecrivains (CNE), the National Writers Committee, whose organ was the underground *Les Lettres Françaises*. This paper engaged in constant attacks on collaborationist writers and periodicals, and its contributors (obliged to remain anonymous) included not only François Mauriac, Albert Camus, and Jean-Paul Sartre, but the leading literary editor of Gallimard, Jean Paulhan, even while Gallimard was publishing the monthly *Nouvelle Revue Française* edited, with German endorsement, by an avowed Fascist, Drieu La Rochelle.

Late in 1943 the National Writers Committee issued a "Warning to Publishers." It declared that the enemy had infiltrated publishing houses, read the manuscripts of patriotic writers, and denounced them to the collaboration press, exercising blackmail, flooding the market with German propaganda. The resistance writers called for a purge of these publishers at the moment of liberation.[27]

Then liberation came. The CNE organ appeared in the open. Its first issue contained a CNE statement committing resistance writers to refuse publication in newspapers, periodicals, book series which published the work of collaboration authors. Significantly, this manifesto did *not* pledge resistance authors to refuse to have their books appear in the same houses which published collaborators.[28]

As with other professions, book publishing soon had a purge committee. Attached to the Ministry of Education, its membership included Jean Bruller, who under the pseudonym Vercors had founded the underground Editions de Minuit, which had published his anticollaboration novella *The Silence of the Sea*. Jean-Paul Sartre, who had been published by Gallimard during the occupation and whose plays were performed on the stage in German Paris, but who was a resistance man at heart, was also a member.[29] He and the other panel members complained that this purge committee had no legal status, no means to enforce sanctions. To protest their helplessness they announced their intention to suspend activity at the end of November 1944, after three months of work. One of the committee's few achievements until then had been the appointment of Jean Paulhan as liquidator of Gallimard's *La Nouvelle Revue Française*.[30] At the beginning of February 1945 the purge of publishers obtained more authority with the creation of a Consultative Commission for the Purge of Publishing, responsible for compiling cases and making recommendations for sanctions to the National Interprofessional Purge Commission (CNIE). Its chairman was Raymond Durand-Auzias, head of a lawbook-publishing house. Vercors remained a member, with resistance publisher Pierre Seghers, CNE member Henri Malherbe (a writer), and the veteran Catholic journalist and publisher Francisque Gay. Editors and lower-echelon staff of publishing houses, and the bookselling trade, were also represented.

Chairman Durand-Auzias understood how difficult their job

was going to be. As he summed up the problem in March 1945 to the CNIE, a publishing company isn't only a business, so publishers couldn't be called to account only for their financial dealings with the enemy—as was happening in other professions. It was the books they published which defined their treason. "A treason quite hard to define in juridical terms ... and yet infinitely more serious in its consequences, immediate and long term, than the simple fact of having sold leather or cement to the enemy." The sanctions provided for did not include a ban on the names of publishers, and yet it would be just as wrong—argued the chairman—to allow names such as Denoël to continue to appear on book jackets as to authorize publication of a periodical with a title used under the Germans, even if run by new people. The imprint of a publisher guilty of treason would hurt the reputation of the author, which author could not, because of contractual obligations, switch publishers or prevent the sale of his book. Even if the head of a publishing house was banned from his profession under the October 1944 decree on the purge of business, another person could step in to use his imprint. Durand-Auzias suggested a range of penalties which would extend to removal of a publisher's name from book covers, and even to liquidation of the firm.[31]

That was the ideal, but it was not to take concrete form. No major publishing imprint, whether or not its owners or directors were indicted or convicted, disappeared from the bookstores. Publishers held on to their authors—to resistance authors too. And indeed few publishers received sanctions proportionate to the services they had rendered to the occupying forces in lending their names to the myth that all was normal in German Paris, that cultural life could go on as usual under Nazi rule.[32]

Cases transmitted by the consultative commission were heard by the CNIE in the presence of publisher Durand-Auzias. Some seemed simple enough—e.g., the collaborationist managers of Ferenczi, a prewar house taken from its Jewish owner during the occupation, were banned from the profession, as was the owner of the promiscuously collaborationist house of Baudinière, accused of having done pro-Nazi books without the obligation to do so. The investigators were in possession of charges that Director Gilbert Baudinière had denounced booksellers who didn't sell enough of his collaborationist books, as well as fellow publishers considered to be insufficiently collaborationist or who published works he considered subversive. But the house of Sorlot, one of the chief targets of resistance invective, received only a "reprimand without publicity." There were extenuating circumstances, for this house was able to show that it had published pro-German books under pressure (although not, the commission felt, under irresistible pressure).[33]

One of the most obvious targets of this purge was Denoël. It had not only flooded the market with the provocative anti-Semitic writings of Louis-Ferdinand Céline during the occupation, together with the pro-Fascist *Les Décombres* of Lucien Rebatet, but publisher Robert Denoël had actually sold 360 of his 725 shares to a German. But Denoël was found dead on a dark street in Paris in December 1945, and to this day it is not known whether the crime was connected with the collaboration, Denoël's private life—or was a random act. But his death ended the case.[34]

Although the major offenders were major publishers—for a prestigious imprint gave more importance to a collaborationist work—the purgers were occasionally to display zeal in running down lesser offenders too. One of these was a young publisher from Marseille, Robert Laffont, cited for having brought out three books containing collaboration doctrine. Laffont, who was then twenty-nine years old, protested that these three titles were part of a total production of sixty in three years of occupation. "During this time not a single translation from the German, not a single work inspired by German propaganda, no propaganda work for Vichy, was published by our house," he explained in a letter to the CNIE in January 1946. "Not a gram of paper, not a franc of subsidy or sales derived from dealing with the Germans was received by our house." He concluded: "This fact is so exceptional that it gives our firm a status which (apart from the underground publishers) no other house can claim no matter how high it may be in the leadership of our profession or in the purge committee." Apparently the panel agreed, for Laffont was acquitted.[35]

But of course the case everyone was waiting for was that of Gallimard, prestigious publisher of many of the greats of between-the-wars France, Gide and Malraux notably. Gallimard, as has been said, was host and sponsor of the German-endorsed *Nouvelle Revue Française.* Like other major houses, Gallimard had continued to publish under German censorship, and thus bowed to the ban on Jews and other writers expressing anti-Nazi sentiments. The investigation determined that in order to prevent a takeover of the company by the Germans, publisher Gaston Gallimard had agreed to turn over the house pride, *La Nouvelle Revue Française,* to the Nazis' candidate for editor, Drieu La Rochelle. In Gallimard's favor it was held that he had published noncollaborating authors when they were not actually banned by the Germans, avoiding Nazi authors. Gallimard produced a file of letters from editors and authors known to be favorable to the resistance. Thus Albert Camus pointed out that his office at Gallimard had served as a meeting place for resistance activists. "Although he did not know the details of this activity, Gaston Gallimard knew it was going on and always protected me in this respect." Camus added that many resistance authors like himself had continued to publish with Gallimard during the occupation, and used this opportunity "to maintain what they felt they had to maintain." Moreover, warned Camus, "any judgment against this house is a judgment against them. And personally I should consider myself, with other colleagues better known than I (Valéry, Gide, Paulhan, Sartre, et al.), as condemned by such a judgment. ..." No less impressive was the statement of André Malraux, a Gallimard author and editor of considerable prestige, an anti-Fascist of the 1930s who had refused to be published in Paris during the occupation—even by Gallimard. At the time of the purge he was de Gaulle's Minister of Information, after having participated in the armed resistance. His affidavit, in the form of a letter to Gaston Gallimard, declared that Gallimard had done the right thing.

And then came Sartre. He pointed out that he had been a member of the first publishing purge body, and that it had found no reason to punish Gallimard. Gaston Gallimard, he said, was a friend who had opposed the Germans and knew his house was being used for secret meetings. Therefore, said Sartre, any blame issued against the house of Gallimard would also stain Aragon, Paulhan, Camus, Valéry, himself, and others—"in brief, all the writers who belonged to the intellectual resistance and were published by him." Sartre added that Malraux, Gide, and Roger Martin du Gard had advised Gaston Gallimard to accept Drieu La Rochelle as editor of *La Nouvelle Revue Française.*

Poet Paul Eluard, a Communist and a CNE militant, also dropped a letter on the pile: "Despite the risk represented by the imposed presence in your house of the miserable editor of [*La Nouvelle Revue Française*], I never felt the slightest suspicion in walking into the building. I felt myself protected courageously, effectively, by you and by those you chose as your associates." All that happened here was that Gallimard could no longer call itself Editions de la Nouvelle Revue Française—its preferred imprint before the war.[36]

The case against Grasset was less ambiguous, because founder Bernard Grasset had personally committed himself to collaboration. In November 1940, for example, he had praised "the creative power of the Führer" in a book he published.[37] Grasset had been arrested at the liberation, was detained at the Drancy camp before being placed on parole in a rest home.[38] But he was the publisher of François Mauriac, and there was an outcry against the threatened closing of the house which had discovered Proust and Malraux. Grasset received a three-month suspension of activity, and it was expected that the case would be dropped so that he could return to run his business.[39] In fact the relatively mild sanction was due to the publisher's health, and the fact that a relatively small number of the books he published under the occupation had contained enemy propaganda.[40] But this was not to be the last of the Grasset case.

For the purge of publishers took two forms: professional sanctions by the CNIE, and then the trials made possible by the decree of May 1945 which also covered newspapers and periodicals. Files had been opened at the Paris Court of Justice against Gallimard, Denoël, and others. Most of these cases were dropped because of lack of evidence of serious collaboration. Even the case against Grasset seemed slight to a magistrate who examined the evidence.[41] But it was the most solid of the cases sent to court, and after two days of trial in June 1948 the Grasset company was found guilty and ordered to be liquidated, with confiscation of 99 percent of its property. The defense had claimed, in vain, that other publishing houses with similar activity during the occupation had not been sanctioned, nor had authors of books which Grasset was blamed for having published. Later the liquidation of Grasset was replaced by a fine, and the verdict pardoned.[42]

FOUR

Writers and Artists I

BUT HOW PUNISH AUTHORS, and their writings? At what point could they be considered to have transgressed the limits of freedom of expression, and how and who was to determine that they had? The problem was compounded by the fact that some ardent collaborators were eminent men of letters, the pride of French culture. "Our glory doesn't weigh much compared to theirs," exclaimed a noted poet (so Sartre reveals) after seeing a list of collaborationist authors which included Henry de Montherlant, Louis-Ferdinand Céline, Jacques Chardonne.[1] Then could talent excuse an author who had served the enemy? A number of influential people seemed to think so, and some of these influential people had been identified with the resistance. Charles de Gaulle, on the other hand, felt that the greater the artist the greater his impact for harm. In the case of those who had chosen "the opposite camp ... one could see too well toward which crimes and which punishments their eloquent instigations had pushed poor gullible people. ..." Being a writer was hardly an excuse. "For in literature as in everything else, talent is a responsibility."[2]

During the occupation, resistance writers of the National Writers Committee (CNE) had used the pages of underground *Les Lettres Françaises* to attack the leading figures of collaboration literature—Drieu La Rochelle, Robert Brasillach, Henry de Montherlant, Paul Morand. They even had words of criticism for an apolitical writer like Colette for contributing an article to a collaborationist newspaper, although in this case the resistance gave

240

her the benefit of the doubt, suggesting that she may not have known in what context she was to be published. "And this maneuver, whose mechanism we have just demonstrated, proves that in giving the occupation press the tiniest article even if it has no political significance, a writer plays his part in the concert of enemy propaganda orchestrated by Goebbels. . . ."[3]

The writers' purge began as a CNE initiative. The first issue of *Les Lettres Françaises* published aboveground in liberated Paris announced that a commission has been founded to draft a list of collaboration authors. Members of the CNE pledged not to write for any newspaper or periodical, not to contribute to any anthology or series, which also published collaborators. Already in its first plenary session on September 4, the CNE organ revealed, a first list of collaborators had been drawn up, which included Brasillach, Céline, Chardonne, Drieu La Rochelle, Jean Giono, Marcel Jouhandeau, Charles Maurras, Montherlant, Morand.[4] The next issue of *Les Lettres Françaises* published a fuller list—94 names in all—including members of the French Academy, the Goncourt Academy, Vichy civil servants, writers who had written regularly for collaborationist periodicals.[5] In October the CNE's purge commission brought in a revised list, and this one contained 158 names. Again the stars of collaboration were included, some of whom would be tried and shot as traitors, such as Brasillach, Paul Chack, and Georges Suarez. There were famous names such as Pierre Benoit, Sacha Guitry, and of course Céline, Chardonne, Drieu La Rochelle, Giono, Jouhandeau, Maurras, Morand.[6] Later the international congress of PEN, the writers' organization, meeting in Stockholm, voted (seventeen to five, with three abstentions) in favor of world circulation of such blacklists. Delegations from countries that had been occupied by the Nazis voted affirmatively, while the United States, Ireland, German-speaking Switzerland, India, and South Africa voted against the proposal. The United Kingdom was an abstainer.[7]

Soon the least conformist of men of letters, Jean Paulhan, reacted against the blacklist. He himself had been an active member of CNE but he was now unwilling to see friends and fellow writers branded as collaborators. He argued that writers were often in the opposition, and that they had the right to be wrong; he refused to be a voluntary gendarme.[8] With irony he described a situation in which resistance veterans would spend all their time writing in newspapers and magazines, since purged writers no longer received space, and so would have no opportunity to create serious literature. "During this time the collaborationist writers, left in peace, will be off working by themselves. In five or six years they'll return in force with ripe works. . . ."[9]

The problem was defined in another way by Jean-Paul Sartre in his new monthly, *Les Temps Modernes,* in an essay significantly called "La Nationalisation de la littérature." In his view, writing was now being judged by the resistance credentials of the author instead of for itself, and there was a danger that critics would go on from there to applaud a work because the author belonged to the same political party as the critic.[10]

Paulhan pursued his campaign against the writers' purge in the months and even the years to come. He was to resign from the CNE, together with Georges Duhamel, Jean Schlumberger, and Gabriel Marcel, persons who in any case had no place in the increasingly political atmosphere of that group (it would soon become an undisguised Communist instrument). In an open letter to those who were resigning, Vercors expressed concern that henceforth publications which had refrained from publishing collaborators for fear of losing more important writers would publish them again, so that those who continued to respect the blacklist would not be able to contribute to these publications. In other words, it was now the CNE writers who were condemned to silence.[11]

Paulhan for his part pointed out that Romain Rolland, who had been a dissenter in the First World War, would have been blacklisted under CNE criteria.[12] In a series of open letters beginning in the spring of 1947 Paulhan argued that it was not for writers to denounce other writers. He observed with irony that "the engineers, contractors and masons who built the Atlantic fortifications [for the Germans] walk among us without fear," and were actually constructing new prisons "for journalists who made the mistake of writing that the Atlantic fortifications were well made."[13] In other words, writers were being treated more harshly than those who had made more tangible contributions to the Nazi war machine.

But blacklisting was a moral sanction, with uncertain financial effects. The purge of writers assumed an official form as well, as it did in all professions. Authors who went before a Court of Justice, as we have seen, were those who had written regularly for the collaborationist press. Indeed, their literary genius was often cited by those who sought to save them from punishment. Thus after the conviction of Robert Brasillach, François Mauriac appealed to fellow writers (on a *Le Figaro* front page) "that they take pity on imagination, even when guilty—especially when it is a young man who incarnates it."[14]

It happens that no outstanding author actually stood trial. Drieu La Rochelle, whom some would place in that category, escaped arrest by committing suicide while in hiding. Jacques Chardonne was arrested and interned. In his writings published during the occupation he had expressed sympathy for the Germans, and he had even joined a delegation of French writers on a visit to Germany. In his own defense he argued that he had made the trip in order to protect other French writers from arrest by the Gestapo, and he claimed to have protected resistance writers Georges Duhamel, Mauriac, Paulhan, and Aragon, to have sought to obtain the release of Colette's Jewish husband, Maurice Goudeket, from detention; he had even tried to save the poet Max Jacob, but Jacob was dead before the rescue efforts got under way.

Before the war Chardonne had been an eminent man of letters and a publisher. He came to his pretrial interrogation armed with impressive testimonials from resistance writers. "Even his errors are noble," Paulhan had written. Mauriac agreed that Chardonne "made a mistake" but certified that "he obeyed no low motive." Even Pierre Bourdan, who had broadcast for the Free French in London, offered support: "Those who possess the facts have the duty to make a distinction between a great mind which went astray for a while and those whose motives had little to do with a crisis of conscience." It didn't hurt that a resistance leader had offered a testimonial to the effect that Chardonne's son had been in the resistance, and had been arrested by the Gestapo. The case against Chardonne was dropped.[15]

The Céline affair could have been tumultuous, thanks to the irrepressible personality of this author, who during the occupation had been as provocative as he had been in the immediate prewar years. He declared, for example, that the Germans were not killing enough Jews.[16] He had joined last-ditch collaborators at Sigmaringen in Germany, then slipped over the border to Denmark at the end of the war. In April 1945 the Seine Court of Justice issued a warrant for Céline's arrest, and the French ambassador in Denmark requested that he be arrested and returned to France. The author was indeed arrested, but kept in jail in Copenhagen for over a year, after which he elected to remain in exile. He knew, he wrote attorney Jacques Isorni, that if he had remained in Paris he should have been assassinated, "either in the night and without a word like Denoël, or at the Palace [of Justice] and with words, like Brasillach." He repeated the then familiar comparison between the harshness of the purge of writers and the apparent leniency shown to businessmen. "With three or four kilometers of the Atlantic wall, I'd be out of it!"[17] The prosecution finally decided to try Céline not for collusion but for the lesser offense of "acts damaging to national defense."[18] The trial was held in the absence of the defendant in February 1950, and Céline denounced it, from Denmark, as a "Dreyfus affair in reverse."[19] In fact Céline had attested in writing to the poor state of his health which made his return to France for trial impossible. But as he made it clear to his lawyer, Albert Naud, he really feared that if he came back he'd be locked up.[20] The sentence was a year of prison and a fine, confiscation of half his property, *indignité nationale* for life—but a year later he was amnestied. "I'll sue the first person who even *alludes* to this," he wrote a friend triumphantly. He was soon back in France.[21]

But courts were for major offenders. The professional purge could deal with acts of collaboration of all kinds and degrees—by factory owners and workers, farmers, salesmen—so why not by writers and artists? But if a factory owner could be considered within the jurisdiction of the Ministry of Production, say, which government office had jurisdiction over creative talent? It would be the Ministry of Education. For writers and artists, as for factory owners and other professionals, punishment was to take the form of financial sanctions. A decree of May 30, 1945, which set up the procedure for the purge of men of letters, authors and composers, painters, illustrators, and engravers explained in its preamble that public opinion "could not accept the fact that works which had as their object or effect to favor the purposes of the enemy or to oppose the war effort of France and its allies can continue to be a source of profit for their creator." So a procedure was established similar to that for other professions. "But if it seems desirable to subject these writers and artists to a ban or limitation of professional activity having the character both of public censure and a financial sanction, we must carefully avoid any system of repression affecting the right of free expression of thought." The decree set up separate purge committees for, on one hand, writers and composers, and on the other, painters, illustrators, sculptors, and engravers. Writers and composers were liable to a ban on works that were responsible for the sanction, as well as to a temporary ban on new works, contributing articles to the press, lecturing, broadcasting, receiving royalties. Artists were liable to a ban on exhibiting and selling works, selling material to the press, lecturing, broadcasting, receiving payment for work. In both cases sanctions were limited to two years, or for persons convicted by a purge court, for the length of the sentence, for a maximum of five years.[22]

The Comité National d'Epuration des Gens de Lettres, Auteurs et Compositeurs was put together at a meeting held at the headquarters of the Association of War Veteran Writers on July 25, 1945. Two members, Francis Ambrière and Simone Saint-Clair, had been delegated by the Société des Gens de Lettres; Charles Vildrac had been chosen by the Société des Auteurs et Compositeurs Dramatiques; composer Joseph Szyfer, then in charge of musical instruction for the government, by the Société des Auteurs, Compositeurs et Editeurs de Musique. Gabriel Audisio came from the National Writers Committee, General Edouard Brémond from the Association of War Veteran Writers. The government appointed the chairman, Gérard Frèche, attorney general at the Paris Court of Appeals. Complaints were processed by three-member examining commissions, which called in an accused author to inform him or her of the charges pending, and then request a verbal or written defense. The accused writer could engage a lawyer. The examining commission passed the case up to a plenary meeting of the purge committee, which could accept the commission's recommendation or reopen the case.[23]

The files of the writers' purge suggest that the committee lacked means. It could hardly be said to have before it the totality of a defendant's writings for the occupation years, or even a fully representative sampling in most cases. But it did dispose of such evidence as lists of German propaganda films and broadcasts to which writers had contributed.[24] In turn the committee would be called on for help by other agencies—e.g., the prefect of police of Paris, before issuing passports or visas to writers or lecturers, had to know if the applicants had been sanctioned.[25] Publishers, newspaper editors planning to assign stories, and authors' associations wishing to know if an author was allowed to receive royalties came to the committee for help. A professor in Scotland who was preparing an anthology of contemporary literature appealed to the committee, for he wanted to avoid including banned authors.[26] The French Cultural Services in New York forwarded a request for similar information from the U.S. Dramatists Guild.[27]

Of course the writers' purge committee had before it the CNE blacklist. It also disposed of batches of questionnaires which authors' societies had sent out to their memberships. The Société des Auteurs, Compositeurs et Editeurs de Musique, for example, had sent out a printed questionnaire asking members to certify on their honor that they were telling the truth; questions covered membership in collaborationist groups, personal relations with Germans, writing songs or scenarios serving German propaganda. Had the author enjoyed the right to use a private automobile during the occupation? (This was an indication of official favor.) Had he participated in broadcasts, performances, visits to Germany? Not surprisingly, members failed to confess to reprehensible behavior.[28]

It can be said that the committee's achievement hardly represented a bloodbath. There were no spectacular cases, and few writers of international standing or worthy of inclusion in an encyclopedia were punished; the list of sanctioned individuals is far less comprehensive, for instance, than the CNE blacklist. One reason for the slim results was the committee's decision not to hear the cases of authors subject to trial.[29] This shortened the list of candidates for purging considerably, and certainly eliminated the most notorious, for they were the ones most likely to be under indictment. Committee files show that when an author faced trial or even investigation by another body, the committee couldn't get its hands on the file anyway, and so it postponed or dropped the case. And by the time an accused collaborator was acquitted by a court, or had obtained dismissal of his case, the committee had all but forgotten his existence. So there was the paradoxical result that sanctions were applied to persons generally considered less offensive, certainly less promiscuously collaborationist, while many persons generally felt to have been more active as collaborators slipped out of the committee's grasp.

Some famous names did get onto the docket. There was a case on Jean Cocteau containing unsupported charges of collaboration.

In his reply to the questionnaire of the Société des Auteurs et Compositeurs Dramatiques, Cocteau himself asserted that his play *The Typewriter* had been banned in occupied Paris, while the pro-Fascists of the PPF had noisily interrupted a performance of *Les Parents Terribles*. Cocteau added that his contributions to the occupation press had been strictly cultural. He failed to appear when summoned, but the panel nevertheless decided that no collaborationist act could be pinned on him.[30]

The file on reclusive and rural Jean Giono was also unhelpful, but it emanated from a Court of Justice (in Aix-en-Provence, which forwarded it to Paris). The worst that could be said about him was that he had written for Drieu La Rochelle's *La Nouvelle Revue Française*. On the questionnaire which Giono had sent in to the Société des Auteurs et Compositeurs Dramatiques, he had replied to the query "Did you help the occupying power recruit workers for Germany?" with a two-page statement describing his sheltering of fugitives from compulsory labor service in Germany; he hid them on his farm where, he added, the first armed group of partisans in his district, the Basses-Alpes, had been founded. He had given refuge to a member of the German Communist Party wanted by the Gestapo for three years, and had hidden so many Jews that a collaborationist sheet had called him "the Jewish Consul of Manosque" (the name of his town). His case was dismissed.[31]

And Pierre Benoit, prolific and romantic, a member of the French Academy: He had been arrested at his home in Dax on charges of collusion with the enemy, brought to Fresnes prison; but the pretrial examination had uncovered no acts of overt collaboration and he was released. The committee took a careful look at the charges. Benoit's publisher certified that none of the author's work had been published during the occupation, that he had rejected offers to work for the German press or movie studios. The committee decided that the charges hadn't been proved.[32]

Of those actually sanctioned, the most prominent was certainly Henry de Montherlant, austere and aristocratic, fascinated by the German mystique of virility. In judging this author the purge committee had before it his replies to the questionnaire of the Société des Auteurs et Compositeurs Dramatiques, in which he claimed to have been censored by German occupation authorities, and said that he had refused invitations to visit Germany. Montherlant submitted a separate thirty-two-page statement on his attitude to Germany before the war, his relations with Vichy and the Germans. There was a file of his articles in the Paris occupation press, including one dated July 4, 1942, in which he spoke of "the struggle of the heroic elite of the new European civilization against the low-Europeans," adding: "Europe would have died of mediocrity without the shock it received in 1939." The committee's punishment of Montherlant took the form of a ban covering a time period which had already elapsed. He was deprived of the right to publish or to receive income from his writings for a year beginning on the first of October 1944, although the sanction was voted on October 29, 1946. So that when it was asked, shortly after this verdict, to define Montherlant's status, the committee declared that "nothing prevents new works of this author from being published or performed." Under the decree, works which had motivated a sanction could be banned permanently; hence the committee's reference to new works.[33]

Decisions of this Comité National d'Epuration des Gens de Lettres, Auteurs et Compositeurs were published in the *Journal Officiel* as decrees of the Ministry of Education. Thus on June 26, 1946, decisions taken during eight sittings between January and April of that year were published; on January 26, 1947, decisions of eight additional sittings between May and October appeared. Then there was a long pause. But in 1948 most of the criminal procedures had been disposed of, and the government thought it was time to take up the job again and to finish it: "Public opinion," as an anonymous Education Ministry official summed it up, "wishes the liquidation of pending business."[34]

FIVE

Writers and Artists II

THAT LOFTY INSTITUTION, the French Academy, had always attracted the most conservative personalities, or rather one may say that the conservative majority regularly selected like-minded candidates to fill vacancies in the forty-member body. At a crucial moment in the ideological wars of the 1930s the Academy had taken to its breast the chief spokesman for the extreme right, Charles Maurras of Action Française, and only shortly after his release from prison for having called for the murder of members of the Popular Front legislature. A number of eminent members of the Vichy government, including Philippe Pétain himself, were academicians. In his recollections Charles de Gaulle speaks of the pressures to which (as traditional protector of the Academy) he was subjected. Some persons desired a renewal of that body's membership; some felt it should simply be shut down. De Gaulle made it clear that he favored the survival of the Academy in its traditional form, although he did agree that the institution needed new blood. Since there were a number of vacancies to be filled, why not suspend the rule requiring that candidates solicit the votes of sitting members, and simply elect some patriots? But when de Gaulle met some academicians he discovered a lack of enthusiasm for renovation. "In the end the Academy, reassured by the return to order, returned to its regular habits."[1]

At the moment of liberation the Academy had shown some energy, for it banned from its sessions "the two Abels" as they were called—Abel Bonnard and Abel Hermant, ardent collaborators about whom there was no ambiguity. The succinct announcement to the press declared that the eleven members of the French Academy present in Paris had voted unanimously; since a quorum was lacking, the members considered their act a ban, not an expulsion.[2] AND PÉTAIN? asked a headline in Socialist *Le Populaire*.[3] We know from his secretary's memoirs that de Gaulle agreed with the Academy for "silence on his case."[4] Charles Maurras? In the pages of *Le Figaro* academician François Mauriac, that body's leading resistance figure and a declared opponent of Maurras's candidacy for the Academy in the prewar decade, explained the problem of the missing quorum. Mauriac saw no need for immediate action, in any case. "Was it urgent to ask a writer under lock and key in a Lyon prison not to take his Academy seat any longer?" As for Pétain: "And for that other colleague whom the Germans abducted from the Hôtel du Parc [in Vichy], is there the slightest chance that we shall see this tragic figure on our doorstep one day?"[5]

The exclusion of Pétain and Maurras was given some support in the purge decrees. Under Paragraph 2 of Article 21 of the December 26, 1944, decree which codified procedures concerning *indignité nationale,* those found guilty were banned from all public functions and bodies.[6] And so the Academy did not have to vote to exclude Maurras; it simply had to read out the decree during one of its sessions.[7] In fact the "Vichy Party" in the Academy—as an analyst called it—remained powerful if dormant. The seats of Maurras and Pétain were not to be filled during their lifetime—a sly homage to them. But as late as 1958 Paul Morand was defeated for election to the Academy because of his "role during the last war," to cite a letter signed by eleven members who protested his candidacy.[8] Times change. Morand presented his candidacy again a decade later and got elected.

Every significant organization of writers carried out its own purge, just as every organization of any kind was expected to do. Thus the Association of War Veteran Writers elected a purge commission and proceeded to exclude from membership Pierre Benoit (who was on the CNE blacklist), philosopher Henri Massis (then in detention), Vichy officials François Pietri (then in Spain) and Georges Scapini (then also a fugitive), Paris journalist André Thérive. The president of this association during the occupation had been none other than Paul Chack, who as we have seen was executed after his conviction for treason.[9]

It has been said that the principal bodies concerned with collecting royalties for authors circulated questionnaires to their members concerning their activities and attitudes during the occupation, and then simply turned them over to the writers' purge committee—whether the replies indicated punishable activity or not; that meant that the purge committee had to screen all two thousand of them.[10] The questionnaire of the Société des Auteurs et Compositeurs Dramatiques began:

> Did you denounce, either directly or indirectly, any person, group, party, or faith?

After a number of similarly direct questions there was a final one:

> Even if you did not actually serve enemy propaganda and if in writing, speech, act, or gesture you were not an active collaborator, do you feel, in your heart, that you did not fail in your duty as a French intellectual empowered with a mission of confidence by the people, and that your attitude, your behavior, in private as in public, conformed to the patriotic dignity that one must observe, after a humiliating defeat, during a materially and morally odious occupation, and in the face of an adversary who, desiring to degrade our nation while pretending to seek its collaboration, starved our people, stifled our thought, our culture, and our freedom, tortured our fellow countrymen, shot our hostages, and behaved like a mortal enemy of our genius and our civilization?

One member added a comment to this question: It was "worthy of the Inquisition or Nazism," commenting that "it must have revolted all those in the committee who have maintained the notion of freedom of thought."[11] The society's own president, playwright and screenwriter Marcel Pagnol, found the question hard to handle, for in his own reply he first wrote "no" and scratched it out to write "yes." He admitted in his reply that he had had use of a private car as director of the Marseille movie studios until 1941; in the same year a book of his film *The Well-digger's Daughter* was published in Paris.[12]

The purge of creative people was bound to be controversial, perhaps more so than the purge of any other category of private citizen. For one always risked the reproach that one was seeking to interfere with the free expression of ideas. A number of members of the Société des Auteurs, Compositeurs et Editeurs de Musique, among them the composer Arthur Honegger, objected to any purge based on the way their work had been utilized in propaganda media during the occupation, on the grounds that they had written music, and music had no political meaning. There had been a decision to refuse to pay royalties to these composers for music written for the pro-German newsreel agency France-Actualités. But the composers argued that the same music written for France-Actualités during the German occupation was now being employed by France-Libre-Actualités. "Thus, the music which accompanied Marshal Pétain on the screen today accompanies General de Gaulle. . . . We thus obtain the absurd result that the same music can be damned or glorious. The same music can receive royalties or not receive them."[13]

In fact the purgers usually judged composers not on the content of their music but on what nonmusical activities they had in their files. Thus Florent Schmitt, then seventy-six years old, a well-known composer in the early years of the century, had lent his name to one of the most overtly collaborationist movements, Collaboration, as honorary president of its music division. He had visited Vienna, then part of Hitler's empire, in a propaganda trip (in 1941, on the 150th anniversary of the death of Mozart); he had dined at the German Embassy in occupied Paris. He was deemed worthy of punishment, but the Comité National d'Epuration des Gens de Lettres, Auteurs et Compositeurs also knew that since the liberation theaters, concert halls, and the radio had refrained from playing his work. So his sanction, issued in January 1946, was ordered for a one-year period beginning just after the liberation, October 1, 1944.[14]

Some seemed to slip through the purgers' net with ease. It was whispered that if a writer with a prestigious signature agreed to contribute to the postwar Communist or fellow-traveling press, his wartime transgressions would be overlooked.[15] In February 1946 an unsigned editorial in daily *Combat,* presumably written by Albert Camus, complained that writers had not really been punished at all. Noting that the activity of the writers' purge committee wasn't being talked about very much, *Combat* observed that even a reporter could remain ignorant of what it was up to. So that there was an "absurd situation," said *Combat:* writers who had collaborated were sending their manuscripts abroad, and since they were better known around the world than were the resistance writers, the former were the ones who were published. France's cultural attachés abroad weren't any help, the paper added, for one of them had confused Albert Camus with Alfred Capus (a journalist and playwright who died in 1922).[16]

Censorship persisted. *Les Lettres Françaises* felt that this was only proper, for the war was still raging. *Les Lettres Françaises* did feel that it was a bit awkward that the head of the publishers' association who circulated a list of censored books was the same person who had circulated the lists of works censored by the Germans during the occupation.[17] Books by famous authors who were notorious collaborators were now banned (among the targets: Céline, Rebatet, Drieu La Rochelle); titles published by well-known houses such as Denoël, Grasset, and Mercure de France were on the list.[18]

Later, one of the purged writers was to say that the works of collaborators had become victims of a conspiracy of silence, and that the police and customs officials were involved in unavowed censorship; he added with irony that the accused collaborators were France's only truly underground writers. (He mocked the writers of the resistance, noting that the poems of Paul Eluard and the plays of Jean-Paul Sartre had been so subtle in their resistance that they were accepted in German-occupied Paris.) Soon the banned writers were at work again, publishing under pseudonyms. Or writers in jail such as Charles Maurras and Henri Béraud were being reprinted in deluxe editions, even if their royalties went to the government. A body of literature was growing out of courtroom and prison experience—some of these books signed, some published with a signature like "X." A few of these books were violent, clearly the work of unrepentant Fascists, anti-Semites.[19]

Painters and sculptors, like musicians, seldom inserted political messages into their works. But as individuals they may have participated in punishable activities, or had lent their famous names to collaborationist causes. Some had participated in German-sponsored cultural events. But the resistance had also had its artists. At the liberation a Front National des Arts under the chairmanship of Pablo Picasso submitted a list of artists to the Paris district attorney and the prefect of police, requesting their arrest and trial. The Front National blacklist included some famous names: Emile Othon Friesz, Paul Belmondo, Paul Landowski, some art critics too.[20]

The same decree which created the writers' purge committee set up an artists' purge committee, as has been seen. The principal objects of investigation of this National Purge Committee of Painters, Illustrators, Sculptors and Engravers were those artists who had traveled to Nazi Germany during the occupation, although what they had actually done there remained a matter of debate. A privileged witness to the journey of France's best-known contemporary painters to enemy territory was a young publisher who himself felt that he had to be nice to the Germans because his own wife was Jewish. He also had had the misfortune of winning a legal suit against a German art collector before the war, which meant that he lost it after Germany's victory; he hoped to be able to settle the matter by a visit to Germany. The publisher was to tell the artists' purge committee that the French painters he had accompanied during the trip felt uncomfortable about being in the enemy's lair. At least one of them, André Dunoyer de Segonzac, felt that the whole thing had been a mistake. And the publisher also observed that André Derain, Maurice de Vlaminck, Othon Friesz, and Kees Van Dongen had looked with contempt at the German art shown to them. Occasionally Derain or Vlaminck would exclaim, "Hell, is that lousy!" On entering the studio of one German artist Vlaminck stepped back, then commented, "Looking at that you see how people lose a war."[21]

In June 1946, twenty-three artists were sanctioned by the purge panel. One of them got the maximum two-year ban—sculptor Charles Despiau. Among those who received one-year sanctions were Derain, Vlaminck, Van Dongen, Othon Friesz, Belmondo; Dunoyer de Segonzac got a three-month ban.[22]

SIX

The Stars

THE WORLD OF SHOW BUSINESS might seem to be a curious place to look for traitors. But in fact the stars of stage, screen, and the concert hall were much in evidence in the otherwise grim occupation years, and what they said and did had certain impact. Some of France's leading entertainers were compromised; theaters and movie companies served enemy propaganda.

The burden of organizing an orderly purge of the entertainment profession fell to a veteran theater man, Edouard Bourdet, then fifty-seven. In between-the-wars France he had been a popular playwright, and director of the Comédie Française, the national repertory company, in the four years preceding France's defeat. His postwar title, in the Secretariat General of Fine Arts of the Education Ministry, was delegate for entertainment. One of Delegate Bourdet's first acts was to order that in the weeks immediately following the liberation no one could take part in a theatrical performance without a temporary permit which was to be granted only after the appropriate union had received written assurance from the applicant that he or she had not collaborated. Acts of collaboration were spelled out, e.g., "I swear on my honor: (1) that I neither denounced nor persecuted anyone. . . ."[1]

And as we have seen, some stars of stage and screen had been targets of a more expeditious form of justice. The most conspicuous collaborators had been picked up by the police, or by resistance squads acting as police; this is the way Sacha Guitry was brought to Drancy and then to Fresnes. But when the same thing happened to

255

actor Pierre Fresnay, who was accused of having starred in movies produced by the German company Continental, and for having displayed pro-German feelings, purger Edouard Bourdet himself intervened, pleading Fresnay's charitable work for fellow actors during the occupation.[2]

Bourdet set up separate panels to handle the various components of the profession—for example, for theater managers, stage directors, performers.[3] Each smaller grouping had its own purge agency—e.g., there was a Purge Committee of the Union of Chorus Members.[4] The Ministry of Education drew up criteria for these temporary panels covering such offenses as the offer of one's services to the enemy, denouncing and persecuting fellow Frenchmen, joining paramilitary formations such as the Militia. Any of these offenses could be grounds for immediate dismissal. In other cases, such as membership in one of the pro-Fascist parties, or taking part in propaganda plays or films, "the sanction to apply will depend on the seriousness of the acts as well as on whether they were habitual or only isolated and accidental." Entertainers who had been forced to collaborate under pressure or whose collaboration was due to "momentary weakness" and who had atoned for their error "by acts of civic courage" could be excused. Sanctions ranged from a permanent ban on exercise of a profession down to a temporary ban—three months to three years.[5]

In carrying out his unprecedented assignment, Edouard Bourdet had the assistance of a panel composed of representatives of all segments of show business—a theater manager, a stage director, a decorator, a playwright, an orchestra leader, a stagehand, and so on. In most cases panel members were nominated by resistance groups, but it was not always easy to persuade them to serve. The panel made use of official lists of collaborators, the card index of Radio Paris (the German-controlled propaganda station), contracts discovered in the files of Continental Films, and similar documentary evidence.[6]

And then the show buiness purge received consecration in a decree of October 13, 1944. It limited the ban on professional activity to one year, while punishing violations of the ban with a year of prison; the manager of a theater in which a banned performer or other member of the profession defied the ban would also be punished, and the theater closed down.[7] At first the Governmental Commission for the Purge of Entertainment was presided over by an actor, but he was soon replaced by a government attorney in order to give the proceedings judicial force. Some 140 sanctions were recommended during the life of this commission.[8]

In the world of show business anything could happen. Anonymous tracts circulated, mocking the resistance credentials of the purgers. "Public, tear off their masks," read one of these. "Boo them, in the name of JUSTICE and of the VERY FUTURE of FRANCE, which they betrayed." The tract went on to ask: "Why do they persist in hunting down entertainers . . . while workers who made shells or rockets or trains for the German army aren't troubled, on the contrary?" It supplied an answer: because the purgers, by getting rid of alleged collaborators, wished to make room for themselves.[9]

The governmental commission dealt with a broad range of cases. The respected actor-director Charles Dullin came before it in February 1945, accused of writing for the violently collaborationist newspaper *La Gerbe,* and for having changed the name of the Sarah Bernhardt Theater (for that actress had been Jewish). Dullin argued that his articles had dealt with purely professional matters, that he had protested when the Germans insisted that the Sarah Bernhardt change its name; he said that he had obtained a compromise, in that he could keep "ex-Sarah Bernhardt Theater" on the door for six months, and in fact he kept the sign until the end of the occupation. He was exonerated.

Famous film actor Fernandel was accused of making movies for Continental. He replied that when he realized it was a German enterprise he sought to postpone fulfillment of his contract as long as he could. He had been a member of a collaborationist club? It was only because he had been invited to use its restaurant. He insisted that he had not been involved in politics, and apparently the commission accepted his story, for he too was exonerated. So was Abbot Fernand Maillet, director of the Little Singers of the Wooden Cross (Les Petits Chanteurs à la Croix de Bois). He had toured Germany with the youth choir, singing for French workers as well as for prisoners of war; he now argued that his intention had been to perform only for the soldier prisoners. And he swore that his choir had never sung for the Germans. Film actor Michel Simon was accused of having made antipatriotic statements while making movies during the occupation. He denied the charge, adding that he had even been denounced to the Gestapo on the false allegation that he was a Jew. Exonerated.[10]

The record manufacturer Pathé Marconi began to badger the purgers as early as October 1944 for guidelines. It was reopening its studios to make phonograph records for Columbia and other labels, and needed to know who could and who could not perform. Only in February of the following year was the governmental commission ready to reply. If fifty-seven Pathé stars were authorized to make records, twenty-six were not, and the latter list included Sacha Guitry, Suzy Delair, Leo Marjane, Tino Rossi, Suzy Solidor. Another twenty-seven performers appeared on a "postponed" list, among them Fernandel, Georges Guétary, Paul Meurisse, Yvonne Printemps.[11]

But the entertainment purge had only begun. On February 17, 1945, a new decree dealt with "the professions of dramatic and musical performers and of performing musicians." The preamble noted that the purge of entertainers, because of the particular nature of that profession, had been the first such measure in a private field. But now that the government had set up procedures for the purge of all professions (by the October 1944 decree for the purge of business), it seemed desirable to harmonize the two systems. So a National Purge Committee of Dramatic and Musical Performers and Performing Musicians was established. Headed by a court officer, it was composed of representatives of government and the entertainment world; the decree further provided that in individual hearings, a representative of the appropriate branch of activity would participate. Sanctions, limited to one year, could involve exclusion from work in a particular theater, a particular branch of the industry (theater, movies, radio, music), or from all professional activity. This last sanction also applied to persons convicted of *indignité nationale,* and for the duration of the sentence.[12]

One important task of the new purge body was to issue certificates requested by theaters, theatrical agencies, and other potential employers, to guarantee that a particular performer had been cleared. Even an applicant for a passport required such a certificate.[13] And now some of France's best-known entertainers were to undergo the process.

Take Mistinguett. The national purge committee had a file which listed the sums she had earned at German-sponsored performances, broadcasts on Radio Paris, as well as testimony concerning her association with German officials, army officers. "They're darlings," she had been heard to say. She was also heard making anti-Semitic threats. So Mistinguett received a reprimand.[14] The film star Arletty was questioned about her *"liaison amoureuse"* with a German. At the time the inquiry was in progress she was in forced residence outside of Paris, accused of having denounced someone who was subsequently picked up by the Germans. She too was recommended for a reprimand.[15] Actress Danielle Darrieux had gone to Germany, although she argued that it had only been because she wished to see her fiancé, the interned Dominican Republic diplomat Porfirio Rubirosa; she added that when she cut short her visit the Germans had made their displeasure manifest. Yes, she had made films for Continental, but she said that she had ceased to do so when Rubirosa was released. No sanction for her.[16]

Maurice Chevalier was not only a French star but an international one. He seemed to be under a cloud at the liberation: There were stories that he had been stoned by Parisians—even killed. He was very much alive, he told the press. "The Germans did me a bad turn. They announced that I sang and acted for them. . . . But all that is false."[17] He was called in for questioning by the police. Hadn't he received special privileges during the occupation? But he remained at liberty.[18]

At the time the national purge committee was looking into his case Chevalier was being solicited to perform for American, British, even French soldiers, as well as for a benefit sponsored by the Communist-dominated Front National. The panel was concerned by the famous singer's performances at events sponsored by collaborationist groups, his visits to Nazi Germany, his broadcasts for German Radio Paris. But he had the solid backing of the show business community, and of the union of vaudeville performers (which made the point that Chevalier had done only eleven broadcasts for Radio Paris, had sung only once for French prisoners of war, and had managed to obtain the release of ten of them). He won the committee over: no sanction.[19]

The purge panel had before it press accounts of Edith Piaf's tours to Germany to sing for French prisoners, for French workers in German factories too. She testified that her first visit to Germany had been forced on her—it was that or a ban on her performing— and that she herself had initiated the second trip, but had turned over all proceeds of the tour to the soldier prisoners. Furthermore, she said that during her trip to Germany she had been able to carry identity cards concealed in a suitcase with a false bottom. (Her half sister would later explain that while in prisoner-of-war camps Piaf had arranged to have her picture taken in the company of French soldiers; then back in Paris the photographs of the soldiers were used to forge identity papers—147 in all—which the singer brought back to the soldiers on the next trip.[20]) Edith Piaf also argued that she had been banned from the Casino de Paris for a month because she sang a forbidden song, and that she had managed to avoid a singing tour of Germany. She provided a list of Jewish friends to whom she had sent money regularly, adding that Jews had made use of her apartment during the occupation. The allegations against her seemed no match for the positive evidence. The panel decided, by unanimous vote: "No sanction and congratulations."[21]

Sacha Guitry's involvement with the courts seemed to have spared him detailed examination of his case by the various purge panels (of playwrights, stage and screen performers). He was indicted on October 15, 1944, for collusion with the enemy.[22] After his release by the examining magistrate the Communist daily *L'Humanité* reported: "The incredible news reached us late yesterday. Sacha Guitry who wallowed at the feet of the invader, Sacha Guitry who banqueted with the torturers, Sacha Guitry who made millions during the occupation, Sacha Guitry has been released. . . ."[23] In rejecting the questionnaire sent to all members of the Society of Dramatic Authors and Composers, Guitry had explained: "I return this questionnaire which has just been sent to me, without any doubt, by error—since I already replied to all these questions in handcuffs." He pointed out that the criminal case against him had been dropped.[24] It had not been dropped entirely, for Guitry was still scheduled for trial by a Civic Chamber. But the case never came up, and the prosecutor admitted that he didn't even know where Guitry's file was.[25] The final disposition of the case would wait until August 1947, at which time Guitry was informed that it had actually been dismissed.[26] A year later the star was in Lyon to present one of his films. Local resistance people stopped his car and obliged Guitry and the actors who accompanied him to observe a moment of silence at the resistance memorial on Place Bellecour.[27]

Serge Lifar, once the Paris Opera's leading dancer, and a ballet master—perhaps the leading figure in prewar ballet in France—had seemed an eager collaborator with the Germans. He had offered a personal tour of the Opera to Adolf Hitler, had called on the Führer during a visit to Germany in October 1942, had published articles praising the Nazis in the occupation press. At the liberation Lifar was discharged without indemnity. In October 1945 the national purge committee banned him from his profession for a year, although dating the ban to begin on November 1, 1944.[28] Nearly a year later, when Serge Lifar was to appear at a benefit for a monument to the liberators of Paris, public protest—manifested in part by ripped-up posters—forced his withdrawal.[29] He was to spend a couple of years as *directeur artistique* of the Ballet de Monte-Carlo before retiring to a less visible job as director of the Choreographic Institute of the Paris Opera.

The Comédie Française, with its permanent troupe, was a world unto itself. Its actors and actresses often appeared in movies, even on other stages. At the liberation this national company received a new administrator general in the person of Pierre Dux, long a member of the troupe. He wished to get rehearsals going, but how to do it before completion of the purge? He explained the dilemma to Edouard Bourdet: "To begin rehearsals with persons I believe unlikely to be sanctioned would point a finger at actors liable to sanctions. ..." A purge commission of Comédie Française personnel was established under the guidance of a retired Paris chief justice, and the first cases were heard on October 28, 1944. That day the famous Raimu (Jules Muraire) appeared. It was agreed that he could not have known in advance that a film he made for Continental would be shown in Germany as anti-French propaganda. He explained that he had even feigned illness to avoid working for that German company. He was absolved. On November 6 other members of the troupe were introduced to the panel one after the other—Madeleine Renaud and Jean-Louis Barrault among them—to be informed that they had been found "correct and loyal." Later that day the purge commission heard the case of two ushers accused of making unpatriotic remarks. Taking account of the role of "feminine rivalry" in the accusations, and the fact that these jobs were their sole livelihood, the women received minor sanctions—suspensions of six and four months.[30]

The film industry was another major terrain of investigation. For the movie business had thrived, and with enemy encouragement and material support, all through the dark years. Actors and actresses had come to fame; directors and screenwriters had created works which in later decades were to be hailed as classics. If radio was a public institution and its utilization had required the approval if not the active involvement of occupation authorities, making a movie required money as well as approval. If the French made more movies than ever during the German years it was largely thanks to the German production company Continental. What to do about all this was debated during the first days of liberation by a Comité de Libération du Cinéma Français, which sought to establish a balance between the demands of justice and the need to put the movie industry back to work as quickly as possible.[31] A commission made up of members of different branches of the profession was set up only days after the liberation, headed by actor Pierre Blanchar.[32] Among the first heads to fall were those of the most famous of the younger generation of directors, such as Henri-Georges Clouzot, whose first important movies had been produced during the occupation (he and several colleagues were suspended from the profession).[33] The Comité de Libération du Cinéma Français drew up a list of movie people it felt deserved to be branded with *indignité nationale.* Later, as the purge became better organized, the investigation of the industry was turned over to the Comité Régional Interprofessionnel d'Epuration dans les Entreprises.[34]

The most controversial case in the movie world was that of Clouzot, who was thirty-five years old when he made *L'Assassin habite au 21* in 1942. Then came *Le Corbeau,* sponsored by Continental, and starring Pierre Fresnay. The theme of this movie—the horrible consequences of anonymous denunciation—could have been taken as subversive during the years of German occupation and Vichy repression. When a critic in *Combat* complained that *Le Corbeau,* although rated as the best movie made during the occupation, still could not be shown at a film festival, the editors of *Combat* stepped in to contest their critic's attitude. It was impossible, said *Combat,* "to accept in an event identified as French a production made by a German company and whose two leading actors behaved so shamefully that they are today under indictment for collusion with the enemy." Perhaps Clouzot showed talent, but "he certainly lacked character."[35]

But when the regional purge body examined the case of Clouzot it had before it a petition initiated by Jean-Paul Sartre, signed by Simone de Beauvoir and others in their circle, which while disapproving of Clouzot's work for Continental, declared that *Le Corbeau* contained nothing that was anti-French. A letter from popular poet Jacques Prévert made the same point (it was even noted that the scenario had been registered two years before the outbreak of war). Sartre's monthly *Les Temps Modernes* attacked the purge of Clouzot as arbitrary, since others who worked for Continental had not been punished. "It's only in the universe of Kafka," said the magazine, "that one finds such preposterous decisions."[36]

But the committee which considered the Clouzot case heard a representative of the Committee of Liberation of the French Cinema, who argued that Clouzot had been the leading French personality in Continental, had maintained good relations with the Germans, defended their interests. By order of the prefect of the Seine district in August 1945 Clouzot had been banned from a responsible position in the industry; the ban was extended for two years in July 1946 on the advice of the regional purge committee. The decision described *Le Corbeau* as a "biased anti-French film."[37]

VII
FORGETTING

"For if they have occasionally
treated crime as weakness they have
also treated weakness as crime."

—JACQUES FAUVET, in *Le Monde*

ONE

The Punished

WHEN THE PURGE IS MENTIONED now, the talk quickly turns to the killings, the court sentences of death or to hard labor for life. The purge shook up the establishment, destroyed reputations, humiliated even those later found innocent; uncounted lives were disrupted for varying lengths of time. Not all the death sentences were carried out, not all prison sentences were served to the end, but enough persons spent long periods in camps and prisons to make a significant mark on history. Five years after the liberation a weekly magazine published a map of France which pinpointed the prisons in which convicted collaborators were still being held. In the Paris region there was of course Fresnes, still employed to detail prisoners awaiting trial. Near Paris at Beauregard-La Celle Saint-Cloud another prison held well-known personalities like the aging scientist Georges Claude, and the Reverend Jean Mayol de Luppé, chaplain of the Légion des Volontaires Français. Saint-Martin-de-Ré on the Ile de Ré off the Atlantic Coast was a well-known penal colony, then employed for some famous collaborationist writers and columnists. Clairvaux, an ancient abbey, held Admiral Jean de Laborde, Charles Maurras, Xavier Vallat, while Jacques Benoist-Méchin was at Fontevrault, near Saumur.[1] An earlier account of the purge prisons focused on Poissy, whose most distinguished collaboration convict of the time was Henri Béraud. In a neighboring cell one found Guy Bunau-Varilla, whose father had owned the collaboration daily *Le Matin*. With a third prisoner, the editor Lucien Combelle, there was an opportunity (so we learn from Combelle's memoirs) for literary talk, reminiscence.[2]

Indeed, a literature grew up around the purge prisons. The irrepressible Xavier Vallat, former Commissioner for Jewish Affairs during the occupation, was a prison mate for twenty-two months of one of France's most experienced debaters, Charles Maurras, and he didn't fail to write a book about the experience. Vallat was given permission to spend an hour a day with the theoretician of Action Française. Admirals Jean Esteva and Jean de Laborde were also confined in this wing of a graceful eighteenth-century building which was used to hold High Court convicts, and exceptionally for Court of Justice convict Maurras. Vallat's book comes to a close with his parole in December 1949.[3]

A less idyllic description of the same establishment can be found in *Les Prisons de l'Epuration* by a convict who was first sentenced to death in absentia for collusion with the enemy, then retried in his presence and sent to prison. Like all those sentenced to a year or more of confinement, author Philippe Saint-Germain is sent to this French equivalent of a penitentiary. His hair is shaved off; he receives kicks (so he tells us); he is even stripped for sleeping because during a search he was found to have tried to conceal his eyeglasses. Some prisoners are put to work; others must march around the courtyard all day, until their feet are bloody. The lame are molested by prison guards. There are constant humiliations, unnecessary tasks. Medical aid lacks, and because of this an inmate dies. The guards are brutal. This author speaks of carrying out tasks "on all fours," of guards who spit in the soup, strike prisoners on the head with keys, kick them in the stomach. He says that Communists keep an eye on the prisoners, and insist on this cruel treatment. And then the author is paroled. But he finds himself subject to a life sentence of *indignité nationale,* meaning that he can't vote, can't work for the government, can't enter a profession or work in the media.[4]

But it is also true—these stories tell us so—that the stiff sentences handed out in the immediate wake of war and liberation were seldom fully served. Those who went to prison could obtain early release—e.g., in 1951, 3,064 prisoners came up for parole in the first ten months of the year, and 1,112 requests were granted. That year the Ministry of Justice began to parole collaboration prisoners sentenced to hard labor, and 406 of the 437 applicants for release got their freedom. In March 1946, 29,401 persons were in prison after sentencing or pending trial; on November 1, 1951, there remained 2,939, of whom 2,826 had been convicted.[5] At the beginning of the

1980s a few collaborators were still in prison. One man who had managed to avoid arrest for over twenty years—he had been sentenced to death in absentia in 1945 for handing resistance fighters over to the Germans—was finally tried in his presence in 1966; he was released in 1982. Another convict, a French member of the Gestapo who had arrested and tortured partisans, had avoided capture until 1962, at which time he was sentenced to death; retried after appeal, he got another death sentence, converted into twenty years of solitary by de Gaulle's successor as President of the Republic, Georges Pompidou. And this prisoner was free in 1983. Another French Gestapo man was apprehended in 1962, accused of responsibility for 430 arrests, 310 transfers to Germany; he got a death sentence in 1966, a sentence commuted by de Gaulle to solitary confinement for life, which Pompidou reduced to twenty years. He too was free in 1983. These three were described as the last collaborators still in prison.[6]

The political opposition to the postwar Fourth Republic, and then to Charles de Gaulle's Fifth, included some of the most articulate of the collaborators. One of the first writers to take a public stand against the purge, and in favor of forgetting, was the brother-in-law of executed Robert Brasillach, Maurice Bardèche. He did it in a privately printed book in the guise of an open letter to François Mauriac; he directed it to Mauriac, he said, because this allowed him to employ a more measured tone—Mauriac, after all, had sought in vain a pardon for Brasillach. Bardèche made a case for the "damned minority," the purged collaborators now banished from society (the book was written in 1947). He explained that the victims of Vichy had been executed once for all time, while the victims of the postwar purge died each day, for they had lost their honor, becoming a caste of untouchables. Bardèche goes on to make the familiar argument that Philippe Pétain was the legitimate chief of state even if he had been in error, so that none of his followers deserved punishment. It was the resistance which was illegal, and the purge only represented vengeance. (In Bardèche's view, even attacks on Communists and Jews in the collaboration press had been lawful.) Bardèche cited the shout of a purge victim at the moment of his execution: "We're not traitors, just minor government employees."[7]

That year, 1947, saw the first overt attacks on the purge by persons who had not been among its targets. Thus a well-known Free

French intelligence agent, "Rémy'—the pseudonym of one Gilbert Renault—called for a purge of the resistance itself, blaming "volunteers of the thirteenth hour" for crimes and other abuses in the name of the resistance.[8] The first author of uncontested talent to join the revisionist camp was Marcel Aymé, whose signature had appeared in notorious collaboration newspapers during the occupation (although the content of his articles was not of the kind which led to treason trials). Aymé chose to sum up the purge in a satirical novel which takes place in an unidentified Norman town heavily damaged by Allied air raids. (The Vichyites laugh, he writes, because the pilots missed real objectives such as the railroad station but instead destroyed nice old houses and killed civilians.) Aymé's heroes are nonconformists who either collaborated or are happy to assist collaborators fleeing the purge. Resistance people are brutes, and Communist resistance people the worst of the lot. Many collaborators were killed at the moment of liberation, and Aymé's novel shows how a harmless and quite sympathetic townsman dies as a consequence of the postliberation purge. In the climax, a band of Communists attacks a returning prisoner of war and no one dares come to his aid.[9]

Beginning in 1950, a monthly magazine called *Ecrits de Paris,* which was serving as a mouthpiece of purge victims and their advocates, began to publish a regular "chronicle" of alleged purge abuses. The compiler, one Jean Pleyber, who revealed not only anti-Gaullist but anti-Jewish feelings, asked his readers to help him by sending him clippings from the regional press concerning "crimes committed in 1944 and 1945."[10] And so this chronicle was to repeat most of the horror stories which circulated in the aftermath of liberation. It reported, for example, that a woman who wished to get rid of her husband had arranged to have him murdered by a partisan who had formerly served in the Germany army auxiliary forces[11]—a story which brought together two of the favorite themes of the opposition, the purge as pretext for crime, the false partisan. Pleyber reported other murders committed in the name of the purge, followed by mild punishment or none at all. Resistance people were shown to have carried out burglaries, holdups, rape, the murder of infants.[12] Murders are often accompanied by other atrocities—e.g., a woman's shorn hair is nailed to the front door of her house.[13] Whole families are wiped out.[14] A woman is killed in her bridal gown.[15] A resistance chief kills a mayor, a notary, a doctor, and a priest who oppose his plan to open a house of prostitution.[16] A woman and her daughter are abducted and the daughter is shot in front of her mother, who is then beaten, her eyes all but torn out, tortured in public, forced to dig her own grave; and then nine months after their deaths mother and daughter are sentenced to *indignité nationale* by a Civic Chamber.[17] The leitmotif is murder by real or alleged resistance people for personal gain, resistance betrayals of other resistance people.[18]

Resistance man Rémy, who had joined the dissidence earlier, as we have seen, now (in 1950) appeared at a meeting called to defend purge victims. While affirming loyalty to Charles de Gaulle, he described his personal evolution in the direction of recognizing the good faith of those who had followed Marshal Pétain in order to serve their country in another way. Rémy followed up with an article in which he claimed that de Gaulle had said to him (and these words were to be repeated frequently by opponents of the purge in the following years), "Look here, Rémy. France always has to have two strings to its bow. In June 1940 it needed the Pétain string as well as the de Gaulle string."[19] De Gaulle immediately contested Rémy's allegation, and wrote the former resistance agent to inform him that his point of view was not de Gaulle's; he expressed regret that Rémy had published such a statement without discussing it with him first.[20]

In the aftermath of liberation and purge there were some feeble attempts to give the dissidence a formal structure. Not surprisingly, the chief organizers were persons who had been collaborators or sympathetic to that position. The writer Jean Galtier-Boissière attended a public debate on amnesty as early as February 1947 in which members of the audience cried out, "Long live Pétain! Long live Maurras! Long live Doriot! Down with de Gaulle! Death to the Jews!"[21] But that same year an association called Défense des Libertés Françaises was founded under the chairmanship of General François d'Astier de la Vigerie, who identified himself as a member of the Gaullist order Compagnons de la Libération. This group published a pamphlet which alleged that the purge had been turned away from its original goals for political reasons. It called for an amnesty for all convicted collaborators who had been under twenty-one years old in 1940, for all minor acts carried out before June 1943 (at which time the Free French received official recognition), for seriously wounded war veterans, and for other persons who had served the nation. The group offered examples of what it felt to be unjust verdicts in the purge courts.[22] Also in 1947, a Union pour la Restauration et la Défense du Service Public was founded to assist purged civil servants. Later Jacques Isorni would admit that the times were not then ripe for such a cause, for even victims of the purge believed that "their own case would have a better chance if dealt with in the absence of publicity." This feeling of apprehensiveness, of insecurity, would disappear among the purged only after the amnesty law was voted in January 1951.[23]

In 1950 this organization submitted a long memorandum to the United Nations in which it denounced what it called "violations of human rights" committed in the purge courts. The union argued that France's government—then the parliamentary Fourth Republic—had created "a repressive apparatus without precedent in our history" which prosecuted free speech, punished political error, stifled freedom of thought and assembly, accepted retroactive legislation, rejected the principle of criminal intent.[24]

This memorandum included an estimate of the number of summary executions of suspected collaborators. It alleged that there had been "at least" 112,000 such killings, explaining that its estimate was based on a U.S. Army report (no source given) that 50,000 persons had been killed in the Mediterranean region in 1944–45, on Vichy police data, and on a remark by Interior Minister Adrien Tixier that there had been 105,000 deaths.[25] These figures were to be heard often, occasionally with variations—e.g., a convicted collaborator in a book he wrote about his own experiences mentioned "105,000 important persons shot down," suggesting that many persons of lesser importance might also have been killed.[26] Minister Tixier was said to have made his statement about 105,000 summary executions to André Dewavrin, who as "Colonel Passy" ran Free French intelligence; specifically, Dewavrin was quoted as having been told by Tixier in February 1945 that "according to information in his possession there had been 105,000 summary executions between the Allied landing in June 1944 and the month of February 1945."[27]

A report given to parliament in 1948 by François Mitterrand, then Minister for Veterans, concerning 97,000 persons who had died of "various causes" was taken by some to refer to these summary executions.[28] Popular historian Robert Aron offered his own estimate: 30,000 to 40,000.[29] But the persistence of the "105,000" figure has troubled historians who avoid using offhand remarks and look for verifiable testimony and documentation. Thus one writer accepted the fact that Minister Tixier spoke of 105,000 dead, but considered that this included all violent deaths of the period—most of them caused by German soldiers.[30] For if Minister Tixier had based the estimate attributed to him on reports of his own prefects and gendarmes, he would have come up with a total only a tenth of the one which has been attributed to him. We can see that for ourselves, for the reports available to him are now available to us.

In truth, there was no easy way then, there is no easy way now to determine the number of persons executed without due process of law by persons acting in the name of the resistance. The months following the liberation were chaotic, but so were the months preceding the liberation. Reports of regional police forces, notably of the gendarmeries which assured law and order outside major cities, do not always indicate whether a victim of a murder was a known collaborator (or a known resistance fighter). In the early years of the Fourth Republic the government did try to find out what had happened. De Gaulle tells us what the investigators came up with. They concluded that there had been 10,842 summary executions, 6,675 of which had occurred during the fighting leading up to the liberation, the balance after the liberation. "A total which in itself was painful," admits de Gaulle, but "quite limited ... considering the number of crimes committed and their frightful consequences"—by which he means crimes attributable to collaborators. De Gaulle notes that the official figure is quite different from the extravagant ones later offered by "the inconsolable lovers of defeat and collaboration."[31]

The 10,842 figure dates back to the beginning of the 1950s, but it was still the best estimate available when de Gaulle published it in 1959. Other figures have been given since, but the Gendarmerie Nationale, in releasing its own estimate of the number of violent deaths in the occupation period, simply made no distinction between murders committed by the German occupation forces, by the Vichy Militia, and by the resistance; thus the 642 victims of the German army in the village of Oradour-sur-Glane are included in the statistics of the Haute-Vienne district.[32]

Scholars continue to dig, to scrutinize available data. At the beginning they even had access to raw gendarmerie records, or to other official records on the village and town level; they also examined registers of deceases, even the local press. By the mid-1970s the survey which had begun under the auspices of a Committee of History of the Second World War attached to the French Premier's office had been completed in fifty-three administrative districts, and the director of the survey, Marcel Baudot (then inspector general of French Archives), was able to announce a total of 5,009 summary executions for the years of occupation and through the early liberation months; if the same averages applied to the rest of France as had been observed in the fifty-three districts for which satisfactory data were available, the national total would be between 8,500 and 9,000 deaths.[33]

A decade later statistics were still to be sifted. The best estimate for summary executions, which includes executions following courts martial and other ad hoc jurisdictions, now approaches the ten thousand figure which de Gaulle had published back in 1959.[34] In any case historians who have taken the trouble to look at the information available dismiss the higher estimates; the bodies simply aren't there; the alleged victims aren't missing. One might also compare the estimate of the number of executed collaborators to the figure which de Gaulle provides for victims of the occupation: sixty thousand executions, two hundred thousand deportations to camps (of which only fifty thousand survived).[35]

Revisionist literature provides other figures calculated to shock: 128,000 sentences by the liberation courts, of which 5,000 were death sentences; 1 million persons condemned to *indignité nationale*.[36] At the time the last Court of Justice was shut down in 1951 the total number of cases tried was in fact 57,954, to which may be added the 69,797 cases dealt with by the Civic Chambers. The results were as follows:[37]

Death sentences in the presence of defendants	2,853
Death sentences in absentia	3,910
Death sentences carried out	767
Sentences to terms of hard labor for life	2,702
Sentences to lesser terms of hard labor	10,637
Sentences to solitary confinement	2,044
Sentences to prison	22,883
Indignité nationale as a main sentence by a Court of Justice	3,578
Indignité nationale by a Civic Chamber (of which sentences 3,184 were excused)	46,145

These are high figures—or low ones, depending on one's feelings about the resistance, about Vichy. In the view of Charles de Gaulle the death sentences actually carried out were as equitable as they could be, while sentences to prison were "on the whole equitable and moderate."[38] Indeed, in a comparative study of other West European nations occupied by the Nazis, historian Peter Novick showed that there had been more arrests, more convictions per capita, not only in Belgium and the Netherlands, but in Denmark and Norway. There were four times as many prison sentences per 100,000 population in Denmark as in France, over four times more in the Netherlands, six times more in Belgium and Norway. If in absolute terms there were more executions in France, there were more such deaths per capita in neighboring Belgium. In the latter nation there had been 50,000 to 70,000 arrests in the first month of liberation, with 40,000 suspects remaining in detention at the end of hostilities, a figure which rose by 50 percent when tensions were stirred up by the return of German camp victims. In the Netherlands there had been between 120,000 and 150,000 arrests, with 96,000 persons in detention at one time. Two years after the liberation of that nation 62,000 persons remained in detention.[39]

In none of the Western nations which had endured Nazi occupation was the prewar legislation concerning treason adequate to the task. In Norway, the Netherlands, and Denmark there was recourse to retroactive laws, while capital punishment, which in each of these nations had been banned years before, was reintroduced. Moreover, in each of these countries, and in Belgium, a milder form of treason was defined, similar to the French *indignité nationale.* "In every country," concluded Novick, "the complex of solutions arrived at was the resultant of all the different forces and pressures brought to bear; legal traditions, popular clamor, political divisions, and many more. In no country were the solutions found satisfactory."[40]

TWO

Forgiving

AMNESTY IS A UNIVERSAL CONCEPT, often covering political crime—or political error. It seemed to Abraham Lincoln and his successor in the White House the way to bring North and South together after the Civil War. In France the purge was still in full swing in 1946 when François Mauriac raised the issue of amnesty for certain forms of collaboration crime, certain categories of offenders. "There are informers, murderers, torturers . . . for whom even the adversary of the death penalty I have always been couldn't imagine anything else but the supreme punishment," the Catholic writer declared in his column in *Le Figaro*. But, in addition to the totally innocent, there was "the crowd of the misled of all ages, and first of all the young people whose milieu condemned to think and to believe what they thought and what they believed." Mauriac felt that it was the duty of Christians to raise the question of amnesty now.[1] In a follow-up column he pleaded for those in prison and penal colonies who in their souls and consciences had not wanted to commit criminal acts. True justice, he argued, requires that the punishment fit the crime. Mauriac appealed not only to Christian pity but to French history. "We must think of today's Dreyfuses, if they exist; it's for these living Dreyfuses that it would be generous to fight and to compromise ourselves."[2]

The amnesty law that was finally passed, on August 16, 1947, did seem to meet some of Mauriac's concerns. It covered minors under eighteen who had acted "without judgment" when they committed minor acts of collaboration, or who had joined a collaborationist movement. (Minors up to the age of twenty-one were covered by this amnesty if they had subsequently served in combat on the Free French side.) These amnesties were automatic. And then minors under eighteen who had been convicted of more serious acts of collaboration, minors up to twenty-one who had belonged to a collaborationist movement without having committed specific crimes, could apply for amnesty, which could be granted by decree. Civil servants who had received the lowest possible penalty in the administrative purge—transfer to another job—also benefited from the 1947 amnesty. As in all amnesty law, the original crime was considered not to have occurred, and reference to it would be removed from court records.[3]

Was this only the beginning? In the following years there were growing demands for a broader amnesty than this one had been. The prisons were full, many prisoners were articulate writers and journalists, politicians and statesmen; some of them had equally articulate allies outside the prison walls. Still, postliberation France was for a long time to come to be proresistance France. If the Gaullists eventually abandoned power they remained active in public life. The first President of the Republic of postwar France was a Socialist and resistance veteran (Vincent Auriol), and the postwar establishment included not only old-line Socialists but the militant Mouvement Républicain Populaire (MRP), that Christian Democratic party which had been born in the resistance and which included Georges Bidault, president of the Conseil National de la Résistance, and de Gaulle's successive Justice Ministers François de Menthon and Pierre-Henri Teitgen.

In the first months of 1948 an opinion poll suggested that the mass of French men and women were hardly prepared to forgive or to forget. Should we let bygones be bygones? The large majority (63 percent) replied no (24 percent yes, 13 percent without an opinion). And 47 percent of respondents felt that the purge courts had not been sufficiently harsh (only 16 percent felt they had been too harsh, and 18 percent saw them as just right, with 19 percent being without an opinion). In the breakdown men were found to be less forgiving than women, the young (twenty to thirty-four years old) less forgiving than the old. Residents of towns of twenty thousand to forty thousand inhabitants were less forgiving than those living in cities of one hundred thousand or more.[4]

A year later the French felt differently. The movement in favor of forgiving and forgetting had hardly become an avalanche, yet amnesty was now out in the open; Mauriac was no longer alone. In the pages of the MRP daily *L'Aube* Georges Bidault made the point that the purge had been necessary "in the name of law, in the name of the nation, and also for public tranquillity and national reconciliation." Those who were now (in 1949) suggesting that the purge had been regrettable, even that it had been scandalous, simply forgot what it had been like under the German occupation, and also forgot the victims of the occupation. Bidault recognized that there was a considerable difference between the harsh sentences of the liberation courts and the milder ones now being handed down. Such disparity was unjust, and clemency could remedy it. It was for those who had resisted, Bidault argued, to say that the hour had come for forgetting what could be forgotten. Those collaborators who had neither killed nor denounced their fellows, those who had not been traitors but who had been led into error, could now be "reintegrated into the nation."

Not all resistance veterans could accept that. The Mouvement National Judiciaire, whose secretary-general was Maurice Rolland, now known as "the father of the judicial resistance," came out flatly against amnesty. It contested the notion that liberation justice had been exceptional: "Aiding the enemy is never political opinion but common crime." The rights of the accused had not been violated by the liberation courts, so there was no reason to go beyond normal procedures for pardon now.[6] Daily *Combat*, whose editor Claude Bourdet had raised the question of clemency a year earlier,[7] opened its columns to the debate, under the title "Clémence ou Réhabilitation?" The majority of those who contributed opinions favored pardons rather than any form of across-the-board amnesty. In that case, commented Bourdet, it was important to speed up the screening process so that prisoners worthy of release were not held in confinement unnecessarily.[8]

President Auriol joined the debate, criticizing those who desired an amnesty but who saw the humane gesture of pardon as rehabilitation, even glorification of crimes which had sent "the best sons of France" to torture and death. He announced that except for traitors, informers, and torturers, convicted collaborators would recover their liberty and their civil rights.[9] A poll taken immediately after Auriol's speech (in May 1949) suggested that the French would follow him. Amnesty was now approved by 60 percent of the population (23 percent opposed it; 17 percent remained without an opinion).[10] But a broad amnesty still stuck in the throats of many opinion makers. In an editorial in *Le Populaire* Léon Blum indicated the dimensions of the dilemma. Perhaps the decrees on *indignité nationale* had not been sufficiently discriminatory, perhaps a measure of amnesty was now in order, but Blum could not accept the idea that a legal amnesty might signify moral amnesty. In his eyes the collaborators remained under a ban. Perhaps not forever, but for a period of time that had not expired. "Between these people and France, who really owes reparation to the other?" asked Blum, who added that discreet withdrawal from the public eye was the least that collaborators owed to their country.[11]

So it is no surprise that the first broad amnesty of the postwar had a painful birth. Many drafts, much argument within the cabinet, inside the majority parties. Some advocates of amnesty were prepared to see the decision postponed until the time came when a thorough amnesty might be possible. Others felt that only a case-by-case examination of court sentences was justified.[12] Summing up the debate, an anonymous correspondent in *The Times* of London wrote: "The growing arrogance of ex-collaborators who either avoided arrest or have been freed has been most remarkable in the last 12 months. Written and spoken disparagement of the Resistance has been plentiful, and a particularly offensive example of this aggressive impenitence came last summer [1949], when a number of friends of the late Philippe Henriot, the Vichy Minister of Propaganda who was shot by the Resistance during the war, attended a memorial mass for him in Paris, dressed in their uniform of the [Militia]. . . ." The *Times* reporter admitted that politics had entered the purge, that amnesty would come sooner or later. But would it apply to Pétain too? "His case is the very heart of the French drama, and the drama is still being played out."[13]

A bill was finally ready just before Christmas, 1949. It called for automatic amnesty for certain offenses, such as sentences of less than ten years of *indignité nationale,* short prison terms for minors under twenty-one, and an amnesty by decree (upon application by the convicted collaborator) for all sentences of *indignité nationale,* for residents of eastern France whose territory had been incorporated into Hitler's Germany, for Court of Justice sentences of three years or less. At this time former Justice Minister Teitgen, now a minister of state, announced that only eight thousand collaborators remained in prison. He added that Belgium, with 8.5 million inhabitants, still had nine thousand such prisoners.[14]

The debate was not over; clearly there was no feeling of urgency on the part of successive cabinets. But in autumn 1950 a bill was placed on the desks of French legislators, and discussion moved to the floor of the National Assembly. "Men of great heart support the project and seek to maintain the discussion on the level of what the Minister of Justice calls 'serene justice and lucid humanity,'" observed a partisan of the bill, Protestant leader Marc Boegner. "But other speakers seem to lower the level of debate without cease. Personal concerns come through in certain speeches, and worries about the forthcoming elections are prejudicial to objectivity."[15] (The National Assembly elected in November 1946 was to be renewed in June 1951.) A headline in *Le Populaire* spoke for the Socialists:

YES TO PARDONS THROUGH AMNESTY

NO TO WHITEWASHING COLLABOS

In fact the bill offered by Justice Minister René Mayer was a compromise between the two possibilities. The main beneficiaries would be persons sentenced by Civic Chambers for relatively minor offenses. Mayer gave the Assembly new data on the prison population: There had been 10,611 collaborators in prison on January 1, 1949, 6,402 on November 1 of that year, and a year later the number was down to 4,784. Of the present total, 539 persons were serving sentences of life at hard labor, 3,060 lesser terms of hard labor, 813 solitary confinement, 362 prison. Ten others waited for decisions on appeals from death sentences.[16]

The debate in the Assembly was bitter that fall. Speech was free, and a legislator could say: "You know as well as I do that selfish and greedy men killed people and slandered families who didn't merit such treatment."[17] There was a reminder of de Gaulle's contested remark about France needing two strings to its bow.[18] Former Justice Minister Teitgen explained once again that in the view of the liberation government *indignité nationale,* if retroactive in a strictly legal sense, had in fact been "a measure of attenuation and indulgence," since it spared those brought before Civic Chambers the stiffer sentences of the Courts of Justice. And if the Courts of Justice had themselves been exceptional jurisdictions, they had been more lenient than the courts martial they replaced. Teitgen attacked those who were now accusing the resistance of crime. If there had been abuses it was because Vichy's collaboration had ruled out the possibility that the Pétainists could remain in place at the liberation, and their departure had created a vacuum. Teitgen also blamed the Communists (France was now a party to the cold war) for the excesses of the purge: That party, he said, had wished to utilize the purge for "political subversion," while the liberation government had sought to maintain legality. He agreed that amnesty was possible for lesser offenses; his party, the MRP, supported the government bill.[19] Privately, Teitgen felt that amnesty was a necessary remedy for the wide disparity of verdicts of the Courts of Justice. (He remembered how a rural or mountain district might sentence a woman to ten to twenty years in prison for "horizontal collaboration"—sexual relations with German soldiers—while a court in the sophisticated Paris region would consider this offense to deserve nothing more than five years of *indignité*.[20])

Both the Socialists and the Communists voted against the amnesty when it came to a vote (at six o'clock one morning in December 1950). In his summing-up in behalf of the bill Minister Mayer promised: "Amnesty doesn't justify anything."[21] The bill passed. Among its chief provisions, this law of January 5, 1951, authorized early release for persons sentenced to prison terms of less than life. *Indignité nationale* would cease to be a criminal offense, and its effects would be limited to deprivation of civil rights, of certain professional activities, including work in the media. Some sentences would benefit from automatic amnesty: This applied to those who had been given fifteen years or less of *indignité*, to minors under twenty-one sentenced to five years or less of prison. Amnesty was also available—but on application only—to collaborators sentenced to minor terms of prison provided that they were not accused of denouncing or responsibility for torture, deportations to camps, or murder. A full amnesty was granted to resistance fighters whose acts had been intended "to serve the cause of the liberation of national territory."[22]

A "timid" law, defenders of the purged were to say. It helped those convicted of *indignité nationale*, but offered less relief to those still in prison.[23] Some months after passage of the bill a critic noted that few persons had been released from prison as a result of the law (he described the behavior of Justice Minister René Mayer—a Jew—as "talmudic."[24])

And so the debate was taken up again. A notable contribution came from a hero of the intellectuals, Jean Paulhan. Ever since he broke with the Communist-dominated resistance writers' organization, the National Writers Committee, he had been involved in polemics on the very foundations of the purge. His argument was summed up in a "Letter to the Directors of the Resistance" in which he took up the cause not only of writers and intellectuals but of all purge victims. He accepted the estimate of sixty thousand summary executions, 1 million arrests. He went so far as to say that none of the four hundred thousand French citizens who had been executed, sentenced to hard labor, ruined, and disgraced had been tried legally. For the Vichy regime had been invested with power by a proper vote, so that those who had accepted Vichy could not be traitors. Paulhan added that the fellow travelers of the National Writers Committee were themselves collaborators—of the Soviet Union.[25] In December 1951 Paulhan tried to publish his open letter in an organ of the Gaullist movement but de Gaulle would have nothing to do with it; he objected to Paulhan's erroneous statistics, and to his plea for the legitimacy of the Vichy regime.[26]

For resistance veterans, a wider amnesty still represented "total rehabilitation" of traitors—so declared an organization of former camp victims.[27] They also feared that amnesty signified "liquidation of the Resistance," and called attention to provisions in a new bill which was before the Assembly which could prevent victims from naming the persons who had tortured them.[28] In fact this broader amnesty was the subject of six different bills, and fifteen days of parliamentary discussion stretched over a period of a year beginning in July 1952. This did not contribute to the unity of the final version enacted into law (as a jurist was to observe), but in the end the campaign promises of the Assembly majority were kept, for candidates had committed themselves to a more comprehensive measure than the January 1951 act.[29] One vocal spokesman for amnesty was a newly elected assemblyman, Jacques Isorni, whom we have already met as attorney for Pétain and many other accused collaborators. Isorni, when he took the floor in the amnesty debate, acknowledged that he had been elected because he had defended Pétain. He said that he agreed that amnesty should not represent a settling of scores or revenge, but had to be seen in terms of a return to civil peace.[30]

None of this was reassuring to resistance veterans. Georges Bidault pointed to articles in the pro-amnesty press which interpreted signs of indulgence as a disavowal of the Free French cause. Once again he pointed to the experience of the other countries occupied by the Nazis, which had jailed more collaborators than France had.[31] The bill finally came to a vote in March 1953, at which time 390 members of the National Assembly accepted it, against 210 negative votes. It was a just law, editorialist Jacques Fauvet commented in *Le Monde,* for there had already been a "de facto amnesty" for all the clever collaborators who had slipped through the hands of justice—notably financial collaborators. It was a wise law, Fauvet added, for it put an end to what Léon Blum had called "internal exile"—the notion of *indignité nationale.* "For if they have occasionally treated crime as weakness they have also treated weakness as crime." Finally it was a generous law, and would require of its beneficiaries "the same sense of national unity of which they are taking advantage today."[32] There were amendments, and a second reading before parliament recessed for the summer. The final vote was 394 to 212, Communists and Socialists in the opposition.[33]

The law of August 6, 1953, as promulgated by President Auriol, began by dealing with its critics:

> Article 1—The French Republic renders homage to the Resistance, whose combat within and without its frontiers saved the nation. It intends to dispense clemency today in fidelity to the spirit of the Resistance.
> Amnesty is not rehabilitation nor revenge, no more than it is criticism of those who in the name of the nation had the heavy task of judging and punishing.[34]

This 1953 amnesty, the final word in the postwar Republic's disposal of collaboration crimes, dealt first of all with the matter of *indignité.* Those who had received this sentence—except as verdicts of the High Court—were now amnestied; High Court sentences to *indignité* could also be effaced, but only by special decree. Those convicted of trading with the enemy, if their sentences did not exceed five years of prison and a twenty-thousand-franc fine, also benefited from the new measure. There was an automatic amnesty for persons sentenced to five years or less—High Court sentences excepted—although those who had been accused of murder, rape, or denunciation, or whose acts or statements had exposed others to torture, deportation to camp, or death, or who had cooperated with the enemy armed forces, police, or espionage agencies, were not covered. Collaborators sentenced to fifteen years or less (twenty years for war invalids, camp victims, decorated resistance fighters) could obtain amnesty on applicaton. The pardon applied to convictions in absentia, even to cases not tried, as well as to prisoners originally sentenced to death but whose sentences were later commuted and reduced.

The 1953 amnesty also dealt with the administrative and professional purge. It did not give civil servants a right to return to their former posts, but made that possible, and restored the all-important right to a pension. The amnesty had among its consequences the removal of the penalty of confiscation of property, except when confiscation had represented reparation. Once again the law offered a protective umbrella to resistance veterans for acts which they had considered in the interests of the country. And Article 45 banned any future reference to amnestied convictions or penalties, which provision a jurist saw as unworkable—since it would make it impossible for convicted collaborators to make use of court records to appeal their own sentences.[35]

Indeed, the provision for elimination of all references to collaboration crime from the files of the convicted was to terrorize historians of the Second World War for years to come.

THREE

The Purge Today

OVER FORTY-FIVE YEARS HAVE PASSED since the armistice of 1940, which opened the door to German occupation and the Vichy regime; the official purge began over forty years ago. For those who were punished then it is over, and well over. But so many collaborators who had done no less than the convicted had avoided punishment. They lived, and some died, in exile, sometimes in internal exile. One of them, Louis Darquier de Pellepoix, who had been a notorious anti-Semitic agitator before becoming Commissioner for Jewish Affairs in the service of Vichy and the Germans, managed to get to Spain, where he lived undetected almost until the end of his life, and then he died there, still untouched. (He had been sentenced to death by the High Court, but in absentia.) Now and then public attention has been drawn to persons fully reintegrated into French society, some of whom enjoy positions of authority and privilege, who passed through the purge without a scar, or who managed to live down a minor punishment, and then to conceal its traces.

But the notion persisted that some kinds of crime had to be sanctioned, no matter how long ago they were committed. Few contested this notion when the Nazi official Adolf Eichmann was tracked down in Latin America, tried and executed in Israel. More recently the French opened a similar case against Gestapo officer Klaus Barbie.

Conforming to decisions of the victorious Allies after the Second World War, notably to the charter of the Nuremberg Tribunal which tried Nazi leaders for war crimes, the French passed a law in

285

December 1964 (by unanimous vote of both houses of the legislature) which eliminated the statute of limitations for war crimes. "Crimes against humanity as defined by the resolution of February 13, 1946, of the United Nations, based on the definition of crimes against humanity in the charter of the [Nuremberg] Tribunal, are by their nature imprescriptible."

The treatment of unresolved purge cases in the post-Gaullist era can be studied through one of the most notorious of them, and perhaps the most enigmatic. Paul Touvier was hardly a national figure, but in the Rhône-Alpes region his name was known. He had been a leader of the Militia in Lyon, a regional chief after September 1943; responsible for intelligence and action, working with the Gestapo in the roundup of resistance partisans and Jews. He was accused of torture, of murder—notably for playing a part in the killing of Professor Victor Basch, who was then eighty-two, president of the prewar League for the Rights of Man, and of his wife, then eighty. Touvier had been tried and sentenced to death while a fugitive by a Court of Justice in Lyon in September 1946, again in Chambéry (Savoie) in March 1947. But Touvier was never found.

Then in 1972, a quarter of a century after the second conviction, the case made the front pages. It was revealed that Touvier had managed to hide with the help of religious institutions, and that a high-ranking church official had intervened in his behalf with the President of the Republic. In November 1971 President Georges Pompidou had signed a pardon which voided the last sanctions still hanging over Touvier's head—a ban on residence in his region and confiscation of his property. At the age of fifty-six he was free to return to his family home in Chambéry.

The press stayed close to the story. Touvier had not been a minor functionary but a particularly active collaborator, the public was told. He had robbed and tortured his victims, had ordered executions without trial. It came out that the secretary of Lyon's Cardinal Pierre Gerlier had taken the initiative to obtain affidavits in Touvier's behalf in the early 1960s. And then in March 1967 the death sentences issued while Touvier was a fugitive were automatically canceled by the statute of limitations (thus leaving only the ban on residence and confiscation). Armed with support of the local clergy, Touvier was received in 1970 by the Catholic philosopher Gabriel Marcel, who was later to admit that he had been gulled by Touvier's rosy version of his activity during the occupation. Marcel was the one who intervened with Pompidou, who despite unfavorable recommendations by the Interior and Justice ministries signed the pardon.[1] (On hearing of Pompidou's act an official of the Lyon Court of Justice wasn't surprised, for he had once examined the Touvier file and found that like many other hastily compiled cases of the liberation era it contained no specific charges, no formal indictment which would have allowed a jury to pronounce a guilty verdict in the presence of the defendant.[2])

The discovery of this "executioner of Lyon" by a Paris newsmagazine inspired protests, demonstrations, one at the very doorstep of Touvier's house in Chambéry.[3] A move began among families of his victims to have him tried again for crimes against humanity, now the only crimes which could still be prosecuted. In October 1975 a Paris court refused to take the case on the grounds that the French law lifting the statute of limitations had been passed only in 1964, while the acts of which Touvier was accused were covered by the cutoff of ten years beginning at the official date of the cessation of hostilities, June 1, 1946.[4] The victims appealed, and the appeals court at once agreed that the statute of limitations was valid, and upheld the plaintiffs in calling for an opinion of the Foreign Ministry on the effects of the Nuremberg Tribunal's decision. And then in July 1979 the Foreign Ministry came down on the side of the victims. The prosecution of Touvier became possible again; pretrial examination began in Paris that very month.[5] When an arrest warrant was issued for Touvier in 1982 he was not to be found; the press had him moving from one monastery to another, and by that time it was thought he might have moved on to a monastery in Italy.[6]

In 1983 the Lyon courts, then preparing the trial of Gestapo chief Klaus Barbie, also began examination of a new complaint against Paul Touvier, this one from the family of murdered Victor Basch.[7] And where is Touvier at this writing? In September 1984 a regional newspaper published his death notice; two days later the same paper ran a report that his grave had been discovered in a village churchyard. But there was no death certificate, no confirmation by the town hall, the church, or the local funeral parlor. The hunt continues.[8] It is thanks to the Barbie case that France's highest appeals court had an opportunity in 1984 to confirm the validity of the law of December 26, 1964, concerning the nonapplicability of the statute of limitations to crimes against humanity.[9]

* * *

The first totally new case to be opened in the second wave of the purge was that of Jean Leguay, secretary-general of the police in occupied Paris, who was believed to be personally implicated in such acts as the rounding-up of Jews at the behest of the Germans (the Jews were transferred to concentration camps, and most were murdered). In March 1979 Leguay was indicted in Paris for "crimes against humanity consisting of illegal arrests, arbitrary detention, abuse of authority, acts of barbarity, abduction and ill treatment of children." The case had been brought to public attention by attorney Serge Klarsfeld, who in the name of a group called Sons and Daughters of Jewish Deportees of France had been compiling evidence of such crimes against humanity, and denouncing their perpetrators.[10] Like so many other high officials of the Vichy police, Leguay had hardly been troubled by the purge. He had been stripped of his duties, but by 1955 he was taken back into the prefectoral corps by decision of the Council of State, which council apparently disposed only of the brief presented by Leguay himself.[11] After the liberation Leguay had gone to the United States as representative of a well-known French perfume manufacturer, and after a dozen years returned to become president of a famous cosmetics firm. When finally indicted he was sixty-nine years old and retired, comfortably installed in Paris and in a villa on the Riviera.[12]

Next on the list of priorities was René Bousquet, who as Vichy's secretary-general of the police had been Leguay's superior. He had received a two-year sentence of *indignité nationale* (as we have seen), a sentence immediately lifted because of evidence of his support for the resistance. With that clean bill of health Bousquet had been able to return to the Interior Ministry, then had moved into banking, ending as a high officer of the Banque d'Indochine, chairman of a film company, member of the boards of a number of other large enterprises. After attorney Serge Klarsfeld brought the Bousquet case to public notice and called for his indictment, Bousquet resigned from his bank position and from the boards to which he belonged as representative of that bank.[13] But Bousquet has not been indicted as of this writing.[14]

A third notable affair was that of a still more public personality of postwar France, Maurice Papon, who in 1958 was prefect of police in Paris, then Minister of the Budget in the cabinet of Raymond Barre under the presidency of Valéry Giscard d'Estaing. During the occupation Papon had served in Bordeaux as secretary-general of the prefecture, but at the liberation he seemed to have support from the local resistance, for the Gaullists' Commissioner of the Republic kept him on the job, even promoting him to be prefect of the Landes. But forty years later the old files were looked into more carefully. Papon's name was found on documents concerning the roundup of Jews at the request of the Germans, an act which seemed to come under the heading of crime against humanity, that crime whose prosecution no longer had a cutoff date. Papon was indicted in January 1983; in March 1984 he was informed by the examining magistrate in Bordeaux that pursuant to seventeen complaints by families of thirty-seven persons who had died in Nazi camps after arrest in Bordeaux, he was the object of another series of indictments.[15] The case is still undergoing pretrial examination.

For now that it is possible to read the heretofore secret archives of the Vichy years, it is likely that evidence will be uncovered which even the most conscientious of investigators could not have found in the tumult of liberation and purge. This is not to say that the cases against Leguay, Papon, and others are certain to hold up in the courtroom. But questions have been raised which call for convincing answers. A decision of a French appeals court in the Barbie case opens the door to further prosecutions, not only on charges of genocide but also for brutal treatment of resisting Frenchmen; in other words, those who escaped the first purge may be subject to a new one, casting aside the statute of limititions, if the will to prosecute exists.

The persistence of strong feelings concerning collaborators who escaped punishment may help us offer a conclusion to this study. For the strong feelings tell us that in the eyes of mainstream public opinion, and of the press which serves it, there is more purging to be done. And this suggests that there had not been too much purging to begin with. Many public officials, many white-collar offenders slipped through the net, as did many unsavory criminals. Most of the worst of them escaped by hiding, by playing dead, or simply by playing off one jurisdiction against another; we have seen examples of each of these in this book. But others, who are now accused of the worst crimes of all, remained safely within the bosom of society. A purge which had so many loopholes, which permitted persons indicted for high crimes to escape untouched, cannot really be called draconian.

If present French law was not so protective, one could name

members of the French elite, including respected authors and artists, famous journalists, statesmen, leaders in business and industry, who went unpurged, or whose purging did not stick. We can remember the complaint of Céline, then facing prosecution for collaboration, that so many worse offenders than himself had gone scot free. One of the examples he gives is fellow writer Henry de Montherlant.[16] Today even Céline's errors seem to have been forgiven: In 1984 the prefect of Paris authorized the placing of a commemorative plaque on the house in which he lived during the occupation. As for Montherlant, there has long been a Henry de Montherlant Square in Paris, near the French Academy to which he was elected in 1960, hardly more than a dozen years after his own sanction. A French government cultural center in Villette Park in north Paris acquired a Cinéma Arletty in 1984; a year later on the centenary of his birth the plays of Sacha Guitry were published in a deluxe twelve-volume set, there were three new books about him in the bookstores, and several of his plays were receiving new productions.

And let it be recalled that a considerable number of lower-echelon civil servants, including policemen who, on order, had arrested political dissidents and Jews, as well as the middle-echelon civil servants who had kept the police departments and the prefectures running, escaped the purge undisturbed. At worst, they were transferred out of sight of their victims. Indeed, no one of any rank was seriously punished for his or her role in the roundup and deportation of Jews to Nazi camps.[17]

Against all this—the undeniable abuses, the regrettable judicial errors. We have taken note of them in many places in this book. It is for the reader to decide whether they were avoidable, whether even if unavoidable in the confusion of the time they are now pardonable. They seem to have been, most of them, the honest errors of very ordinary men and women in the villages and towns of France, even if some of these ordinary people were Communists.

We may also ponder the observation of one of the most responsible figures of the purge years, law professor and Catholic layman Pierre-Henri Teitgen, former Minister of Justice. When the first comprehensive amnesty was promulgated in January 1951 it contained a clause which allowed victims of the unofficial purge—families of victims of resistance executions, for example—to file claims for war reparations.[18] There were no notable claims.[19]

As for the official purge, is it really necessary to remind readers of the evidence found earlier in these pages that it was planned and carried out by the most enlightened of French jurists, the most democratic of statesmen, who later were to rule France from the moderate center? Should they be blamed for failing to control outbursts of village anger, murders in the woods and fields of France? For this book contains ample proof that the Free French in Algiers and then in Paris, with their Commissioners and their prefects, were on the side of law and order from the moment they took responsibility for their respective territories. The message seems to be that the French need not be ashamed of their purge, as they often seem to be, even today.

Notes

Abbreviations

AN   Archives Nationales
ITP   Institut d'Histoire du Temps Présent (Paris)
JO   *Journal Officiel*
JORF   *Journal Officiel de la République Française*
SH   Service Historique de l'Armée de Terre

Prologue

1. Yves Farge, *Rebelles, Soldats et Citoyens* (Paris, 1946), 229.
2. Etienne Fournial et al., *Saint-Etienne: Histoire de la Ville et de ses habitants* (Roanne, 1976), 330ff.
3. Maurice Toesca, "L'Occupation," in *Vie et Mort des Français (1939–1945)*, (Paris, 1971), 126, 131f.
4. Talk with Charles-Fournier Bocquet, Association Nationale des Anciens Combattants de la Résistance.
5. Abbé [Jean-Marie] Desgranges, *Les Crimes masqués du Résistantialisme* (Paris, 1948), 13.
6. Maurice Bardèche, *Lettre à François Mauriac* (Paris, 1947), 111.
7. *Rivarol* (Paris), August 23, 1951.
8. Jean Pleyber, "Les Travaux et les Jours," *Ecrits de Paris* (Paris), June 1950.
9. *Ibid.,* August 1950.
10. *Ibid.,* February 1951.
11. *Ibid.,* October 1950; *Rivarol* (Paris), August 23, 1951.
12. *Ecrits de Paris,* June 1952.

13. *Ibid.*, February 1951.
14. *Ibid.*

Part I
Chapter One. Resistance Justice

1. AN W-III 303 (High Court); text also published in Philippe Pétain, *Actes et Ecrits* (Paris, 1974), 605ff.
2. Jacques Delperrie de Bayac, *Histoire de la Milice* (Paris, 1969), 268f., 278f.
3. Ministère de l'Intérieur, Synthèse des Rapports des Préfets, May 1943. Archives Départementales de la Haute-Savoie 12 M 364.
4. Préfet de la Région de Lyon, Compte-rendu mensuel d'information, June 10, August 7, September 9, October 11, 1943. AN F1C III 1200.
5. Préfecture du Rhône, Rapports d'Information, November 5, 1943; January 5, 1944. AN F1C III 1183.
6. FTP-MOI, *Carmagnole Libérté* (Villeurbanne, 1982).
7. Talk with Henri Krischer, Nancy.
8. *Les Voix de la Liberté: Ici Londres (1940–1944)*, IV (Paris, 1975), 49f.
9. Talk with Claude Urman (regional military commander of the 35th Brigade). Cf. *Cérémonies en hommage à la 35ᵉ Brigade/Marcel Langer* (Toulouse, 1983); Claude Lévy, *Les Parias de la Résistance* (Paris, 1970), 177ff.
10. *L'Echo d'Alger* (Algiers), December 31, 1943.
11. *Alger Républicain* (Algiers), January 10, 1944.
12. Charles de Gaulle, *Discours et Messages,* I (Paris, 1970), 15.
13. *Voix de la Liberté,* I, 268 (July 24, 1941).
14. *Ibid.,* 280.
15. *Ibid.,* 295.
16. *Libération* (south zone) No. 21, January 10, 1943.
17. *Voix de la Liberté,* IV, opp. 224.
18. *Le Populaire* (clandestine), March 1943, reproduced in *Journaux du Temps Passé* No. 20, "La Résistance" (Paris, n.d.).
19. *Bir Hakeim* (clandestine) No. 5, August–September 1943.
20. *Voix de la Liberté,* III, 203f.
21. Charles de Gaulle, *Mémoires de Guerre,* II, *L'Unité (1942–1944),* (Paris, 1956), 134.
22. *La Dépêche Algérienne* (Algiers), October 10, 1943.
23. *Voix de la Liberté,* IV, 127.
24. *Ibid.,* 245f.
25. *Le Pilori,* December 1943, reproduced in Louis-Frédéric Ducros, *Montagnes ardéchoises dans la guerre,* II (Valence, 1977), Appendix VI.

26. Reproduced in *Bulletin d'Information du Front National de Lutte pour la libération de la France* No. 5, February 1944.

Chapter Two. The Battle for France

1. *Voix de la Liberté,* IV, 157f.
2. *Editoriaux prononcées à la radio par Philippe Henriot* Nos. 11, 12 (Vichy, 1944), May 3, 4, 8, 14, 1944.
3. *Voix de la Liberté,* V, 91.
4. *Ibid.,* 78.
5. July 13, 1944. ITP 72 AJ 49.
6. From Pierre Péré.
7. Archives Départementales du Rhône: Archives of the Commission d'Histoire de la Guerre 1939–1945, file C 1.
8. Marcel Baudot, "La Répression de la Collaboration et l'Epuration Politique, Administrative et Economique," in *La Libération de la France* (Paris, 1976), 760, 769.
9. AN 72 AJ 1. Cf. Waldeck Rochet on London radio: *Voix de la Liberté,* V, 6. De Gaulle on London radio had said on April 18, 1942: "National liberation cannot be separated from national insurrection." De Gaulle, *Discours et Messages,* I, 182.
10. Comité d'Action du CNR, Ordre d'opération, June 1944. ITP 72 AJ 49: AN 72 AJ 3.
11. AN F1A 3734.
12. AN 72 AJ 1; ITP 72 AJ 49.
13. Ducros, *Montagnes Ardéchoises,* II, 389; Roger Bellanger, *Dordogne en armes* (Périgueux, 1945), 187; ITP 72 AJ 56.
14. *Voix de la Résistance,* V, 7, 144.
15. *France d'Abord* (clandestine) No. 58, July 15, 1944, reproduced in *Journaux du Temps Passé.*
16. AN 72 AJ 158 (ITP).
17. *Ibid.*
18. Talk with Jean Chaintron.
19. *Voix de la Liberté,* IV, 149.

Chapter Three. The Clandestine Planners

1. ITP 72 AJ 49; Henri Michel, *Les Courants de pensée de la Résistance* (Paris, 1962), 338ff.
2. Jean Larrieu, "L'Epuration judicaire dans les Pyrénées-Orientales," *Revue d'Histoire de la Deuxième Guerre Mondiale* (Paris), October 1978, 29.

3. Charles-Louis Foulon, *Le Pouvoir en province à la libération: Les Commissaires de la République (1943–1946)*, (Paris, 1975), xiv f., 51ff., 57ff., 63, 66f.

4. *Voix de la Liberté*, V, 38.

5. *JORF* (Algiers), July 6, 1944, 534.

6. Foulon, *Le Pouvoir en province*, 86.

7. For fuller information on the CGE: Diane de Bellescize, *Les Neuf Sages de la Résistance: Le Comité Général d'Etudes dans la clandestinité* (Paris, 1979); Foulon, *Le Pouvoir en province*, 53f.; Jacques Charpentier, *Au service de la liberté* (Paris, 1949), 221ff.; Michel Debré, *Mémoires*, I, *Trois républiques pour une France* (Paris, 1984), 189ff.

8. Talk with François de Menthon, Menthon-Saint-Bernard.

9. Note, France Combattante (BCRA), February 17, 1943, in AN F1A 3733. See Foulon, *Le Pouvoir en province*, 53ff.; Michel, *Les Courants de pensée*, 347ff.

10. Talk with Maurice Rolland.

11. Talk with Charles Zambeaux.

12. From Maurice Rolland. Cf. Henri Faucher, "L'Indignité Nationale," *La Semaine Juridique* (Paris) No. 454, 1945.

13. From Maurice Rolland. Debré, *Mémoires*, I, 208, attributes the invention of *indignité nationale* and the Courts of Justice to the CGE.

14. From François de Menthon, Maurice Rolland.

15. Debré, *Mémoires*, I, 209.

16. Michel Debré, "Préparé dans la clandestinité," *Echo de la Résistance* (Paris), August–September 1955; Debré, *Mémoires*, I, 230ff.

17. Debré, *Mémoires*, I, 426.

Chapter Four. Algiers

1. De Gaulle, *Mémoires de Guerre*, II, 149f.

2. Gaston Schmitt, *Toute la vérité sur le procès Pucheu* (Paris, 1963), 30ff.

3. *Ibid.*, 37ff.; de Gaulle, *Mémoires de Guerre*, II, 134.

4. *JORF*, July 10, 1943, 24.

5. *JORF*, September 11, 1943, 116.

6. *JORF*, September 23, 1943, 140.

7. *JORF*, October 9, 1943, 183.

8. AN BB 30 1730.

9. AN BB 30 1730.

10. Préambule, January 5, 1944. AN BB 30 1729.

11. AN BB 30 1729.

12. François de Menthon, "L'Epuration," in *Libération de la France*.

13. Emile Garçon, *Code Pénal annoté*, I (Paris, n.d.).

14. *JORF*, January 15, 1944 (Débats de l'ACP), sessions of January 11, 12.

15. De Gaulle, *Mémoires de Guerre*, II, 155.

16. *JORF*, April 22, 1944, 325ff.

17. *JORF*, October 7, 1943, 164.

18. Schmitt, *Toute la vérité*, 37.

19. AN BB 30 1730.

Chapter Five. The First Trials

1. Schmitt, *Toute la vérité*, 42.

2. *La Dépêche Algérienne* (Algiers), October 27, 1943.

3. Marcel Peyrouton, *Du Service public à la prison commune* (Paris, 1950), 193ff., 230ff., 244.

4. *Ibid.*, 244f.

5. AN BB 30 1730.

6. *Voix de la Liberté*, IV, 142.

7. *Foreign Relations of the United States: Diplomatic Papers,* 1943, II (Washington, D.C., 1964), 193–201.

8. Jean Pierre-Bloch, *Le Vent souffle sur l'histoire* (Paris, 1956), 208ff.

9. Peyrouton, *Du Service public*, 247ff.

10. Pierre Pucheu, *Ma Vie* (Paris, 1948), 343, 358f.

11. Schmitt, *Toute la vérité*, 54f.; *JORF,* January 8, 1944, 27.

12. Schmitt, *Toute la vérité*, 65ff.

13. *Ibid.*, 68ff., 97ff., 103ff.

14. *Ibid.*, 108.

15. *Ibid.*, 124ff.

16. *Ibid.*, 186ff., 197ff., 230, 237.

17. *Ibid.*, 240ff., 254.

18. March 24, 1944. Charles de Gaulle, *Lettres, Notes et Carnets* (*Juin 1943–Mai 1945*), (Paris, 1983), 174ff.

19. De Menthon, "L'Epuration," 792.

20. *Voix de la Liberté*, IV, 207.

21. March 13, 1944. *Foreign Relations of the United States: Diplomatic Papers,* 1944, III (Washington, D.C., 1965), 654.

22. Service de Sondages et Statistiques, *Sondages de l'opinion publique française pendant l'occupation,* April–September 1944 (Paris, n.d.). Some of the original material is in AN Papiers Gernahling.

23. *Echo d'Oran* (Oran), March 21, 1944.

24. *La Dépêche Algérienne* (Algiers), March 23, 1944.

25. *Alger Républicain* (Algiers), March 30, 1944.

26. *La Tunisie Française* (Tunis) May 10, 1944; *L'Echo d'Alger* (Algiers), May 10, 1944.

27. AN BB 30, 1728.

28. AN BB 30 1730.

29. *La Dépêche Algérienne* (Algiers), May 13, 1944.

30. De Menthon, "L'Epuration," 792.

Part II
Chapter One. Taking Over

1. Ducros, *Montagnes ardéchoises,* III, 418ff.

2. Report by Lt. Yole, maquis de l'Ardèche. Archives Départementales du Rhône: Archives of the Commission d'Histoire de la Guerre 1939–1945, C 1.

3. *Ibid.,* D 4.

4. Guy Labedan, "La Répression à la Libération dans la région de Toulouse," *Revue d'Histoire de la Deuxième Guerre Mondiale* (Paris), July 1983, 105ff.

5. Col. Henri Monnet, *Mémoires d'un éclectique* (Paris, 1980), 128f.

6. From Pierre Péré.

7. From Pierre Péré.

8. ITP 72 AJ 137.

9. From Suzanne and Paul Silvestre; Suzanne Silvestre, "Intervention," in *Libération de la France,* 808f.

10. ITP.

11. July 17, 1944. *Voix de la Liberté,* V, 114.

12. Jeanne Grall, "Statistique de la Répression à la Libération (Calvados)," *Bulletin du Comité d'Histoire de la Deuxième Guerre Mondiale* (Paris), January–February 1977.

13. Ministère de la Justice, Inspection des Services Judiciaires, Historique; Note sur la Justice, Commissaire de la République (Bayeux), July 3, 1944. Courtesy of Maurice Rolland.

14. Talk with Pierre Laroque.

15. Coulet to Koenig, June 19, 1944. AN F1A 4007.

16. Note, July 22, 1944, from secretary-general of police to deputy director of Sûreté Nationale. AN F1A 4007.

17. Statement by Yves Grasset, mayor of Marmande, 1949. ITP.

18. Elsa Triolet, "Les Routes de la Drôme," *La Drôme en Armes* (Romans), September 5, 1944.

19. *Combat* (Paris), September 2, 1944.

20. Jean Galtier-Boissière, *Mon Journal depuis la libération* (Paris, 1945), 11.

21. Jacques Chastenet, *Quatre fois vingt ans* (Paris, 1974), 368.

22. James Wellard, in *Voix de la Liberté,* V, 191f.

23. Abbé Roger More, *Totor chez les FTP* (Chambéry, 1974), 120ff. A

similar conclusion is proposed by Peter Novick, *The Resistance Versus Vichy* (New York, 1968), 69.

24. *Le Monde* (Paris), October 22, 1983.

Chapter Two. Swift Punishment

1. Foulon, *Le Pouvoir en province,* 136
2. *JORF,* July 6, 1944, 534; Garçon, *Codé Pénal annoté,* 266.
3. Papiers Ingrand AN 72 AJ 521. See Henry Ingrand, *Libération de l'Auvergne* (Paris, 1974), 157.
4. Papiers Ingrand AN 72 AJ 521.
5. Report by Ingrand, March 23, 1946. Papiers Ingrand AN 72 AJ 524.
6. *L'Appel de la Haute-Loire* (Le Puy), August 31, September 3–4, 1944.
7. *Ibid.,* September 5, 6, 1944.
8. *Ibid.,* September 5, 1944.
9. *Ibid.,* September 16, 17–18, 1944.
10. *Ibid.,* September 22, 23, 1944.
11. Jean Lacipieras, *Au Carrefour de la trahison* (Paris, 1950), 114f., 125ff.
12. Louis Rougier et al., *L'Epuration* (Paris, 1957; supplement to *Défense de l'Occident,* January–February 1957).
13. *Le Travailleur Alpin,* September 3–4, 1944, quoted in Michel Chanal, "La Milice française dans l'Isère (février 1943–août 1944)," *Revue d'Histoire de la Deuxième Guerre Mondiale* (Paris), July 1982.
14. Minutes, May 24, 1945. Archives of the Assemblée Nationale, Paris.
15. *JORF,* Assemblée Nationale, November 9, 1951, 7835.

Chapter Three. Paris

1. *Front National* (Paris), August 27, 1944.
2. Paul Léautaud, *Journal littéraire,* XVI (Paris, 1964), 44f., 57, 84.
3. Jacques Isorni, *Je hais ces impostures* (Paris, 1977), 170f.
4. *Combat* (Paris), August 30, 1944.
5. *Combat* (Paris), September 4, 1944.
6. *Le Figaro* (Paris), September 1, 1944; *Libération* (Paris), September 1, 1944.
7. Henri Denis, *Le Comité parisien de la libération* (Paris, 1963), 172ff.
8. *Ibid.,* 237ff.
9. *Le Populaire* (Paris), August 29, 1944.
10. *Le Figaro* (Paris), September 5, 1944.
11. *Le Figaro* (Paris), September 12, 1944.
12. Pierre Taittinger, . . . *Et Paris ne fut détruit* (Paris, 1948), 233ff.

13. Claude Mauriac, *Un Autre de Gaulle: Journal* (*1944–1954*), (Paris, 1970), 42.

14. Mary Marquet, *Cellule 209* (Paris, 1949), 43ff.

15. *Le Populaire* (Paris), September 1, 1944.

16. Taittinger, . . . *Et Paris ne fut détruit*, 239.

17. *Ibid.*, 254.

18. *L'Humanité* (Paris), September 28, 1944.

19. AN F21-1

20. Marquet, *Cellule 209,* 51ff.

21. Taittinger, . . . *Et Paris ne fut détruit*, 249ff.

22. Galtier-Boissière, *Mon Journal depuis la libération,* 16ff., 31, 33, 47, 71.

23. Jean-Paul Abel, *L'Age de Caïn* (Paris, 1947).

24. Jean-Henri Roy, "Les Deux Justices," *Les Temps Modernes* (Paris), June 1948, 2261ff.

Chapter Four. France Takes Charge

1. Robert Aron, *Histoire de la libération de la France* (Paris, 1959), 454ff.; Robert Aron, *Histoire de l'Epuration*, I (Paris, 1967), 576ff.

2. Ingrand, *Libération de l'Auvergne,* 167.

3. *JORF,* November 20, 1943.

4. *JORF,* October 5, 1944.

5. *Libération de la France,* 769ff., 787.

6. Albert Chaudier, *Limoges* (*1944–1947*): *Capitale du Maquis* (Paris-Limoges, 1980), 124.

7. *Libération de la France,* 769ff.

8. Foulon, *Le Pouvoir en province,* 143.

9. November 18, 1944. Papiers Ingrand AN 72 AJ 524.

10. Ministère de la Guerre, Direction de la Gendarmerie, Synthèse pour la période du 15 septembre au 15 octobre 1944. AN 72 AJ 384.

11. AN F7 14968. (Intérieur to Commissaires Régionaux.)

12. AN F7 14968.

13. Charpentier, *Au Service de la liberté,* 251ff. On July 31, 1945, the government decided to cease to employ administrative internment except for treason or black market activity, although suspects could still be placed in forced residence or banned from a district. AN F1A 3311.

14. From Charles Zambeaux.

15. AN 72 AJ 92 (ITP).

16. Jean Pleyber, "Les Travaux et les Jours," *Ecrits de Paris* (Paris), March–August 1950.

17. Chastenet, *Quatre fois vingt ans,* 368f.

18. Desgranges, *Les Crimes masqués,* 69.

19. Marcel Baudot, *L'Opinion publique sous l'occupation* (Paris, 1960), 264.

20. *Le Populaire* (Paris), September 28, 1944.

21. *L'Humanité* (Paris), September 28, 1944.

22. Jacques Bounin, *Beaucoup d'imprudences* (Paris, 1974), 194; Ministère de la Guerre, Direction de la Gendarmerie, Synthèse pour la période du 15 décembre 1944 au 15 janvier 1945. AN 72 AJ 384.

23. Bounin, *Beaucoup d'imprudences,* 197f.

24. Charles de Gaulle, *Mémoires de Guerre,* III, *Le Salut* (Paris, 1965), 127, 421.

25. Ministère de la Guerre, Direction de la Gendarmerie, Synthèse pour la période du 15 décembre 1944 au 15 janvier 1945. AN 72 AJ 384.

26. *Ibid.,* 15 janvier–15 février 1945.

27. *Ibid.,* 15 février–15 mars 1945.

28. June 3, 1945, letter to Minister of Interior. Papiers Ingrand AN 72 AJ 521.

29. May 27, 1945. François Mauriac, *Journal,* IV (Paris, 1950), 66.

Chapter Five. Attitudes

1. *Bulletin d'Informations de l'Institut Français d'Opinion Publique* (Paris), October 16, 1944. The sampling was made from September 11 to 16.

2. *Ibid.,* November 16, 1944.

3. Conseil National de la Résistance, Association Nationale des Comités départementaux de la libération, *Resolutions* (Paris, 1944).

4. From Pierre de Chevigné.

5. *L'Année politique,* I (Paris, 1946), 444.

6. *Combat* (Paris), October 10, 1944 (speech of October 8).

7. De Gaulle, *Discours et Messages,* I, 454.

8. C. Mauriac, *Un Autre de Gaulle,* 58ff., 61.

9. *Le Monde* (Paris), February 24, 1945.

10. Talk with Pierre-Henri Teitgen.

11. De Gaulle, *Mémoires de Guerre,* III, 117ff.

12. *Ibid.,* 119; *Année politique,* I, 92.

13. De Menthon, "L'Epuration," 788f. Cf. Charles de Gaulle, *Mémoires de Guerre,* I, *L'Appel* (Paris, 1954), 231f.

14. Denis, *Le Comité parisien,* 167.

15. *Ibid.,* 136, 231.

16. *Discours prononcé à la radio par M. Jean Chaintron le 29 janvier 1945* (Limoges, 1945).

17. *Discours prononcé à la Radio par M. Jean Chaintron le 2 Août 1945* (Limoges, 1945).

18. *Année politique,* I, 72f.

19. From Geoffroy de Courcel.

20. Denis, *Le Comité parisien,* 164.

21. Jean-Louis Panicacci, "Le Comité départemental de Libération dans les Alpes-Maritimes (1944–1947)," *Revue d'Histoire de la Deuxième Guerre Mondiale* (Paris), July 1982, 99ff.

22. Ministère de la Guerre, Direction de la Gendarmerie, Synthèse pour la période du 15 décembre 1944 au 15 janvier 1945. AN 72 AJ 384.

23. Abbé Jean Popot, *J'étais aumônier à Fresnes* (Paris, 1962), 119f.

Part III
Chapter One. Capital of the Resistance

1. *France Automobile en un volume* (Guide Bleu), (Paris, 1938), 200.

2. Henri Michel, *Histoire de la Résistance* (Paris, 1958), 20, 60.

3. For example see Henri Amoretti, *Lyon Capitale (1940–1944)*, (Paris, 1964), 368ff.

4. "Situation à Lyon," September 13, 1944. AN F1A 4022.

5. Département du Rhône, Rapport du 16 février 1945 (période du 15 janvier au 15 février); Rapport du 16 mars 1945 (période du 15 février au 15 mars). AN F1C III 1225.

6. "Situation à Lyon," September 13, 1944. AN F1A 4022.

7. Claude Morgan, *Yves Farge* (Paris, 1954), 54, 67ff., 72ff., 173ff.

8. *Ibid.,* 78.

9. Debré, *Mémoires,* I, 352f.

10. Note Fouché, AN F1A 4022.

11. Foulon, *Le Pouvoir en province,* 93; Morgan, *Yves Farge,* 85.

12. Report by Gregoire (Farge) quoted in Morgan, *Yves Farge,* 94ff.

13. Talk with René Tavernier.

14. Farge, *Rebelles,* 190f.

15. Fernand Rude *Libération de Lyon et de sa région* (Paris, 1974), 134.

16. Farge, *Rebelles,* 207ff.

17. *La Marseillaise de Lyon et du Sud-est* (Lyon), September 23–24, 1944.

18. AN F1A 4022.

19. Farge, *Rebelles,* 216ff.

Chapter Two. Punishment in Lyon

1. AN 72 AJ 186 (ITP).

2. *Journal Officiel du Commissariat de la République (Région Rhône-Alpes),* September 4, 1944.

3. *Ibid.,* September 11, 1944.

4. Farge, *Rebelles,* 226f.; *La Voix du Peuple* (Lyon), September 11, 1944.

5. *La Voix du Peuple* (Lyon), September 16–17, 1944.

6. *La Marseillaise* (Lyon), September 16–17, 1944.

7. Talk with Jean Bernard, Lyon.

8. *La Marseillaise* (Lyon), September 16–17, 1944.

9. *La Voix du Peuple* (Lyon), September 16–17, 1944.

10. From Jean Bernard.

11. Farge, *Rebelles,* 227f.

12. From Jean Bernard.

13. AN F1A 4022.

14. *La Marseillaise* (Lyon), *La Voix du Peuple* (Lyon), September 21, 1944.

15. Report of Procureur Général, Lyon, to Ministre de la Justice, December 7, 1944. Archives Départementales du Rhone: Archives du Parquet 3U-2040.

16. Rapport du Commissaire de la République concernant la période du 16 au 31 janvier 1945, Archives Départementales du Rhône.

17. *La Marseillaise* (Lyon), October 7–8, 14–15, 1944.

18. Rapport du Commissaire de la République concernant la période du 16 au 31 janvier 1945, Archives Départementales du Rhône.

19. Farge, *Rebelles,* 229f.

20. *Ibid.,* 257f.

21. Département du Rhône, Rapport du 16 février 1945, AN F1C III 1225.

22. Farge, *Rebelles,* 242ff.

23. Archives Départementales du Rhône: Archives du Commissariat de la République.

Chapter Three. Around Annecy

1. Report for December 25, 1943–January 23, 1944. Archives Départementales de la Haute-Savoie 12 M 364.

2. Pierre Mouthon, "La Répression de la Collaboration dans le Département de la Haute-Savoie" (unpublished manuscript), ITP.

3. Archives Départementales du Rhône: Archives of the Commission d'Histoire de la Guerre 1939–1945, C 1.

4. Alban Vistel, *La Nuit sans ombre* (Paris, 1970), 506.

5. Henri Noguères, *Histoire de la Résistance en France,* IV (Paris, 1976), 431.

6. Henri Noguères, *Histoire de la Résistance en France,* V (Paris, 1981), 646.

7. *La Résistance Savoisienne* (Annecy), August 19, 1946.

8. *Ibid.*

9. Jean Truffy, *Les Mémoires du Curé du Maquis de Glières* (Paris, 1979).

10. Henri Bordeaux, *Histoire d'une vie,* XII, *Lumière au bout de la nuit* (Paris, 1970), 253f.; *Lectures Françaises* (Paris), August–September 1964: "Le Livre Noir de l'Epuration," 37f.; Jean Pleyber, "Les Travaux et les Jours," *Ecrits de Paris* (Paris), March 1950, 29; June 1951, 19f.

11. Report by Capt. Peccoud ("Quino"), AN 72 AJ 181 (ITP).

12. Talk with Jean Comet, Annecy; minutes, courtesy of Joseph Lambroschini.

13. From Jean Comet.

14. Talk with Robert Poirson, Annecy.

15. From Jean Comet.

16. From Jean Comet; testimony in possession of Pierre Mouthon.

17. From Jean Comet, Robert Poirson.

18. From Pierre Mouthon.

19. From Robert Poirson.

20. Minutes, from Jean Comet.

21. From Jean Comet.

Part IV
Chapter One. Justice Before the Railroads

1. De Gaulle, *Mémoires de Guerre,* III, 47.

2. Talk with François de Menthon.

3. From François de Menthon.

4. Ministère de la Justice, Inspection des Services Judiciaires: Historique. Courtesy of Maurice Rolland.

5. Talk with Maurice Rolland.

6. *JORF,* July 6, 1944.

7. *JORF,* September 15, 1944.

8. Pierre-Henri Teitgen, *Les Cours de Justice* (Paris, 1946), 25ff.; talk with Raymond Lindon.

9. *Le Monde* (Paris), January 10, 1945.

10. Report of chief of mission Justice R. Fournier to M. le Garde des Sceaux, Marseille, September 8, 1944. Courtesy of Maurice Rolland.

11. Talk with Raymond Aubrac.

12. C. Mauriac, *Un Autre de Gaulle,* 31.

13. *Bulletin Officiel du Commissariat Régional de la République à Marseille,* September 6, 1944, 32.

14. *Ibid.,* September 8, 1944, 48.

15. Talk with André Cellard.

16. Talk with Raymond Aubrac.

17. From Raymond Aubrac.

18. From Raymond Aubrac; Decree 704 of November 6, 1944, in *Bulletin Officiel du Commissariat Régional de la République à Marseille,* November 9, 1944, 351.

19. Mission de liaison administrative de Groupe d'Armée pour le Théâtre d'Opérations Sud-Justice, Rapport à M. le Garde des Sceaux sur les Cours de Justice de la Zone Sud, September 30, 1944. Courtesy of Maurice Rolland.

20. L'Inspecteur Général de la Magistrature à M. le Garde des Sceaux, September 23, 1944. Courtesy of Maurice Rolland.

21. *Ibid.,* September 26, 1944.

22. Rapport sur la Cour d'Appel de Limoges, November 6, 1944. Courtesy of Maurice Rolland.

23. From Charles Zambeaux.

24. Garçon, *Code Pénal annoté,* 268.

25. Teitgen, *Le Cours de Justice,* 29.

26. Minutes of Commission de la Justice et de l'Epuration, November 24, December 1, 1944. Archives of the Assemblée Nationale.

27. Jean Bracquemond, "Intervention," *Libération de la France,* 803; Garçon, *Code Pénal annoté,* 266.

28. Teitgen, *Les Cours de Justice,* 30f.

29. *JORF,* November 29, 1944, 1543.

30. From Charles Zambeaux.

Chapter Two. The Paris Trials

1. Talk with Robert Vassart.

2. René Floriot, *La Répression des faits de collaboration* (Paris, 1945), 5.

3. Yves-Frédéric Jaffré, *Les Tribunaux d'exception (1940–1962),* (Paris, 1962), 167.

4. Affidavit of October 4, 1944, AN C.J. 1.

5. Sténographie René Bluet, AN 334 AP 8.

6. *Ibid.*

7. AN C.J. 1.

8. *JORF,* August 28, 1944, 767f.

9. *JORF,* December 27, 1944, 2076ff.

10. Charpentier, *Au Service de la liberté,* 257.

11. *Combat* (Paris), September 28, 1944.

12. Sténographie René Bluet, AN 334 AP 8.

13. Talk with Raymond Lindon.

14. Sténographie René Bluet, AN 334 AP 10.

15. From Raymond Lindon.

16. Sténographie René Bluet, AN 334 AP 10.

17. Galtier-Boissière, *Mon Journal depuis la libération*, 97.

18. François Mauriac, *Le Baillon dénoué* (Paris, 1945), 220f.

19. Henri Béraud, *Quinze jours avec la mort* (Paris, 1951), 221f.

20. *Ibid.*

21. *Le Monde* (Paris), April 21, 1950.

22. Jacques Isorni, *Le Procès de Robert Brasillach* (Paris, 1956), 35ff.

23. *Ibid.*, 53, 59ff.

24. *Ibid.*, 86.

25. *Ibid.*, 146ff., 152.

26. *Ibid.*, 155, 168f., 175f., 177, 186, 189ff., 203.

27. Robert Brasillach, *Lettres écrites en prison (octobre 1944–février 1945)*, (Paris, 1952), 185; Isorni, *Procès de Brasillach*, 212.

28. Brasillach, *Lettres*, 185.

29. Isorni, *Procès de Brasillach*, 218ff.

30. Herbert R. Lottman, *Albert Camus* (New York, 1979), 349.

31. Simone de Beauvoir, "Oeil pour oeil," *Les Temps Modernes* (Paris), February 1, 1946, 823f.

32. C. Mauriac, *Un Autre de Gaulle*, 79ff., 85ff., 88, 92, 99, 247.

33. Isorni, *Procès de Brasillach*, v f.

34. Pierre de Boisdeffre, "Apologie pour un condamné," *Le Monde* (Paris), February 18, 1975.

35. Jacques Isorni, *Mémoires*, I, *1911–1945*, (Paris, 1984), 324ff.

36. C. Mauriac, *Un Autre de Gaulle*, 75, 78.

37. Sténographie René Bluet, AN 334 AP 15; *Les Procès de la Radio: Ferdonnet et Jean Hérold-Paquis* (Paris, 1947).

38. *Ibid.*, 201ff.

39. Sténographie René Bluet, AN 334 AP 17; *Les Procès de collaboration* (Paris, 1948).

40. AN C.J. 255.

41. Jean Galtier-Boissière, *Mon Journal dans la grande pagaïe* (Paris, 1950), 31f.

42. Lottman, *Camus*, 349.

43. Lucien Rebatet, *Mémoires d'un fasciste (1941–1947)*, (Paris, 1976), 240f.

Chapter Three. Justice and Charity

1. F. Mauriac, *Le Baillon*, 24ff.

2. *Combat* (Paris), October 18, 1944.

3. F. Mauriac, *Le Baillon*, 87ff.

4. *Combat* (Paris), October 20, 1944.

5. F. Mauriac, *Le Baillon*, 91ff.

6. *Combat* (Paris), October 25, 1944.

7. C. Mauriac, *Un Autre de Gaulle,* 62.

8. *Le Figaro* (Paris), November 14, 1944, in F. Mauriac, *Le Baillon,* 131ff.

9. *Le Figaro* (Paris), December 12, 1944, in *ibid.,* 171ff.

10. *Le Figaro* (Paris), December 27, 1944.

11. *Combat* (Paris), January 5, 1945.

12. *Le Figaro* (Paris), January 7–8, 1945, in F. Mauriac, *Le Baillon,* 222ff.

13. *Combat* (Paris), January 11, 1945.

14. *Le Figaro* (Paris), July 26, August 16, 1945, in F. Mauriac, *Journal,* IV, 113ff., 128ff.

15. "L'Incroyant et les Chrétiens," in Albert Camus, *Essais* (Paris, 1965), 371f.

16. *Le Figaro* (Paris), October 19, 1944, in F. Mauriac, *Le Baillon,* 90.

17. *Bulletin d'Informations de l'Institut Français d'Opinion Publique* (Paris), March 1, 16, 1945.

18. Roger Secrétain, "Echec de la Résistance," *Esprit* (Paris), June 1945, 4f.

19. *Le Figaro* (Paris), October 26, 1944.

20. *Combat* (Paris), August 30, 1945, in Camus, *Essais,* 290.

21. Sténographie René Bluet, AN 334 AP 10; Galtier-Boissière, *Mon Journal depuis la libération,* 84ff.

22. *Combat* (Paris), December 27, 1944.

23. Teitgen, *Les Cours de Justice,* 37.

24. From Raymond Lindon.

25. From Raymond Lindon.

26. Case of Joseph Amblard, Sténographie René Bluet, AN 334 AP 17.

27. *Combat* (Paris), December 23, 1944; *Le Monde,* December 21, 1944.

28. *Le Monde* (Paris), April 11, 1945.

29. *Le Monde* (Paris), May 5, 1945.

30. *Le Monde* (Paris), December 12, 1945.

31. "Statistque de la répression à la libération (Département de la Seine)," *Bulletin du Comité d'Histoire de la Deuxième Guerre Mondiale* (Paris), November–December 1972.

32. Ministère de l'Intérieur, Bulletin sur la situation dans les Régions et les Départements, April 3, 1945. AN F1A 4028.

33. Larrieu, "L'Epuration Judiciaire," 35ff.

34. Labedan, "La Répression," 110ff.

35. Procureur Général à Montpellier à M. le Garde des Sceaux, November 17, 1944. Courtesy of Maurice Rolland.

Chapter Four. The Lyon Trials

1. AN C.J. 171.
2. Sténographie René Bluet, AN 334 AP 9; AN C.J. 171.
3. *Les Nouvelles* (Lyon), December 3, 1944.
4. *Le Progrès* (Lyon), December 4, 1944.
5. *Le Figaro* (Paris), December 7, 1944.
6. AN C.J. 170; Exposé des faits complémentaires, AN 334 AP 9.
7. *Le Figaro* (Paris), December 10–11, 1944.
8. Exposé des faits complémentaires, AN 334 AP 9.
9. AN C.J. 170
10. C. Mauriac, *Un Autre de Gaulle,* 52.
11. L'Inspecteur Général des Services Judiciaires à M. le Garde des Sceaux, February 17, 1945. Courtesy of Maurice Rolland.
12. *Le Progrès* (Lyon), January 25, 1945.
13. L'Inspecteur Général à M. le Garde des Sceaux, February 17, 1945. Courtesy of Maurice Rolland.
14. Sténographie René Bluet, AN 334 AP 10; see also *Le Procès de Charles Maurras* (Paris, 1946).
15. L'Inspecteur Général à M. le Garde des Sceaux, February 17, 1945. Courtesy of Maurice Rolland.
16. Galtier-Boissière, *Mon Journal dans la grande pagaïe,* 79.
17. *Journal de Genève* (Geneva), October 21, 1949.
18. *Le Figaro* (Paris), April 10, 1952.
19. Archives Départementales du Rhône: Cour de Justice No. 1.
20. *Ibid.;* also Archives du Parquet 3U-2058.
21. Archives Départementales du Rhône: Cour de Justice Nos. 2, 3, 4.
22. Le Premier Président et le Procureur Général de Lyon à M. le Garde des Sceaux, December 20, 1944. Courtesy of Maurice Rolland.
23. Commissaire Régional de la République au Ministre de l'Intérieur, February 2, 1945. AN F1A 4022.
24. *Le Progrès* (Lyon), January 11, 1944.
25. *Le Progrès* (Lyon), July 24, 1945.
26. Archives Départementales du Rhône, Cour de Justice No. 1924.
27. *Le Monde* (Paris), September 26, 1946.
28. Archives Départementales du Rhône, Cour de Justice No. 2030.
29. Talk with Roland Blayo, Lyon.

Chapter Five. Problem Solving

1. De Gaulle, *Mémoires de Guerre,* III, 127.
2. From Charles Zambeaux and Pierre-Henri Teitgen.
3. C. Mauriac, *Un Autre de Gaulle,* 79f.
4. From Pierre-Henri Teitgen.
5. *Le Monde* (Paris), April 2, 1947.

6. Talks with Adolphe Touffait and Charles Zambeaux.

7. *L'Humanité* (Paris), October 18, 1944.

8. *L'Humanité* (Paris), October 24, 1944.

9. From Raymond Lindon.

10. Larrieu, "L'Epuration judiciaire," 41ff.

11. De Menthon, "L'Epuration," 788.

12. Marcel Baudot, "La Résistance française face aux problèmes de répression et d'épuration," *Revue d'Histoire de la Deuxième Guerre Mondiale* (Paris), January 1971. See tables in Novick, *The Resistance Versus Vichy,* 220f.

13. Ministère de la Guerre, Direction de la Gendarmerie, Synthèse pour la période du 15 janvier au 15 février 1945. AN 72 J 384.

14. *Le Monde* (Paris), March 22, 1945.

15. *Le Monde* (Paris), May 4, 1945.

16. *Combat* (Paris), August 1, 1945.

17. *Le Monde* (Paris), October 6, 1945.

18. *Le Monde* (Paris), September 14, 1946.

19. *Le Monde* (Paris), December 11, 1946.

20. L'Inspecteur des Services Judiciaires à M. le Garde des Sceaux, July 9, 1945. Courtesy of Maurice Rolland.

21. Charpentier, *Au Service de la liberté,* 264.

22. *Ibid.,* 264f.; *Le Monde* (Paris), October 20, 1945.

23. Ministère de l'Intérieur, *Bulletin sur la situation dans les Régions et les départements,* December 9, 1944. AN F1A 4028.

24. February 1, 1947. AN 72 AJ 158 (ITP).

Chapter Six. Courts and Chambers

1. *Le Monde* (Paris), February 15, 1949.

2. *JORF,* July 30, 1949; *Le Monde* (Paris), July 31–August 1, 1949.

3. *Le Monde* (Paris), July 31–August 1, 1949.

4. From Roland Blayo.

5. January 31, 1950. Archives Départementales du Rhône: Archives du Parquet 3U-2046.

6. *Le Monde* (Paris), December 21, 1944.

7. *Le Monde* (Paris), January 10, 1945.

8. *Bulletin hebdomadaire d'informations judiciaires* (Ministère de la Justice), June 2, 1945.

9. Teitgen, *Les Cours de Justice,* 33ff.

10. *JORF,* Assemblée Nationale Constituante, August 7, 1946 (session of August 6), 3000ff.

11. Baudot, "La Repression," 722. Cf. *JORF,* Assemblée Nationale, December 13, 1951, 9100; March 24, 1952, 1213.

12. *L'Humanité* (Paris), October 20, 1955.

13. *JORF,* December 26, 1944, modified in *JORF,* February 10, 1945.

14. Faucher, "L'Indignité Nationale," 453ff.

15. Jaffré, *Les Tribunaux d'exception,* 208.

16. Henri Saubel (Dr. Henri Balmelle), *Mon Crime* (Moulins, 1952), 80ff., 112ff., 123ff., 150ff.

17. AN: card file.

18. AN Z511 No. 776.

19. AN Z521 No. 1041.

20. AN Z521 No. 1033.

21. AN Z522 No. 1089.

22. AN Z557 No. 2227.

23. AN Z548 No. 1871 I.

24. *Le Monde* (Paris), June 5, 6, 1946.

25. Jaffré, *Les Tribunaux d'exception,* 207.

26. *Le Monde* (Paris), July 3, 1946; AN Z5137 No. 6051.

27. AN Z5148 No. 6294.

28. AN Z5270 No. 8492.

29. AN Z5279 No. 8580.

Part V
Chapter One. The High Court

1. De Gaulle, *Mémoires de Guerre,* III, 129.

2. *JORF,* November 19, 1944, 1382ff.

3. Talk with Pierre-Henri Teitgen.

4. *L'Humanité* (Paris), September 12, 1944.

5. Louis Noguères, *La Haute Cour de la libération* (Paris, 1965), 46.

6. *Combat* (Paris), October 10, 1944.

7. *Le Monde* (Paris), December 31, 1944–January 1, 1945.

8. Charpentier, *Au Service de la liberté,* 266.

9. Maurice Guérin, "La Haute Cour de Justice" (manuscript), AN 72 AJ 180 (ITP).

10. De Gaulle, *Mémoires de Guerre,* III, 130.

11. Sténographie René Bluet, AN 334 AP 31.

12. De Gaulle, *Mémoires de Guerre,* III, 130.

13. Sténographie René Bluet, AN 334 AP 31.

14. Anonymous, *Prisons de l'Epuration* (Paris, 1947), 209ff.; de Gaulle, *Mémoires de Guerre,* III, 131.

15. De Gaulle, *Mémoires de Guerre,* III, 131f.

16. December 28, 1944. Quoted in Noguères, *La Haute Cour,* 80.

17. *Ibid.,* 87.

18. Herbert R. Lottman, *Pétain: Hero or Traitor?* (New York, 1984), 353ff.

19. Guérin, "La Haute Cour," 20.
20. Lottman, *Pétain*, 362ff.
21. *Le Procès du Maréchal Pétain*, II (Paris, 1945), 951.
22. *Ibid.*, 954.
23. Lottman, *Pétain*, 368.
24. *Procès de Pétain*, II, 1123.
25. Lottman, *Pétain*, 369, 371ff.
26. Noguères, *La Haute Cour*, 95ff.
27. AN 334 AP 34.
28. *Le Procès Laval* (Paris, 1946), 7f.
29. Albert Naud, *Pourquoi je n'ai pas défendu Pierre Laval* (Paris, 1948), 244.
30. *Procès Laval*, 112.
31. *Ibid.*, 10ff.
32. *Ibid.*, 12.
33. *Ibid.*, 97.
34. *Ibid.*
35. *Ibid.*, 109
36. *Ibid.*, 116f.
37. *Ibid.*, 208.
38. *Ibid.*, 301f.
39. Naud, *Pourquoi*, 265ff.
40. Noguères, *La Haute Cour*, 100ff.
41. *Le Monde* (Paris), November 3, 1945.
42. Sténographie René Bluet, AN 334 AP 34.
43. Noguères, *La Haute Cour*, 105.
44. *Ibid.*, 103ff, 109ff.
45. *Ibid.*, 122.
46. Sténographie René Bluet, AN 334 AP 36.
47. Noguères, *La Haute Cour*, 157.
48. *Ibid.*, 149.
49. *Ibid.*, 152.
50. Sténographie René Bluet, AN 334 AP 36; for Laborde: 334 AP 39.
51. Jaffré, *Les Tribunaux d'exception*, 154.
52. *Ibid.*, 155.
53. Sténographie René Bluet, AN 334 AP 37.
54. Sténographie René Bluet, AN 334 AP 40.
55. Noguères, *La Haute Cour*, 199; Sténographie René Bluet, AN 334 AP 40.
56. Robert Dufourg, *Adrien Marquet devant la Haute Cour* (Paris, 1948), 63f.
57. Sténographie René Bluet, AN 334 AP 47; Peyrouton, *Du Service public*, 278.

58. Sténographie René Bluet, AN 334 AP 47.

59. Noguères, *La Haute Cour*, 224.

60. *JORF*, Lois et Décrets, March 4, 1954, 2142 (law of March 3).

61. Sténographie René Bluet, AN 334 AP 36.

62. *Ibid.*

63. *Le Monde* (Paris), July 22, 1955.

64. Sténographie René Bluet, AN 334 AP 39.

65. *Le Monde* (Paris), February 1, 1958.

Chapter Two. The Politicians

1. AN BB 30 1729.

2. *JORF.* September 23, 1943, 140.

3. Foulon, *Le Pouvoir en province*, 222ff.

4. *Année politique*, I, 44f.

5. *JORF*, Assemblée Consultative Provisoire, November 18, 1944, 296ff.

6. *JORF*, April 7, 1945, 1914.

7. *Le Monde* (Paris), November 8, 1945.

8. *JORF*, October 14, 1945, 6512f.

9. *Le Monde* (Paris), November 8, 1945.

10. *Année politique*, I, 316ff.

11. *Le Monde* (Paris), December 22, 1945.

12. *Le Monde* (Paris), July 6, 1946.

13. *L'Aube* (Paris), July 6, 1946.

14. *JORF*, July 19, 1946, 2694ff.

15. Novick, *The Resistance Versus Vichy*, 104.

16. *Ibid.*, 107ff.

17. *Le Populaire* (Paris), August 31, 1944.

18. Marc Sadoun, *Les Socialistes sous l'occupation: Résistance et Collaboration* (Paris, 1982), 228ff.

19. Henri Dubief, *Le Déclin de la IIIe République (1929–1938)*, (Paris, 1976), 204.

20. Herbert R. Lottman, *Pétain* (Paris, 1984), 466.

21. Note à propos de l'existence légale de l'Union Interfederale du PSF non dissoute, courtesy of Gilles de La Rocque. Interior Minister Tixier maintained that the PSF was illegal; in 1937 a Paris court had fined its leaders for reconstitution of a banned organization, and this decision was upheld on appeal. Le Ministre de l'Intérieur à MM les Commissaires Régionaux de la République, April 6, 1945, AN F1A 3238.

22. Archives des Yvelines.

23. Letter from La Rocque to PSF leaders, January 10, 1946, courtesy of Gilles de La Rocque.

24. From Charles Zambeaux.
25. AN F1A 3239.
26. From Gilles de La Rocque.
27. Archives des Yvelines.
28. *Ibid.*
29. *Ibid.*
30. La Rocque to Prefect Léonard, July 17, 1945. Archives des Yvelines.
31. August 23, 1945. Archives des Yvelines.
32. AN Papiers La Rocque, 451 AP 21; from Gilles de La Rocque.
33. October 9, 1945. Archives des Yvelines.
34. October 11, 1945. Archives des Yvelines.
35. Archives des Yvelines.
36. AN Papiers La Rocque, 451 AP 21.
37. June 11, 1945. From Gilles de La Rocque.
38. AN Papiers La Rocque, 451 AP 21.
39. Archives des Yvelines.
40. December 28, 1945. Archives des Yvelines.
41. From Gilles de La Rocque.
42. From Gilles de La Rocque.
43. Decision of July 26, 1947. AN Papiers La Rocque.
44. From Gilles de La Rocque.

Chapter Three. Administrations: At the Top

1. *JORF,* January 8, 1944 (decree of December 21, 1943).
2. *JORF,* July 6, 1944 (decree of June 27).
3. AN F1A 3809.
4. C. Angeli and P. Gillet, *La Police dans la politique* (*1944–1954*), (Paris, 1967), 137.
5. Talk with Maurice Rolland.
6. *Bulletin hebdomadaire d'informations judiciaires* (Ministère de la Justice), June 2, 1945.
7. Report of Commission d'Epuration, November 15, 1944. Dossier Epuration, Archives du Ministère des Relations Extérieures, Paris.
8. Decree of October 3, 1944, Notes, Direction du Personnel, Dossier Epuration, Ministère des Relations Extérieures.
9. Note from Secretary-General Raymond Brugère to Minister Bidault, October 4, 1944. Dossier Epuration, Ministère des Relations Extérieures.
10. *Combat* (Paris), September 15, 1944.
11. Letter from Ministre des Affaires Etrangères, June 13, 1945. Dossier Epuration, Ministère des Relations Extérieures.

12. AN F72 bis 689.

13. Dossier Epuration, Ministère des Relations Extérieures.

14. Morand statement, Papiers Jacques Chardonne, courtesy of André Bay.

15. Talk with Roger Peyrefitte; Roger Peyrefitte, *Propos secrets,* I (Paris, 1977), 101.

16. *Ibid.,* 98.

17. Roger Peyrefitte, *La Fin des ambassades* (Paris, 1953), 356ff.

18. Galtier-Boissière, *Mon Journal depuis la libération,* 299.

19. *Résistance* (Paris), July 3, 1945.

20. From Roger Peyrefitte.

21. Peyrefitte contre le Ministre des Affaires Etrangères, May 25, 1960 (1218/55). The ministry's appeal of this decision was rejected by the Council of State: Ministre des Affaires Etrangères contre Peyrefitte, November 28, 1962, No. 51 619.

22. Peyrefitte contre le Ministre des Affaires Etrangères, May 25, 1960, No. 476/54.

23. Ministre des Affaires Etrangères contre Peyrefitte, session of November 14, 1962, No. 51 618. See *Recueil des décisions du Conseil d'Etat statuant au Contentieux, Année 1962* (Paris, 1962), 637.

24. Session of April 26, 1978.

25. From Roger Peyrefitte.

26. Raymond Brugère, *Veni, Vidi Vichy* (Paris, 1953), 155ff.; de Gaulle, *Mémoires de Guerre,* III, 55.

27. Andre Latreille, "Les Débuts de Monseigneur Roncalli à la Nonciature de Paris," *Revue de Paris* (Paris), August 1963, 66ff.

28. André Latreille, *De Gaulle, la libération et l'Eglise Catholique* (Paris, 1978), 21.

29. *Bulletin d'informations de l'Institut Français d'Opinion Publique* (Paris), December 16, 1944.

30. Latreille, *De Gaulle,* 20f.; Latreille, "Les Débuts," 67.

31. Latreille, *De Gaulle,* 26ff.

32. *Ibid.,* 48f., 54.

33. Latreille, "Les Débuts," 71ff.

34. Charles de Gaulle, *Lettres, Notes et Carnets (8 mai 1945–18 juin 1951),* (Paris, 1984), 19f.

Chapter Four. Administrations: At the Base

1. AN, Inventaire, Versements du Ministère de l'Education Nationale 1958–1968.

2. AN F17 16701.

3. *L'Humanité* (Paris), September 3, 1944.

4. André Basdevant, "L'Epuration administrative," in *Libération de la France,* 798.

5. AN F72 bis 689.

6. XXX, "L'Université épurée," *Ecrits de Paris* (Paris), July 1949, 81ff.

7. Basdevant, "L'Epuration administrative," 798.

8. March 12, 1944, note, Archives SH 7 P 209.

9. Archives SH 9 P 133.

10. Jacques Vernet, *Le Réarmement et la réorganisation de l'Armée de Terre française (1943–1946),* (Vincennes, 1980), 121ff.

11. September 22, 1944. *JORF,* September 29, 1944, 842.

12. *JORF,* September 26, 1944, 835.

13. Vernet, *Le Réarmement,* 206.

14. Archives SH 6 P 11.

15. Vernet, *Le Réarmement,* 123.

16. C. Mauriac, *Un Autre de Gaulle,* 59.

17. Archives SH.

18. Vernet, *Le Réarmement,* 124.

19. *Ibid.,* 127.

20. *JO,* Assemblée Consultative Provisoire, June 21, 1945, 1156ff.

21. Vernet, *Le Réarmement,* 128.

22. Baudot, "La Répression," 777f.

23. AN 72 AJ 91 (ITP).

24. Ministère de l'Intérieur, *Bulletin sur la Situation dans les Régions et les départements,* December 9, 1944. AN F1A 4028.

25. Commissaire de la République à Bordeaux, Rapport Bi-Mensuel, November 15, 1945. AN F1A 4020.

26. *Bulletin d'informations de l'Institut Français d'Opinion Publique,* January 16, 1945.

27. *JORF,* Assemblée Nationale, January 26, 1951, 408; August 3, 1948, 5230.

28. *JORF,* Assemblée Nationale, January 26, 1951, 408.

29. *Recueil des arrêts du Conseil d'Etat statuant au Contentieux, Année 1948* (Paris, 1948), 599.

30. *Ibid.,* 600.

31. *Recueil des arrêts du Conseil d'Etat statuant au Contentieux, Année 1949* (Paris, 1949), 712.

32. G. E. Lavau, "De quelques principes en matière d'épuration administrative," *La Semaine Juridique* (Paris), 1947, I, 584, 1–5.

33. *Recueil des arrêts du Conseil d'Etat,* 1949, 715.

34. Ibid., 712

35. Basdevant, "L'Epuration Administrative," 797.

36. René Tunc, "La Loi d'Amnistie du 6 août 1953," *La Semaine Juridique* (Paris), 1953, II, 1123, 4.

Part VI
Chapter One. Engineers and Contractors

1. Talk with Raymond Aubrac.
2. Foulon, *Le Pouvoir en province*, 233ff.
3. Jérôme Ferrucci, *Vers la Renaissance française*, preface by Raymond Aubrac (Paris, 1945); Foulon, *Le Pouvoir en province*, 233f. See notes by Raymond Aubrac in Pierre Guiral, *Libération de Marseille* (Paris, 1974), 205.
4. From Michel-Henry Fabre.
5. *JORF*, October 17, 1944, 965f.
6. Georges Capdevielle and Jean Nicolay, *La Confiscation des profits illicites* (Paris, 1944), 5ff.
7. *Le Monde* (Paris), January 10, 1945.
8. AN F12 9596.
9. Bracquemond, "Intervention," 804.
10. *Le Figaro* (Paris), December 13, 1944.
11. *Le Monde* (Paris), February 9, 1945.
12. *Le Monde* (Paris), September 6, 1945.
13. *Le Monde* (Paris), October 20, 1945.
14. Pierre Mouthon, "La Répression de la Collaboration dans le Département de la Haute-Savoie" (unpublished manuscript), ITP.
15. Pierre Berteaux, *Libération de Toulouse et de sa région* (Paris, 1973), 204f.
16. AN F12 9554.
17. *Ibid.*
18. AN F12 9623.
19. AN F12 9554.
20. AN F12 9556.
21. *Ibid.*
22. AN F12 9555, 9565.
23. AN F12 9554, 9555.
24. AN F12 9555, 9578.
25. AN F12 9554.
26. AN F12 9555.
27. *Ibid.*
28. AN F12 9556.
29. AN F12 9629.
30. AN F12 9631.
31 Baudot, "La Répression," 780.
32. Charpentier, *Au Service de la liberté*, 262.
33. Foulon, *Le Pouvoir en province*, 171.
34. Talk with Pierre-Henri Teitgen.

Chapter Two. The Renault Affair

1. *L'Humanité* (Paris), October 28, 1944.
2. De Gaulle, *Mémoires de Guerre,* III, 113f.
3. *Le Monde* (Paris), May 31, 1945.
4. *Le Monde* (Paris), April 13, 1945.
5. *Année politique,* I, 76–83; *Le Figaro* (Paris), November 29, 1944.
6. Saint-Loup, *Renault de Billancourt* (Paris, 1956), 196.
7. *Ibid.,* 184.
8. Anthony Rhodes, *Louis Renault* (London, 1969), 131.
9. *Ibid.,* 157.
10. *Ibid.,* 160ff.
11. *Ibid.,* 170ff.
12. Saint-Loup, *Renault* 313ff.
13. *L'Humanité* (Paris), September 19, 1944; AN 9 SP.
14. Saint-Loup, *Renault,* 313ff.
15. AN 9 SP.
16. *Ibid.*
17. *Ibid.*
18. *Combat* (Paris), September 26, 1944.
19. *Combat* (Paris), September 28, 1944; AN 9 SP.
20. *JORF,* January 17, 1945, 222f. (decree of January 16).
21. Saint-Loup, *Renault,* 320ff.
22. AN 9 SP; Isorni, *Mémoires,* I, 363.
23. Rhodes, *Renault,* 198ff.
24. Isorni, *Mémoires,* I, 345ff., 385ff.
25. *Le Monde* (Paris), December 17, 1957.
26. Rhodes, *Renault,* 202f.
27. *Recueil des arrêts du Conseil d'Etat,* 1949, 720f.
28. Ibid., 1948, 610.
29. *Recueil des arrêts du Conseil d'Etat statuant au Contentieux, Année 1952* (Paris, 1953), 732.
30. *JORF,* August 30, 1944, 776f.
31. Georges Lefranc, *Les Expériences syndicales en France de 1939 à 1950* (Paris, 1950), 130ff.
32. *Le Populaire* (Paris), October 29–30, 1944.
33. Lefranc, *Les Expériences syndicales,* 136.

Chapter Three. Ideas in Print

1. Bellescize, *Les Neuf Sages,* 178ff.
2. *Ibid.,* 183f.; Pierre-Bloch, *Le Vent souffle,* 287ff.
3. AN F1A 4004.

4. August 11, 1944. Jean-Jacques Mayoux, in *Voix de la Liberté,* V, 157f.

5. Bernard Lebrun, "La presse du Calvados à la libération," in colloquium "Normandie 1944" (Caen, 1984).

6. *JORF,* July 8, 1944, 550.

7. Debré, *Mémoires,* I, 322.

8. *JORF,* October 1, 1945, 851.

9. *JORF,* February 18, 1945, 851.

10. *Ibid.*

11. Ministère de l'Information, Les Séquestres de presse. AN 72 AJ 383.

12. *JORF,* October 1, 1944, 851.

13. *Combat* (Paris), October 11, 1944.

14. *Ibid.*

15. De Gaulle, *Mémoires de Guerre,* III, 134f.

16. Jean Mottin, *Histoire politique de la presse (1944–1949),* (Paris, 1949), 32ff.

17. Chastenet, *Quatre fois vingt ans,* 369.

18. Claude Hisard, *Histoire de la Spoliation de la presse française* (Paris, 1955).

19. Anonymous, "Ote-toi de là que je m'y mette!" in *Lectures Françaises* (Paris), August–September 1964; "Le Livre Noir de l'Epuration," 54.

20. *JORF,* May 6, 1945, 2571ff.

21. Affaires de presse en cours d'examen à la Cour de Justice de Paris, 14–18 janvier 1946, by Inspecteur Général Maurice Rolland. Courtesy of Maurice Rolland.

22. AN C.J. 492.

23. *Le Petit Journal acquitté en Cour de Justice* (Paris, 1948).

24. Mottin, *Histoire de la presse,* 51ff.

25. *Le Monde* (Paris), June 16, 1948.

26. ZN C.J. 492 (L'Oeuvre): C.A. 4628.

27. *Les Lettres Françaises* (clandestine), November 1943.

28. *Les Lettres Françaises* (Paris), September 9, 1944.

29. *Les Lettres Françaises* (Paris), September 30, 1944.

30. *Les Lettres Françaises* (Paris), November 25, 1944.

31. AN F12 9640.

32. Galtier-Boissière, *Mon Journal depuis la libération,* 218.

33. AN F12 9554, 9640.

34. AN F12 9640.

35. AN F12 9642.

36. AN F12 9641.

37. Bernard Grasset, *A la recherche de la France* (Paris, 1940), 51.

38. AN F12 9641.

39. *Les Lettres Françaises* (Paris), October 25, 1946.
40. AN F12 9554.
41. Examen de l'Etat des affaires de presse en cours d'instruction à la Cour de Justice, April 6, 1946. Courtesy of Maurice Rolland.
42. *Le Monde* (Paris), June 19, 1948.

Chapter Four. Writers and Artists I

1. Jean-Paul Sartre, "La Nationalisation de la littérature," *Les Temps Modernes* (Paris), November 1, 1945, 205.
2. De Gaulle, *Mémoires de Guerre,* III,135f.
3. *Les Lettres Françaises* (clandestine), December 1942.
4. *Ibid.,* November 1943.
5. *Les Lettres Françaises* (Paris), September 9, 1944.
6. *Ibid.,* October 21, November 4, 1944.
7. *Ibid.,* June 21, 1946.
8. Correspondence of Paulhan with François Mauriac, Claude Morgan, Vercors, 1944. Archives of Mme J. Paulhan.
9. *Les Lettres Françaises* (Paris), May 12, 1945.
10. Sartre, "La nationalisation," 206.
11. *Les Lettres Françaises* (Paris), December 27, 1946.
12. *Ibid.,* March 21, 1947.
13. Jean Paulhan, *Oeuvres complètes,* V (Paris, 1970), 328ff.
14. F. Mauriac, *Journal,* IV, 13.
15. Papiers Chardonne, courtesy of André Bay.
16. Herbert R. Lottman, *The Left Bank* (Boston, 1982), 172f.
17. August 10, 1947, September 4, 1947. Isorni, *Mémoires,* I, 334f.
18. *Le Monde* (Paris), December 9, 1948.
19. Galtier-Boissière, *Mon Journal dans la grande pagaïe,* 284.
20. L.-F. Céline, *Lettres à son avocat* (Paris, 1984), 138.
21. Les Cahiers de l'Herne I, *L.-F. Céline* (Paris, 1963), 139, 148, 338. A lawyer obtained an amnesty from the Military Tribunal under a 1947 provision which granted an amnesty to the seriously war wounded, but the military judges apparently did not know that the applicant "Destouches" was actually the person who wrote under the name "Céline." Céline, *Lettres à son avocat,* 181.
22. *JORF,* May 31, 1945, 3108.
23. AN F21 13
24 An F21 18.
25. AN F21 13.
26. AN F21 22.
27. AN F21 13.
28. *Ibid.*
29. *Ibid.*

30. April 26, 1946. AN F21 23.
31. AN F21 24.
32. AN F21 22.
33. AN F21 24.
34. Note, April 20, 1948. AN F21 13.

Chapter Five. Writers and Artists II

1. De Gaulle, *Mémoires de Guerre,* III, 136: C. Mauriac, *Un Autre de Gaulle,* 24ff.
2. *Le Figaro* (Paris), September 1, 1944.
3. September 1, 1944.
4. C. Mauriac, *Un Autre de Gaulle,* 26.
5. September 1, 1944. F. Mauriac, *Journal,* IV, 6.
6. *JORF,* December 27, 1944, 2078.
7. Bordeaux, *Histoire,* XII, 292ff.
8. ***, "Les Elections à l'Académie Française," *Revue Française de Science Politique* (Paris), September 1958.
9. *Le Figaro* (Paris) September 16, 1944; AN F21 13.
10. Letter from Gérard Frèche to Ministre des Affaires Estrangères, March 11, 1946. AN F21 13.
11. AN F21 14.
12. AN F21 16.
13. April 4, 1945. AN F21 18.
14. AN F21 25.
15. Galtier-Boissière, *Mon Journal depuis la libération,* 299f.
16. *Combat* (Paris), February 1, 1946.
17. *Les Lettres Françaises* (Paris), October 7, 1944.
18. Circulaire Hachette No. 1, March 1945. AN 72 AJ 383.
19. André Thérive, "La Littérature clandestine sous la IVe République," *Ecrits de Paris* (Paris), January 1949, 53ff.
20. *Le Figaro* (Paris), October 5, 1944.
21. Minutes, January 22, 1946. AN F21 13.
22. *JORF,* June 26, 1946, 5745.

Chapter Six. The Stars

1. An F21 1.
2. AN F21 3.
3. September 6, 1944. AN F21 1.
4. AN F21 1.
5. *Ibid.*
6. Rapport sur l'Epuration, Union National du Spectacle, in *ibid.*

7. *JORF,* October 14, 1944, 937.
8. AN F21 1.
9. *Ibid.*
10. AN F21 2.
11. AN F21 11.
12. *JORF,* February 18, 1943.
13. AN F21 4.
14. AN F21 12, 4.
15. AN F21 4.
16. AN F21 7.
17. *L'Echo d'Alger* (Algiers), October 6, 1944.
18. *Combat* (Paris), October 18, 1944.
19. AN F21 6.
20. Simone Berteaut, *Piaf* (Paris, 1969), 211.
21. November 30, 1945. AN F21 11.
22. Sacha Guitry, *Quatre ans d'occupations* (Paris, 1947), 34ff.
23. *L'Humanité* (Paris), November 14, 1944.
24. November 7, 1945. AN F21 24.
25. *Le Monde* (Paris), March 5, 1946.
26. Guitry, *Quatre ans,* 9.
27. *Le Monde* (Paris), May 27, 1948.
28. AN F21 9.
29. *Le Monde* (Paris), September 12, 15–16, 1946.
30. AN F21 3.
31. *Le Populaire* (Paris), August 31, 1944.
32. *Le Figaro* (Paris), September 5, 1944.
33. *Libération* (Paris), September 12, 1944.
34. An F21 1; *Le Monde* (Paris), April 6, 1946.
35. *Combat* (Paris), December 22, 1944.
36. "A la Kafka," *Les Temps Modernes* (Paris), October 1, 1945.
37. AN F21 23.

Part VII
Chapter One. The Punished

1. *Carrefour* (Paris), November 14, 1949. AN 72 AJ 615.
2. Lucien Combelle, *Liberté à huis clos* (Paris, 1983), 23ff.
3. Xavier Vallat, *Charles Maurras n° d'écrou 8.321* (Paris, 1953).
4. Philippe Saint-Germain, *Les Prisons de l'épuration* (Paris, 1975), 119ff.
5. *Le Figaro* (Paris), December 11, 1951.
6. *Le Monde* (Paris), February 14, 15, 1984.
7. Bardèche, *Lettre.*

8. Galtier-Boissière, *Mon Journal dans la grande pagaïe,* 136.

9. Marcel Aymé, *Uranus* (Paris, 1948).

10. *Ecrits de Paris* (Paris), April 1950. On Pleyber's opinions: *ibid.,* March 1950, 26; April 1950, 39.

11. *Ibid.,* March 1950, 28.

12. *Ibid.*

13. *Ibid.,* 31.

14. *Ibid.,* April 1950, 38.

15. *Ibid.,* 41.

16. *Ibid.,* 40.

17. *Ibid.,* May 1950, 21.

18. *Ibid.,* June 1950, 16.

19. Rémy, *Dans l'ombre du Maréchal* (Paris, 1971), 72, 91f.

20. De Gaulle, *Lettres (1945–1951),* 416.

21. Galtier-Boissière, *Mon Journal dans la grande pagaïe,* 51.

22. *Cahiers de la France Libérée: L'Epuration arme politique* (Paris, 1947).

23. Jacques Isorni, "L'Epuration Administrative," in Rougier, *L'Epuration,* 89f.

24. *Requête aux Nations Unies* (Paris, 1951) 13.

25. Ibid., 24ff.

26. Saint-Germain, *Les Prisons,* 13.

27. Jean Pleyber, "Les Travaux et les Jours," *Ecrits de Paris* (Paris), August 1950, 32.

28. Jean Pleyber, "L'Epuration insurrectionnelle," in Rougier, *L'Epuration,* 33f.

29. Aron, *Histoire de la libération,* 655, 723.

30. Baudot, "La Répression," 764.

31. De Gaulle, *Mémoires de Guerre,* III, 48.

32. Baudot, "La Répression," 765f.

33. *Ibid.,* 767f.

34. Talk with Marcel Baudot.

35. De Gaulle, *Mémoires de Guerre,* III, 126.

36. Saint-German, *Les Prisons,* 14ff.

37. Garçon, *Code Pénal annoté,* 266.

38. De Gaulle, *Mémoires de Guerre,* III, 127.

39. Novick, *The Resistance Versus Vichy,* 159, 186f.

40. *Ibid.,* 209ff.

Chapter Two. Forgiving

1. March 7, 1946. François Mauriac, *Journal,* V (Paris, 1953), 5ff.

2. *Ibid.,* 44ff. (April 30, 1946).

3. *JORF,* August 17, 1947; Henri Faucher, "Amnistie et Collaboration

avec l'Ennemi," *La Semaine Juridique* (Paris), 1947, II, 658.

4. *Sondages* (Paris), April 1, 1948.

5. *L'Aube* (Paris), March 5, 7, 1949.

6. *Le Monde* (Paris), April 14, 1949.

7. *Combat* (Paris), February 19, 1948.

8. *Combat* (Paris), May 7, 1949.

9. *Le Monde* (Paris), May 31, 1949.

10. Service de sondages et statistiques, in *Le Figaro* (Paris), June 21, 1949.

11. "A propos de l'Amnistie," *Le Populaire* (Paris), July 5, 1949.

12. *Le Monde* (Paris), June 11, 12, 1949.

13. *The Times* (London), November 18, 1949.

14. *Le Monde* (Paris), December 22, 1949.

15. *Le Figaro* (Paris), November 10, 1950.

16. *Le Populaire* (Paris), October 4, 1950.

17. *JO*, Assemblée Nationale, November 5, 1950, 7469.

18. *Ibid.*, 7472.

19. *Ibid.*, 7475ff.

20. Talk with Pierre-Henri Teitgen.

21. *Le Monde* (Paris), December 6, 1950.

22. *JO*, Lois et Decrets, January 6, 1951; *Le Monde* (Paris), January 4, 1951.

23. Bernard Vorge, "L'Amnistie," in Rougier, *L'Epuration*, 140.

24. Jean Pleyber, "Les Travaux et les Jours," *Ecrits de Paris* (Paris), August 1951, 16.

25. Paulhan, *Oeuvres complètes*, V, 429ff.

26. C. Mauriac, *Un Autre de Gaulle*, 350.

27. *Combat* (Paris), December 29, 1951.

28. *L'Humanité* (Paris), January 4, 1952.

29. Tunc, "La loi d'Amnistie," 1123.

30. *La Croix* (Paris), October 22, 1952.

31. *JO*, Assemblée Nationale, October 29, 1952, 4500f.

32. *Le Monde* (Paris), March 12, 1953.

33. *Le Monde* (Paris), July 26–27, 1953.

34. *JO*, Lois et Decrets, August 7, 1953, 6942.

35. Tunc, "La Loi d'Amnistie," 1123.

Chapter Three. The Purge Today

1. *L'Express* (Paris), June 5, 26, 1972.

2. From Roland Blayo.

3. Paul Touvier, *Mes Crimes contre l'humanité* (1979), 25; *Le Figaro* (Paris), June 17–18, 1972; *Le Monde* (Paris), June 20, 1972.

4. *Le Monde* (Paris), October 29, 1975.

5. *Le Monde* (Paris), June 12, 1976; July 29, 1979.

6. *Le Canard Enchaîné* (Paris), March 23, 1983.

7. *Le Monde* (Paris), March 20–21, 1983.

8. *Le Monde* (Paris), September 23–24, November 17, 1984.

9. David Ruzié, "Crimes contre l'humanité," *La Semaine Juridique* (Paris), May 9, 1984.

10. *Le Monde* (Paris), March 14, 1979.

11. Serge Klarsfeld, *Vichy-Auschwitz* (Paris, 1983), 540.

12. *L'Humanité* (Paris), March 13, October 10, 1979. For more details on the Leguay case: David Pryce-Jones, *Paris in the Third Reich* (New York, 1981), 233.

13. *L'Humanité* (Paris), January 30, 1949; *Le Monde* (Paris) March 14, 1979.

14. Klarsfeld, *Vichy-Auschwitz,* 539f.

15. *Le Monde* (Paris), October 8, 29, 1983; March 10, 1984. *Le Canard Enchaîné* (Paris), May 4, 1983.

16. Céline, *Lettres à son avocat,* 113.

17. From Serge Klarsfeld.

18. *JO*, Lois et Decrets, January 6, 1951, 262.

19. Talk with Pierre-Henri Teitgen.

Index